Trying to Fix

Stupid

The Autobiography
of a Maverick Professor

D1737241

GERALD NEWMAN

Published by Wheatmark®
2030 East Speedway Boulevard, Suite 106
Tucson, Arizona 85719 USA
www.wheatmark.com

ISBN: 978-1-62787-893-7 (paperback)
ISBN: 978-1-62787-894-4 (ebook)
LCCN: 2021910388

Bulk ordering discounts are available through Wheatmark, Inc. For more information, email orders@wheatmark.com or call 1-888-934-0888.

CONTENTS

PREFACE

They say "YOU CAN'T FIX STUPID," but educators try. Yes, and make a living out of it. But, really, you *can* fix stupid. We're all born stupid, right? And, with help, don't we get less so? So stupid is fixable. Why the pessimism, then? I think "YOU CAN'T FIX STUPID" refers to beliefs held so rigidly that they won't budge under any fact or argument. Unfortunately they're often acquired at the mother's knee, along with the more innocent stupidity of simply knowing nothing at birth. So stupidity can be not-knowing, or knowing-too-much; the first is the stupidity of a potato, the second that of a jihadi. Often you find the two together, and then you've got a real problem—or maybe (I hear you say) a politician of a certain party?

Ordinarily the day job of the educator is, first, to fix the potato, implanting information from the real world, and, second, to fix the jihadi, implanting protective habits of critical thinking. You try to fill blank minds, and promote open ones. That seems doubly important now, when any crackpot carrying a phone can set off a stampede. But isn't there a third stupidity to fix, maybe even the most important one?

Doesn't the educator have another, more properly civic obligation, to undermine shibboleths that prevent folks from seeing the flawed assumptions of groups they belong to? Stupidity can belong to communities too, and manifests itself, for example, as blindness to monumental anachronisms like stoning, cannibalism, and the United States Senate. More generally, it's the stupidity of organisms unaware of their imprisonment, like cattle in a boxcar, or fish in a tank. Call it group-blindness stupidity, or simply bubbled stupidity.

However, the answer to the above question is No. It's not, strictly speaking, in the teacher's job description to undermine shibboleths. Dispensing information and assisting critical thinking is about all an educator can do. You can try to attack group misconceptions, but it's rarely productive to do it head-on. And so, you may well ask, does fixing stupid entirely prohibit the teaching of values? I don't think so, but you've got to be careful. The main job is to train people to think clearly, but, along the way, you can try to implant the idea of our common humanity. That's a shortcut to clearer thinking anyway.

I'm a very old guy, 82, an educator, so I've often tried to fix all those stupidities, the birth-stupidity, the know-it-all stupidity, and the bubble stupidity. Of course I've tried to fix my own stupidity too, and that has meant taking stock of myself. An extended stock-taking may amount to an autobiography, and that's what this book is.

But a certain feeling of helplessness may arise, because writing your autobiography is surveying your life when it's too late to change it. It's like locking yourself to an escalator going down to your birth, then up again to your present. If you're attentive, you see where you should have gotten off at the third floor rather than the fourth, or maybe spent more time in "Men's Furnishings" than you did, or picked up more silly putty instead of whoopee cushions on the fifth, or simply have gotten off altogether and taken the back stairs.

Writing your autobiography is an exercise of memory, research, discovery, and sometimes of guided imagination too. It ought to be a literary exercise, but the most important thing is to get the story right, because at an advanced age you want to see yourself as you really were. "Know Thyself" was the command of the ancient Greeks: try to find your place in the great order of things. From which it follows that writing your autobiography is humbling. But it can be fun, too. It can be entertaining to summon stuff from memory that faded decades ago. Sometimes I've laughed out loud at things discovered on the second floor, or the seventh.

What sort of book resulted from all this upping-and-downing? With my life story as its foundation it's a narrative of tales and anecdotes, observations and lessons, a volume, I hope, of amusement, unusual experiences, sundry observations, and cracker-barrel philosophy, all tending to illustrate the making and life's work of a professional teacher. I've lived a boring life but met many unusual people, and educators, in particular, will see here a jolly parade of familiar types.

Beyond that, this book might be regarded as a record of an American family that immigrated from Ireland, settled in the eastern U.S., moved West in the 1860s, made its home in a beautiful valley in Washington State, did well enough there, moved from agriculture and blacksmithing into modern professional life, and then partly moved East again. But at its core, it's simply my life-story, an account of the making and baking of a 20th-century American teacher-professor, and of the pleasures and hardships encountered along the way.

I began writing this book about six years ago and was nearing its end when I started wondering whether it might have wider interest beyond some 25 targeted sufferers, my family and few remaining old friends. It started as a purely personal attempt to sift the details of my 82 years and try to find the shape of them. But perhaps others might find something curious, or at least worth a chuckle? If you think so, please pass the word. I can't afford paid advertising, but every reader gets a sucker.

You'd like a brief tour. Well, I review my advantages as a baby born somewhat accidentally in Singapore, my halting progress and disciplinary issues as a youngster in Washington State, my awakening interest in girls, sports, and intellectual subjects in the college town of Ellensburg, my grab-ass membership in a college fraternity at the University of Washington in Seattle, my encouragement by several fine teachers, my growing intellectual proficiency, the typical liberal-arts crisis of my college years in which I found my career path, my first taste of the pleasures of teaching at Western Washington University in Bellingham, my variable adventures into marriage and fatherhood, the grueling period of further preparation in graduate school at Harvard University, and then my career as a more or less annoying and mavericky professor of history at Kent State University in Ohio. All along the way I tried to fix stupid, but once I had my credentials and found myself in those green Ohio pastures, I totally buckled down to work—not to say I accomplished anything much, but there you are.

While wandering through all that I've sketched my youthful follies and amours, pranks and kerfuffles, fellow students and zany faculty members, curmudgeons, administrators, foreign study programs, disputatious encounters with biggies like David Landes, W.K. Jordan, Henry Kissinger, Augie Meier, and R. K. Webb. I describe my moving but hilarious visiting professorship in Communist Poland, and a return tour to Singapore with my family. At last, after an exciting run at sexual harassment, I reach my geezerly retirement.

Included too are stories about recreation in Washington, tips on teaching, professional wisdom about the role of historical lies in political propaganda, and a running commentary on American politics. As I spent half my life in the shadow of the Cold War, my story conveys the general pattern of liberal-to-radical academic opinion during that entire period—or, returning to the "Fixing Stupid" idea, it revisits blasts from my own little Bureau of Public Corrections.

For better and often worse, it's a true story. Since 1958 I've written 15 fat diaries and never read any of them till about six years ago, when I began this book. All along I saved them for my old age, which, I find, is now. Also I've worked from photos and a giant pile of memorabilia, so my problem has not been too few materials, it's been a felt obligation to weed through all that stuff in order to see my own life steadily, and see it whole. I would have had more fun if I'd made it all up, and maybe I'll do that for the CliffsNotes.

Honesty is vitally important to a good memoir, and everything that follows is true except for one or two tiny exaggerations, and every quotation is verbatim except for itty-bitty tweakings, and every name is the real McCoy except for real McCoys whose names I've blurred to avoid defecation of character. So this is the genuine article. It's my stupid life, trying to fix stupid.

April Fool's Day, 2021
Tucson, Arizona

PART ONE

Growing Up

1

Master Gerald

SINGAPORE, 1938-1941

First, think of me as a fertilized egg. I entered the world as a gorgeous baby in December, 1938, but, if you please, just picture a cute little egg somewhat earlier that same year. Most memoirs start with a hatching, but mine needs to begin a bit earlier in the college town of Pullman, Washington, in the good old USA—not nine months later, almost a world away, being pushed howling into existence amongst Malays and Chinese, elephants, tigers, snakes, and fancy-pants British imperialists.

So there we are in a placid town near the Idaho border. Pullman, in the southeast corner of the state, was the seat of Washington State College, a "cow college" specializing in training veterinarians. The town lies in beautiful terrain, the rolling hills of the "Palouse" country, colorfully striped with crops planted in many directions; in the fall, during the harvest season, that farmland is stunningly beautiful. Farmers, many of them artists at heart, consciously plant it that way.

An associate veterinarian teaching classes in that college was my father, Leonard Laverne Newman, 25 years old. He could treat all animals, but his expertise lay mostly in doctoring cows and horses. He even had a side job with horses: he owned a Model A Ford, and in summertime drove back and forth across the state, from Pullman to the "Longacres" race track near Seattle, where he drug-tested racehorses. By 1938 he'd already been a prosecution witness in a doping scandal. So there's one leading actor in my little story. We're picturing Leonard

Leonard Newman

3

Newman on the teaching faculty at Washington State. Photos show him as a handsome young man with a broad brow and big, capable hands. He was the son of farmers, Fred and Nellie Newman. They lived some 200 miles west, near the small agricultural town of Thorp in the foothills of the Cascades. Thorp stood near the highway between Pullman and Seattle, so Len, my dad, could easily drop in on his parents when motoring west to the race track.

～

In Thorp the Newman family enjoyed a certain prestige due to the fact that John Miles Newman, Len's grandfather, had been a prominent pioneer. He'd arrived in 1878 when there were very few white people in the area. In these pages I'm going to call him "The Valley Patriarch" (or JMN), to distinguish him from all the other dead Newmans in the Thorp Cemetery. But first just a word about *his* father, the man who brought our family to the West in the first place. That was Michael Piper Newman, born in 1820 in Virginia. (*His* father had immigrated from Ireland—my lineage is mostly Anglo-Irish.) In the 1840s he became a blacksmith, married and moved to Missouri, then to Texas, then back to Missouri. I wish I could have met him; probably, like his son and grandson, he was a disciplinarian and a joker. Anyway, in early 1864 he decided to pack up his blacksmith's tools and hit the Oregon Trail. He must have felt uneasy: great hardships awaited him. There were vast mountain ranges, wide rivers, horseflies, mud. He waited for the grass.

"The grass is up!" was the cry that every year heralded the beginning of westward movement. In May, with the snow melted and grass growing to feed their animals, pioneers boarded wagon trains for the 2,000-mile trek. The Newmans traveled with a certain Captain Wadkins. A contemporary described "mothers tucking away in the wagons their

John Miles and Isabel Newman

small boxes and bundles, a tiny bag of seeds, a slip of some beloved plant; children, big and little, helping or getting in the way of the grown-ups; fathers looking to the last-minute details for the endless days of travel over the Oregon Trail; all with high hopes and longing for the new home in the lush valleys by the Western Sea." Michael Piper Newman settled in Oregon, then farmed and did his blacksmithing there till he died in 1890 and was buried in Kings Valley. A wanderer, he'd lived 70 eventful years and come a long way. *He* was the ancestral parent of the Newman family in the American Northwest.

His son, the star we've been waiting for, John Miles Newman, was born in Missouri in 1851 and then as a 13-year-old traveled west on the journey I've just described. I can imagine him walking behind oxen and cattle, carrying a stick and idly switching bushes as he follows the family wagon. He spent his teens and early 20s in northern Oregon, growing up lean, muscular, and brown-haired, with a steady gaze. He married a solid-looking girl, Isabel Forgey, who brought him his first child in 1874; he named her Olive after his dead mother. In 1875 their second child, my great aunt Lillie, was born (she was stunningly beautiful); in 1876 came Otis (in the 1930s he blew himself up in a dynamite accident); in 1878 came Minnie (very assertive, and later such a terrible cook that dogs threw up after filching her fried chicken); then in 1880 my grandfather Fred (of whom more later), and then in succession were born three more sons, John (accidentally he cut off three of his own fingers when dressing a deer), Jake (a baby-faced sweetie), and Jess—much loved, very handsome, the only family soldier in World War I, a free-thinker who swore he'd never go to church because he couldn't stand the people who did.

In 1878 JMN moved with his growing brood to the Kittitas Valley in central Washington. They came by wagons over the sagebrush road from The Dalles, on the Columbia River. The Kittitas Valley was just then beginning to calm down after its last "Indian War" (1878), and was suddenly open to settlement. JMN was then 27, aggressive, an empire-builder, and soon became one of the biggest landholders in the area. He acquired a large spread on Thorp Prairie, and another on the outskirts of Thorp, including a large island in the Yakima River, "Newman's Island." He liked to hold big Fourth of July celebrations there—such celebrations were still being held by his sons and daughters when I was a kid in the early 1950s. One night I stayed in the sprawling lovely Victorian farmhouse that he built there.

The Patriarch and his Children; my grandfather Fred at lower left

He founded Thorp in 1895, laid it out and platted it. He was prosperous and popular, an agricultural experimenter, philanthropist, and promoter of local education. He became Justice of the Peace and a County Commissioner—the most important elective office in the County. He was a Democrat and a supporter of "The Grange," an organization to promote farmers' prosperity. Besides farming he also ran his own blacksmithing shop and livery stable. He knew many Native Americans of the Kittitas tribe who'd surrendered to American soldiers and who now sparsely populated Thorp, and he learned to speak their Chinook language. His children did, too. His daughter Minnie would stop on the street to talk to local Native Americans, and his son Fred, my grandfather, had "Indian Tommy" as a friend; he also taught my father to count to ten in Chinook, and even passed some phrases down to me—for example, "Hiya Kunchuck Chinook Wa-Wa!" (I think it means "Do you speak Chinook?")

There's more on my family's interaction with Native Americans in a charming book by Barton Porter about early Thorp, *Listen to the Mill Race* (Seattle: Stone, 1978). Porter, discussing his own youth, treats JMN as a major community leader and extols his generosity, observing that "Mr. Newman never acted as though he owned the millrace near our home, or all the land where birds and chipmunks lived between it and the river. He let us use it as though we owned it."

Porter's book contains many stories about my great-grandfather, but the one I like best is about how he got dressed down by Lavina Wyneco, the Native American woman who washed his family's clothes and otherwise helped out. Dressed in her bright, red-fringed blanket and beaded moccasins, she came to his house and asked him to bring his horse team to help her and her husband haul some firewood: "Newman, me need wood. You bring team come haul 'em?" His reply: "Oh, Lavina, I wish I could haul you some wood but I been so doggone busy butchering hogs and picking fruit and getting things done for winter, I don't have time." Her response: "You have no time! Lavina have time wash baby dities. Scrub. Wife sick. Me come help. Uh! Lavina cold. Newman no have time bring em wood. Me no come more. No have time! Uh!" That did it. Properly chastened, he replied: "Oh well, all right, Lavina. I owe it to you. Have Masterson get your wood ready. I'll bring a team and haul it next week."

The good man died on Nov. 2, 1922, after a life of work, invention, and service. It was a heart attack; it happened while he was bringing home his milk cows one evening. He now lies buried under one of the largest stones in the Thorp Cemetery. It makes me a little proud to see it. On Memorial Day I always snip the grass around it and dress its base with flowers. When he died, the local newspapers were outspoken in his praise: "His many friends admired him for his public spirit, keen sense of honor and devotion to high standards."—*Evening Record*. "One of the most widely known and highly respected men of the Kittitas Valley."—*Ellensburg Capital*. That's a send-off anyone might envy.

～

His second son, born in Thorp in 1880, was my grandfather, Fred Piper Newman—whose name, you see, bore the stamp of his own grandfather, the wanderer born in Virginia in 1820. His boyhood was that of a farmer's son. The Newmans grew hay, wheat, oats, barley, fruit, and vegetables, and they had cows for milk, and sheep for meat and wool. Young Fred drove sheep up the grassy Taneum Canyon in springtime, and learned to shear them in fall. Growing up, he learned blacksmithing, house-painting and general repair work. When he was 18 he organized a village reading and debating society where a dozen young people came together to socialize, read poems, sing songs, and argue about such current topics as American imperialism and intervention in the Philippines.

He was, like his father, respected for honesty and judgment. His 1948 obituary states that "throughout his residence in the Kittitas valley he was active in many community affairs. He was a charter member of the Thorp Farm Bureau and helped to organize the Farm Bureau in this county. He was one of the organizers of the Thorp Cemetery Association, served as a member of the Thorp school board, as a county road supervisor, and as head of the committee for the Kittitas county booth at the Western Washington Fair." That last came to me as a surprise. I've always known my grandfather had an aesthetic bent, but it seems that at the annual fairs in Yakima he regularly handled the ornamental arrangement of huge display cases of fruits and vegetables. In pioneer days that was an art-form much admired, the display on giant inclined beds of all sorts of garden crops, brightly waxed and laid out in triangles or squares. Country women excelled in quilting; Fred Newman practiced something similar in which apples, pears, eggplants and peppers were displayed like jewelry.

This all figured into the lineage of Leonard Newman, my father, the young teaching veterinarian at the cow college on the state's eastern border, the handsome 25-year-old with the Model A Ford and the side job at the racetrack near Seattle. His background taught him to be useful, to lead when leadership was called for, and to work as tirelessly as any dirt farmer anywhere. His parents, Fred and Nellie, had taught him order and exactitude and responsibility—he had to measure up, to "be a man," to do so much more than most boys today. On the farm you couldn't spend your mornings in pajamas, twiddling some digital device. Farm work taught him the beauty of good work well done, and work's importance to the enjoyment of life.

But I should note that there was more to farm kids' lives than that. They played, mostly out of doors—baseball, and horseshoes, and sometimes they'd ride their pigs or sheep, or just invent outlandish stuff. Most events at rodeos today were invented by farm kids. The Newman boys loved to horse around, and some were famous for cooking up barnyard-style practical jokes. Not just "cow-tipping" or doing crazy things with outhouses—nailing them shut, rigging up trapdoor seats—but sometimes really outlandish stuff like going out in the middle of the night and, with block and tackle, hoisting somebody's buggy atop his barn. Imagine an old farmer trudging out at six a.m. to do his chores and sighting his wagon 40 feet up, resting on his hay loft!

Some practical jokes were dangerous. Dana Miles Newman, my dad's favorite cousin (you see he bears part of the Patriarch's name), was famous for his. In his teens he'd stowed away on a boat to Alaska, got a cooking job with the Civilian Conservation Corps, and lived in Anchorage in a tiny cabin with one bed but two roommates. His obituary explains that "according to a family story, they would take turns shooting at a lit candle in the doorway to see who got the bed that night." I can't imagine which was more dangerous, the gunsmoke, the splintered candle, or whatever godawful stuff they must have been drinking. Later in life he'd trick little kids into believing that he knew black magic, then fool them into believing they'd become possessed by demonic forces!

My dad inherited that Newman tomfoolery. For my ninth birthday he gave me a giant crate triple-wrapped with heavily knotted rope and filled with packing material. It was so heavy I couldn't lift it! After removing the rope I discovered inside a very heavy anvil. (It had belonged to his blacksmithing ancestors.) Was *that* my gift? No. My gift, he told me, was *underneath* the anvil. At last I managed to budge it a little, but still found no gift! After more prompting I managed to push the anvil over, and there I found, taped to its bottom, a five-dollar bill! That was a kid's fortune in 1948!

He was still at it many years later. One time—I was middle-aged, and home for the summer—I laughingly jeered at his purchase, at the Bi-Mart discount store, of disgusting stuff that came in a generic white can with the sole word BEER on it. The whole family, eating lunch at the family home, witnessed our verbal jousting about high-quality beer. "All right, smart guy," he said, "why don't you get some fancy beer and *let's see* whether you can taste the difference?" That was a ridiculous challenge, an easy victory for me, so I charged out to the cooler in the garage and grabbed some of the Löwenbräu I'd stashed there. I handed him a bottle, he opened it, he also opened a can of BEER, then ordered me out of the kitchen so I couldn't watch him fill the two glasses he'd brought out for the testing. On my being called to return, he said, "OK, smart guy, Mr. Sophisticated Beer-drinker, which is the better beer, mine or your fancy stuff?" With a vicious laugh, knowing what embarrassment lay in store for him, what triumph lay in store for me, I tasted the one sample, then the other. Smacking my lips, I tasted them each again, just to be sure of my choice. . . . And, um, actually, to tell the truth, I couldn't detect much difference between them! Everybody waited. "WELL?" he said. "WHICH IS WHICH?" Triumphantly I pointed at the glass on the left: "THAT," I testified with a flourish, "is good beer; the other one is pure bilge water!" Everybody broke out laughing. He'd poured BEER into both glasses.

～

My mother, Frances Loree Wood, was a crackerjack of a different sort. She wasn't a practical joker but did see the funny side of things, and as a gifted storyteller made the most of it; she came from a line of amusing talkers, southerners with an eye for colorful tales and an ear for the ringing phrase. Her background was quite unlike my father's. His was rural, hers urban; his was northern, hers southern. His people, most of them, were quiet country workaholics, farmers and ranchers; hers were loquacious urbanites and salespeople. His were indifferent to religion, hers conventional Methodists. His people loved to hunt, fish, and gather berries; hers were into golf and tennis and movies.

She was born in 1916 in Kansas City, Missouri, moved to Memphis, lived there till she was 14, then moved to Spokane with her mother, Ruby Ann, and her stepfather, C.E. Wood. She was the birth child of a handsome but wayward character named Edward Johnson who had split with her mother when she was a baby. About all Loree knew of him was that he was Catholic and a philanderer; later I learned that he'd gone through several wives, leaving behind a trail of debt and woe. But her bloodline was better on her mother's side. There, she was of highly respectable descent through the wealthy and aristocratic Graves family of Illinois. Her Graves grandmother, Lu Ella (1850-1943), who she always called "Bombom," could remember when Abe Lincoln had come to their Illinois home to confer with Absalum Graves, her father, a lawyer like

Loree Wood at 16, in 1932

Lincoln himself. Bombom's husband, Ruby Ann's father, was James Montgomery, of Scots-Irish descent, from the Shenandoah Valley. He'd enlisted in the Confederate Army, fought under Stonewall Jackson at Gettysburg, been captured at Harper's Ferry, held at Elmira, New York, till 1865, then freed after swearing loyalty to the Union.

My grandmother, born in 1895, "never forgot that her father fought on the Confederate side of the Civil War," as my mother ruefully recalled. Ruby Ann considered herself a southerner, and, though very kind and soft-hearted, never quite outgrew the paternalistic racism of her Virginian forebears. An only child, she too had only one child, my mother. My grandmother when young and pretty was a bit of a coquette. She married three times, always unsuccessfully, and spent her later life living alone with outrageously spoiled dogs and cats. But although her married life was disappointing, the bond with her child, my mother, was strong almost to the point of being possessive. To me she was a very dear person. I loved her, I enjoyed listening to her talk, and she always made it clear that she adored me. She was generous and had a heart of gold.

She was also very colorful. Even as an old woman she was considered pleasantly eccentric. She liked to wear unusual hats. She made friends easily. She was a sympathetic listener and entertaining talker who employed colloquial expressions like "not on your tin-type!" or "you're darn tootin'!" She played the piano marvelously well, and passed her gift down through four more generations to my own granddaughter, Katie. Also, she adored animals and as an old lady living in Ellensburg was tortured by the thought of cattle doomed to stand outside in the below-zero cold and winter snow. Although she had very little money she spent huge sums overfeeding the birds shivering in her small back yard. In later life I dubbed her "Gramlin," a play on "Gram" and "Gremlin." Everybody else adopted the term, and I'll begin to use it here.

My Mother and Gramlin

It was with this forceful and colorful

character, her mother, Gramlin, that my own mother spent her youth and early teen years in Kansas City, then Memphis, then Spokane. Loree had a trim figure and fine angular face, with wide-set hazel eyes and curly hair that remained almost black till late middle age. Though a good listener and a sympathetic personality, she had a remarkable toughness that never left her. It was characteristic of her rather brash personality that, arriving in Spokane at the age of 14, she created a little splash in the newspaper by taking out an ad that apparently led to the founding of the first Girl Scout troop there. A Campfire Girls organization already existed in Spokane, but she scorned Campfire Girls as "prissy little things who didn't really learn to do anything. We Scouts learned to do everything, tie knots, we had merit badges for everything under the sun."

Frances Loree—she favored "Loree" to forestall the possibility that people might call her "Fanny," the common nickname for Frances—had the normal experiences of a high school girl. She went to movies, fell in love, got jilted, did baby-sitting "for ten cents an hour!" She took Latin for four years under a disapproving female teacher, excelled in English, and then, on graduating in 1934, declared her intention to go to college. That seemed a highly irresponsible step, especially in hard times, and her stepfather, she wrote, "was just furious with me: I had a chance to be secretary for the Superintendent of Schools, and it was Depression time, and he felt that I was an idiot to turn down the permanent job. But I had a single-minded purpose that I wanted to get some higher education, so I overrode him!"

She borrowed $100 from a cousin in San Diego and headed off to Washington State in the Fall of 1935. Very poor but resourceful, eager but untested, she arrived in Pullman with enthusiasm and determination. At the same time, separated from her mom living 75 miles away, she began her easy lifelong practice of letter-writing. That would, of course, endear her to her mother still living in Spokane—but also, later, to me and many others. Letter-writing is a gift to its recipient, a sign of attachment and concern. With my mother it was something she perfected with every experience she wrote about. I still have boxes of her letters, the paper now dry, her distinctive, beautiful, energetic handwriting now fading; I have her letters that will never again be read by anyone, letters that once contained not only the news but her love and her vigorous, adventuring spirit.

～

So now at last, after sorting through their bloodlines, we've got both our leading actors there in Pullman, at Washington State, in 1936. My mom was 19, my Dad 23; she was a pert freshman, he was a handsome veterinarian teacher in the vet school. My mother recalled how poor she was: "I didn't have any money from home. I remember one time stealing a bar of soap from the girls' gym because I could not afford the nickel for a bar of soap!" So she worked at two jobs when she was in college, one on weekends, the other on work days. On weekends at fraternity "firesides" she performed as an entertainer, playing the piano—she'd started taking lessons at the age of five and was now a versatile pianist who, like her mom, could play any popular song "by ear." During the work-week, however, she worked as secretary for the Dean of Pharmacy. It was through that connection that she knew Mack McCrory, a professor in the veterinary lab, and it was he who proposed a double date with his friend, Len Newman. Len, she later exclaimed, "was a catch." He was "very likeable, a very laid-back person, really a very nice guy, everybody liked him. He was handsome, an older man, a professional man. He dressed well. He had a car and a decent income of $150 a month when people were just starving to death."

But didn't he see that she was a catch, too? She was pretty, clever, adventurous, unafraid, and never at a loss for something interesting to say. Her fidelity and depth of family feeling were clear from her devotion to her mother pining away in Spokane. And, it must be remembered, she also spent her weekends playing the piano in frat houses, laughing and bantering with the boys while her fingers flew over the keys. She was a dish *and* a catch, and he wasn't alone in thinking so. Maybe he should make a move before somebody else grabbed her? A lot would depend on that first date. Here, in her words, is what happened. McCrory called her and said,

My friend [meaning Len] has just washed his car. "How would you like to go for a ride? Can you get a date for me, too?" I said okay, and got Gladys Morez, and the four of us went off for a drive. In the course of it we got out, and I was crawling under a fence, and I was wearing a navy blue corduroy jacket and skirt to match; and I got the sleeve caught in barbed wire and tore a little piece out of it. I sadly got back in the car, and Len put his arm around me, and kissed me! And I knew right then—in fact I told the girls at the dorm when I got back that night—that I was going to marry him some day. I had already made up my mind.

That was on Sunday, May 10, 1936, Mother's Day. Once Loree had made up her mind, and Len had too, they needed to meet each other's parents. First they went to Spokane where they told Gramlin they had some news for her, and advised her to sit down. "She began to cry, and said, 'Oh No!' She knew what was in the wind." Then, second, were Len's parents. The young couple stopped off in Thorp while making their way to the Longacres racetrack. "We pulled into his folks's place in Thorp, on their farm. It was about two o'clock in the morning! Len led me into their bedroom, turned on the light, and said, 'Hi, Mom, Dad, this is Loree. Is there any cottage cheese?' And he went off looking for cottage cheese with them sitting up in bed and looking at me and blinking!"

Loree, Len, and Gramlin, December 1936.

I *said* she had a knack for storytelling. It didn't fail her when she described the marriage proposal itself. Back in Pullman one evening, they drove to the top of Lewiston Hill. They were listening to the radio, "listening to a song called 'For a Nickel I would Run Away with You.'" She continued: "I've never heard the song again. I said to Len, referring to nickels, 'I don't have one, but can I borrow one?' He said 'I don't have one, but will a dime do?'" From that exchange, privately whispered on a faraway hilltop, my own existence hove into view.

~

Dr. Len Newman and young Loree Wood got married on December 18, 1936. And so, to return to that egg pictured in my opening sentence, in early 1938 it got poached. Nine months later I was born on the other side of the world. Now, how did *that* happen? It's a curious story. In early 1938 a call went out from the Singapore Dairy Farm, Ltd., the only dairy on Singapore island, seeking to hire a skilled veterinarian. The British-owned company was managed by a San Francisco firm, Getz Brothers. Its milk cows had been imported from the American Northwest, and a veterinarian from the Northwest was now urgently wanted to look after them—they were suffering from sterility and other tropical disorders. The company sent out an emergency job offer to vet schools, and my father mentioned it to his young wife. Her response: "Len, let's take it!" She was no fence-sitter when it came to decision-making.

The news was very distressing to Gramlin. "It was bad enough to tell Mom that we were going to Singapore, going to the ends of the earth. So I didn't tell her I was already pregnant. That would be the end of her." In July they packed up and boarded the ship "Empress of Asia." They were off on their great adventure to the far side of the Pacific. But that was a dangerous place. World War II had already begun there; the Japanese conquest of the Far East was already underway. Manchuria had been annexed, eastern China was aflame. The couple, after staying briefly in Yokohama, went on to Shanghai where they saw dead Chinese everywhere, lying in the streets and floating in the harbor. The Japanese armies, my mother wrote, "were very arrogant, insufferable. They carried their bayoneted guns with them everywhere and loved to give orders to the Europeans." From Shanghai they sailed to Hong Kong, and from there to Singapore. To me that name, Singapore, has an exotic ring. Like "Shangri-la" or "Xanadu" it seems musical and mysterious, it summons visions of rickshaws, parrots, jungle, orchids.

Singapore is a small island, about 15 miles by 25, at the southeastern tip of the Asian land mass. For its size it's probably the most strategic location in the world. Beyond it, surrounded by water, lie Indonesia, Australia, New Zealand, and the Philippines—it's the jumping-off spot to all those countries. It's also the critical way-station on the shortest waterway between India and China. Britain annexed the island in 1819, fortified it with huge cannons pointed out at the Straits, and made it the chief British naval base in the South Pacific. It became a key possession of the British Empire—which means, you see, that I was born in a British colony. A small, powerful British elite ran the show. Their job was to rule the colony, command the naval base, and facilitate trade.

Beneath them, Singapore's population was 80% Chinese. There was also a mixture of Indians, Malays and Europeans who managed trading relations for their countries or directed native laborers in the production of rubber. There weren't many Americans—only three or four dozen of them, mostly executives from Goodyear and Firestone. The island stood almost on the Equator; its average temperature was 80 degrees. Much of it was covered with bamboo, rain trees, elephant grass, and thick jungle—ideal for bird-watching, but also for snake-bite. The terrain is flat near the coastline, but there are some steep, rolling hills, and even a small mountain called Bukit Tima. That's where my parents were headed; the Getz representatives, all smiles and cordiality, escorted the delighted new veterinarian and his pregnant wife to their new hilltop home there.

Singapore Dairy Farm, 1938.

Because of Bukit Tima's elevation, the dairy farm was cooler than anywhere else on the island. Comfort was essential for the cows. There were 225 of them, black-and-white Holsteins, tended by 108 workers in barns that sprawled across a green hilltop surrounded by jungle. The cattle were well cared for; in old photos they look very happy, and, even when chewing the cud, smile. The new vet and his wife smiled too. They were delighted to find themselves taken to a large and beautiful villa with a grand garden. They had four house servants to cook, clean, polish the floors, and care for the place. After I was born I acquired a pretty Chinese amah, Ah Tie, with responsibility to look after my every need. There was also a sweet young man, a "house boy," who doted on me and let me ride around on his back whenever I liked.

In order to converse with servants and dairy workers, my parents learned Malay. Before long they were calling for "a minim," a whiskey, from the house boy—he'd answer, "bye, Tuan" (yes, boss)—or they'd request the cook to "Kossy makanan" (bring the food). It was a wonderful life for my parents, and it kept getting better. The farm's managers were so satisfied with my father's work—he fixed the cows' sterility and eating disorders—that, knowing my parents liked swimming, they built for them a 30-foot pool with diving boards and a filter system, and for me a kiddie pool, ten feet long. They surrounded both pools with hedges to keep the help from goggling at the white sahib, the memsahib, and little "Tuan," the little master—me.

Is it necessary to point out that this was a giant step up from everything my parents had experienced before? Formerly a rather ordinary young couple, an unsophisticated horse-doctor from tiny Thorp with his provincial little wife, scratching a living during the Great Depression, they now found themselves catapulted into a sophisticated ruling class running an important outpost of the British Empire. And they weren't just members of the literate professional elite, for in that caste society marked by skin color they were members of the *Raj*. Of course they were still very nice people, imbued with the honest values they'd acquired in youth. But, treated well, they naturally became used to enjoying respect, even command. How could they not? They increasingly mixed with the white, educated, well-to-do people near the top of the social pyramid. They golfed, swam, went yachting, went sailing, danced, played bridge, went out to dinner. They wore white linen suits and fine leather shoes; they drove into the high hill country in summers to escape the heat; they bought ivory and jade figurines, camphorwood chests and silk rugs, teak and porcelain, wooden masks, silk kimonos. When they could, they traveled and filmed exotic customs—the Tamil religious rituals of Thaipusam and Depo Valley, for example, in which penitents endured dozens of barbed needles, and walked barefoot through beds of hot coals.

Slowly, the farm boy from Thorp and the penniless Spokane secretary became well-to-do cosmopolites. There was no need any longer to take two jobs or steal a nickel's worth of soap. They prospered, their tastes were immensely broadened, their sense of themselves transformed. The world was their oyster, Singapore their pearl. They'd stay there forever, they thought.

Such was the feathered nest prepared for me. Accordingly, I arrived. Equipped with the approved numbers of fingers, toes, ears, noses, tongues, cheeks, buttocks, and reproductive gizmos, I was in good working order and ready to roll! According to the birth certificate, Gerald Gordon Newman,

alias "Jerry," was born at 4:25 a.m. on December 8, 1938, in General Hospital, Singapore, Straits Settlements (the official name of the British colony), to Leonard Laverne Newman, Caucasian, Veterinarian, Age 26, from Thorp and Pullman, Wash., and Frances Loree Newman, Caucasian, Age 22, from Kansas City, Mo., Memphis., Tenn., and Spokane, Wash.

Just for the record I should mention that the day inscribed on my birth certificate, December 8, 1938, was *the same day as December 7, 1938,* in the U.S., thanks to the effect of the International Date Line. So, because my birth certificate dictates what must go onto other documents like my passport and driver's license, I'm officially stuck, so long as I live in the U.S., with a birth date that actually *follows* my day of birth by one day! *The exact time of my birth, 4:25 a.m. on Dec. 8, was, in Washington State, 1:25 p.m. on Dec. 7.* I solve this double-birthday problem by celebrating and accepting gifts on both days. I see it as a twofer.

In her letters back to the States my mother wrote all about my wonderful arrival, and there were many replies. I like Gramlin's best for its inverted logic and wit. She addressed me as "Master Gerald Gordon Newman," welcomed me into "this great universe," and expressed her gladness that "you chose us for your family." Unfortunately I have no certain memories of those Singapore years but there are, anyway, lots of photos; not every memoir-writer has such an advantage. I see photos of me being held by my smiling parents, my smiling amah, the smiling house boy; there are pictures of me growing through those early years, from a mere rug-rat in

a blanket to a crawler barely able to lift its head, then to a wobbler being helped by his doting mother, then to a confident and self-consciously cute toddler playing independently in his sand-box, or laughingly preparing, on the lawn, to stand on his head. There are pictures of me in my little swimming pool, flapping my arms in the water like a turtle, held by my smiling young dad in his bathing trunks. There are pictures of my birthday parties with other little kids around, pictures of my toys like the giant wooden Mickey Mouse rocker. In many photos I'm dressed in tropical white shorts with pretty sandals, but in others I appear in a white linen play suit. My mother teased my curly black hair into a peak, making me look like a rapper with a mohawk.

There are other interesting documents. It's curious to see, among the rude pictures I drew with crayons, several of airplanes—we could easily spot planes from our aerie atop Bukit Tima. Some look like bombers, with gun turrets for waist gunners, and German swastikas and Japanese "zeros" on their wings. It's a reminder that World War II had already begun in Asia and Europe. I was born in 1938, the year of the *Anschluss* and the Munich Crisis; 1939 saw Hitler's invasion of Poland and the Japanese Imperial Army's attack on Changsha, the capital of Hunan Province; 1940 was the year of the Battle of Britain and the Japanese military advance into French Indochina.

The letters, photos and drawings all prove that I was a very ordinary little boy, but certainly not living in anything like ordinary circumstances. Instead I was the petted only child, surrounded by smiling servants and doted upon by my parents. A story is told about how I might waken in the middle of the night and yell, "BOY! KOSSY LIME-SQUASH!"—waking up the house boy and demanding that he bring me a limeade, and make it pronto! (The story also indicates that I too was learning Malay.) I mentioned earlier that I rode on his back when he was polishing the floors; my mother admonished him to unsaddle me, but he'd just smile and reply, "But he likes it, Mem" (Memsahib).

So I suppose this must have been the sweetest period of my entire life. The pictures are there as proof. Didn't I smile a lot? Didn't everybody else smile a lot? I played in my sand box, I paddled in my pool, I gave orders like a little general. I flourished under benevolent influences all around. Everything nourished my ego. There I was in my garlanded sphere of flowers and plants and rolling lawns, looking around from my blissful, leafy hilltop onto a protecting universe. My mother later recalled that "the four years we had in Singapore were wonderful!"

But outside that little world, the sky was falling in. People were being bombed, machine-gunned, gassed, burned alive, raped, tortured, drowned, shot, executed. Ships, buildings, railroads, mines, oil wells, airports, ancient churches and shrines, docks, piers, libraries—all were being obliterated. World War II was coming closer and closer to us while we sang and danced and played on our little hilltop. The war in Asia, raging through the 1930s as the Japanese sought to extend their Pacific empire, and the war in Europe, fed by Hitler, Mussolini, and Stalin as they sought to extend theirs—the two wars came together in the Rome-Berlin-Tokyo pact of September, 1940.

Emboldened by this "Axis," the slaughtering heartless Japanese armies—and they *were* slaughtering and heartless—battled their way farther and farther down the Asian coastline, annexing parts of China and Vietnam, moving ever closer to the Malay Peninsula. Meanwhile Germany swept through western Europe while the Italians careened into north Africa. The French empire staggered, also the Dutch, ditto the Belgian. The biggest empire, the British, remained. Increasingly the aggressors coordinated their activities until finally only two major democratic world powers stood in their way, the British Empire and the American Republic.

The British had been fighting since 1939, and by 1941 were in a desperate position. The Americans, though nominally neutral, had been intervening more and more, not only against Germany with convoys and arms to help the embattled British Isles, but also against the Japanese, by imposing heavy embargoes on their importation of steel and oil. To Japan, this last was intolerable. And so Japan, with the encouragement of Germany, decided to strike both Britain and America simultaneously. It would be a sneak attack upon their major installations in the Pacific. Across 1,000 miles of water the Japanese would, at the same hour, without any preliminary declaration of war, bomb the military installations at Pearl Harbor and Singapore. The day chosen for the surprise attack was the day of my third birthday.

My birthday party on the afternoon of December 7, 1941, was a big event, with lots of kids and grownups in attendance. As a present, my father had told the servants to build me a large playhouse. All that remained of the work was the job of wood-burning its name above its door—it would be called "Chateau Jerry." My mother later related what happened. That evening, after my birthday party, she and my dad went to a dinner party.

We came back, and Len got his woodworking tools ready so he could make the engraving over the playhouse door. We didn't get to bed until after midnight. It seems to me that we had barely gotten to sleep when Len got up suddenly and went out onto the veranda. I followed him. I said 'What's the trouble'? He said, 'Look at that!' There was anti-aircraft fire all over the sky, the sky was all lit up, and there was this great group of bombers heading steadily over the island with no variation at all. I said, 'My, the British are really having their maneuvers tonight!' He said, 'Maneuvers, hell, this is war!' I didn't know it was war, but he did. Before long we were enduring incessant bombing by the Japanese—they bombed the island every four hours.

Suddenly we were plunged into the maelstrom. There could be no staying on in Singapore forever. The only priority now was to escape with our lives as soon as possible. We left three weeks later, on New Year's Eve, on a refrigerated cargo ship, the Orion, which miraculously escaped the mines laid in the harbor by the Japanese. Two other ships that sailed at the same time were sunk. We reached Australia, where, in Perth, according to my mother, we exhausted three had a sort of victory bath together—"Rub-a-dub-dub, three men in a tub," she recalled. Then it was on to New Zealand where we transferred to another ship, the Cefalu, and made sail for the Panama Canal; we transited it and sailed on to New Orleans on a banana boat. I first set foot on American soil on Feb. 23, 1942, a week after Singapore's surrender to the Empire of Japan. From New Orleans we rode by bus back to Washington State. "It was," observed my mother, "a long, drawn-out trip!" But we survived. We got out alive even though my reign as master of "Chateau Jerry," never even begun, was now gone with the wind.

2

Just Another Idiotic Kid

COFFEYVILLE AND LAKE SAMMAMISH,

1942–1946

The Second World War was the most wide-ranging and destructive event in history. Everywhere, millions died because of it. Millions more were wounded, disfigured, handicapped for life. Everyone alive during the war years, the early 1930s to 1945, was affected. But history's outcomes are always mixed. Not all the war's effects were bad. It led to epoch-making scientific and medical breakthroughs, it produced the breakup of oppressive empires and the liberation of subject peoples; more civilized rules of international law were established, more advanced legal tribunals founded, the United Nations was created to deter aggression and forestall the outbreak of later wars. New agencies of international economic cooperation and more enlightened racial and human-rights policies emerged.

Some effects were both bad and good. For example, the war resulted in mass migrations. Great numbers of soldiers, captives, detainees, slave laborers, and ordinary civilians were forced this way and that; the worst example in the U.S. was the internment of Japanese citizens with the vicious expropriation of their farmlands and property. But also there were voluntary large-scale movements of soldiers and sailors, military families, field hands, munitions workers, factory and transport workers. Sometimes this led to fuller and happier lives, as when the demand for munitions workers in the northern U.S. led to the resettlement there and technical education of many poor and only semi-literate Blacks from the Deep South. The war also brought many braceros from Mexico to the U.S., to fill up the workforce depleted by Americans' army service; many of them made new lives in better conditions.

What about the war's effect on the world's children? That was a misfortune with no silver linings. Many millions of them, even those never physically injured, were damaged. They were more vulnerable than older people because more susceptible and impressionable. Children during the war years, young people who were at that most formative stage of their lives, experienced turmoil, uncertainty, dislocation, separation from parents, and major disruptions of those healthy attachments and developmental processes that occur normally in a world at peace.

In a small way, my own experience exemplifies that point. I say that only to bring into focus an important aspect of my youth. Earlier I said we left Singapore on the last day of 1941. After leaving that snug nest, the only one I knew, I got moved around a lot. First to Washington, then to Kansas, then to a different place in Washington, then to another, then to still another. Moreover, I lost my father for an extended period. He, like so many others, went overseas to play the soldier. I didn't see him for more than two years, when I was five and six—the very time that many psychologists believe to be crucial in a boy's normal development. Altogether, in the eight years from 1942 to 1950, I moved five times and tried to make new friends and attachments in five different milieus. That's not the stuff of a normal childhood.

~

We left Singapore at the end of 1941 and wound up in Washington State. I was still three when I met Gramlin for the first time. Somebody photographed me with her wonderful black cocker, Rumpus. Also, maybe to create something worth remembering at that tender age, I broke the window of a passing bus with a rock. Soon my father's military commission arrived and he became a second lieutenant in the army. Promptly we moved 2,000 miles to a military base outside Coffeyville, Kansas. We were there from late 1942 to late 1943, when I was around four years old.

What I remember most are four traumatic scenes. First, I have the very scary recollection of a large, white, instructional placard in the wood shop of the Coffeyville army base. My father, for some reason, took me there. On the wall, high above a table saw, was a placard of warning that pictured an arm severed in half by the saw, gushing a waterfall of blood! That memory has stayed with me all my life. Second, there's the memory of being baby-sat by some teenage girl. With my parents gone, she got into bed with me and put her hand on my little sex organ and kept it there for a very long while. Perhaps we even fell asleep that way, I can't recall. Doubtless she was only exploring the unknown—after all, she was growing up too. Third, there was that little boy who threw something at me, I think it was a lug wrench, and hit me in the face. I remember bleeding a lot, walking home, and being treated with ice. Fourth, I remember that a carnival came to Coffeyville and that my mother and I got onto a ride called the "Octopus" that made me very dizzy and very sick, but the operator wouldn't stop it. I've hated those things ever since.

Another memory, more pleasant, is of playing kick-the-can with neighborhood kids. I loved that game and can still visualize how I'd hide behind a tree or house, wait for the right moment, then run to kick the soup can, the "base," freeing all the prisoners waiting for rescue. "Ally-ally-alsinfree!" was the cry. ("Everybody gets to come free back to the base!") That's a great game, combining suspense and derring-do with cunning and a wild foot-race. Today I couldn't run ten paces,

but today's soup cans are so miniscule I'd miss one anyway.

Beyond those fragments there's nothing left of my short Coffeyville experience. There are a few photos. There's one of me looking cute in a little man's army uniform with some kind of decoration on the shoulders;

I even wore a short tie! Maybe that was a social-class thing, something to show that my father was an officer? There's another of, I suppose, my kindergarten class, which shows me smiling broadly and wearing (unlike other boys who were wearing grubby overalls or suspenders) another sharp military-style blouse with a short tie—the little boy beside me seems offended by it.

My mother, contemplating my entry into kindergarten, faced a dilemma by virtue of my birthday being in December, three months after opening day. Should she hold me back to next September in 1944, which would install me as one of the oldest, most mature kids in my class? Or should she enter me early, making me one of the very youngest and least mature? She decided to enter me early, sealing my fate as an insecure jackass. But I don't think I minded. In all the surviving photos I see myself smiling broadly as if I didn't have a care in the world. It's a sunny smile, self-confident, the expression of a kid who has neither fears nor enemies. I think that was a carry-over from my Singapore days. Didn't we live in an okay house, and wasn't I enjoying this new life? Weren't my mom and dad still there, caring for me and engaging with me every day?

So, what can be said about those first two years in my American homeland? Well, certainly they greatly broadened my experience of life. Formerly I had lived as a pampered fledgling in a luxurious oriental nest. The voyage to America carried me to all these people called "my family," especially my grandparents. I saw the vastness of the U.S. and began taking in the common sight of white people everywhere. Kindergarten began my initiation into the lore and symbols of my country, teaching me to recognize and pledge allegiance to my flag. I heard for the first time my national anthem. I had my first experiences of schoolrooms, teachers, authorities outside the home, unrelated people I had to listen to and obey. I began to learn about baseball, trains, radios, highways, motor cars. My education in manners continued, and like other normal kids I began learning about polite interaction with others assumed to be equal to myself in rights and responsibilities. I was no longer "little Tuan." I was pretty much done with being waited on.

In late 1943 my father's new military orders came through: he was directed to return to Washington and catch a troop ship headed for New Guinea. I wouldn't see him again for 26 months. My mother and I were to wait for him with my grandparents, Fred and Nellie, outside Issaquah. My last memory of that period comes from that long trip back to Washington in late 1943, a trip by rail. It's vividly audio-visual. There I was, in my seat beside the window of the railroad car, looking up through that window at hundreds of small blue dome-shaped glass insulators whizzing by. They were on orderly racks atop tall posts running beside the track for miles and miles, and as I stared at them I heard the train's wheels rocketing along on the rails, clickitty-CLACK, clickitty-CLACK, clickitty-CLACK as it pushed on to my next destination, my next home, my next set of brand-new friends.

And my next set of clothes too, because in the northwest woods I'd look ridiculous in little-kid soldier suits showing off the rank of my daddy. My mom would have to give up dressing me that way, and forget the short military neckties too. She'd have to dress me like a regular kid, a civilian kid, a farmer's grandson. Soon I'd be in grubby overalls. I was descending in status, sinking from the hilltop of my early childhood to become just another idiotic kid smudged with the common clay. I was on my way to rural Issaquah, where one kid would rub his own do-do on my face and another force me to kiss his thingamabob.

Issaquah is about eight miles east of Seattle, spread out around one end of a very large lake, Lake Sammamish. It's on I-90, the highway from Seattle to the eastern U.S., in one of the fastest-growing urban regions of the west, famous for production of airplanes, ships, software, high-tech instruments, coffee, and many services. Most of Issaquah's buildings were constructed after 1980 as a response to all that growth. The result is that there's really no historic center to the place. Instead there are long parkways linking businesses, eateries, construction companies, car dealerships, boat-storage facilities. Seen from I-90, Issaquah presents a picture of high-rise condos blanketing the hills and then blending into tracts of expensive private homes spreading down to the lake itself. The whole place is extremely crowded. At rush hour it's a mad-house.

That scene was very different when I arrived in 1943. What's blanketed now with houses was blanketed then with trees. A few small two-lane roads ran uncertainly from the town into the forests and clearings where country people lived. Postal addresses sometimes included only the person's name, the town, and "RR," the abbreviation for "Rural Route." Fred and Nellie Newman lived on one such route. Their house stood on a forested hillside that led down toward the lake. Next-door was a gas station with just one pump; it was also a small grocery and had the area's only telephone. There were no other neighbors.

I try to remember my grandparents' house, which disappeared long ago. Let's see, there was the forest above, where I hid during that awful Thanksgiving, then the road, then the brown shingled house with its front door that my dad came through two years later with that big smile and the giant Japanese sword, and inside was the bathroom where I got my mouth washed out with soap for expressions learned at school, and then downhill behind the house was the trailer where my mother and I slept and she slapped me once for asking about girls' private parts, and behind that was the fruit tree I got spanked for whittling on, and then, trailing down farther behind the house, was the blackberry bramble which inclined another two hundred feet or so, by a steep trail, to the lake, which is where fat trout lived and got fished for by granddad smoking his pipe and me rowing.

In the front room was the 1940s "Entertainment Center," a floor-model Zenith radio. TV didn't exist; the internet hadn't been invented; and if you needed to use a phone, you went to the gas station. Is there an opportunity here for a short history lesson? That phone at the gas station wasn't just a tin can attached to a wire, but to any person born later, having to run to the gas station to use a phone would seem incredibly primitive. It's important, though, to understand that American life in the 1940s was much more rural than it is now. There were no superhighways, and very few four-lane roads. Lots of people had outhouses. Even in cities, chickens wandered about. Large areas in the U.S. had only recently received electricity. Ordinary pastimes were pursued out-of-doors much more often than now. What I call device-isolation or, humorously, "Device-o-lation," something today's kids plunge themselves into, was impossible. Life without modern electronics meant that work and play were often performed under the sun or stars. Hunting, gathering, and gardening weren't hobbies, they were, for most people, the first step in eating. You had to dry, can, pickle or freeze much of the stuff that was hunted, gathered and gardened.

The same went for butchering. I remember seeing slaughtered chickens flapping around my uncle Rowland's yard with their heads cut off, the neck stumps spattering blood; and seeing a pig with its throat cut, hanging upside-down to let the blood run out; and slaughtered animals' hearts and livers simply lying in people's kitchen sinks, slowly bleeding till they could be attended to. That was all part of my youth. Today we buy our meat pre-killed, pre-washed, pre-plucked, and neatly packaged in plastic wrap, and we buy our vegetables packaged the same way, with no worms in the radishes or dirt on the carrots. Gradually, for the sake of sanitation and convenience, we've largely unplugged ourselves from Nature and so never miss its lessons. We carry on without it, rarely wondering what it might teach us. *Mais autres fois, autres moeurs:* "But in other times, other cultural norms." That's something a lot of young people today might try to remember.

I used to wonder why my grandparents were living near Issaquah. Their own parents had been noted personalities in Thorp, and when I met them in Issaquah they still had many relatives and friends farming in the Kittitas Valley. Why had they forsaken it and gone over the mountains? It's an interesting story. My grandfather Fred, who, as I mentioned earlier, was born in 1880 and who therefore was 60 years old in 1940, was getting pretty worn out from farm work. He felt he was getting too old for it, but believed that when my dad, his son, returned from Singapore, he would take possession of the farm. So he resolved to stick it out till Len and Loree returned. But then in early 1941 they decided to stay longer in the Orient. According to my mother, "we sent him a letter saying that Len was going to sign up for another three years in Singapore, that he was going to continue on to 1944 for another term."

That did it. That, according to her, was the reason Fred sold the farm and moved to the West Side. But there's a tragic twist to the story. When, some months later, the Japanese bombed Singapore, my parents reversed course and rapidly prepared to return to the States. This led my grandfather to turn around and approach the man, Raymond Thompson, to whom he'd sold the farm. "I'd like to take back my offer to sell the ranch because my son's coming home and I think he'd like to take it and stay." And Raymond said, "You gave me your word, Fred." And Fred said, "Yeah, you're right, I did." So he stuck by it and sold the ranch. The Newman men, my mother remarked, "made a point of being good on their word." That's commendable, but I can't help reflecting that if Mr. Thompson had relented, my entire childhood would have been a lot better. Historians notice turning-points, and that certainly was one. If, that day, he'd said yes rather than no, then I'd have lived continuously for 13 years in the Kittitas Valley from kindergarten through high school, rather than bouncing around as I did. A yes or a no can change everything.

Anyway, if Fred and Nellie moved because they had to, there are good reasons why they moved to the Lake Sammamish area: their other two children, my dad's older siblings, lived in the vicinity. My dad's brother,

Rowland, lived straight across the lake with his wife, Hope, and her two sons, Bill and Claire. They too dwelt on a forested slope and owned several long red chicken coops, from which they made a living by selling eggs and chickens. Meanwhile Ruth, my father's sister, lived south of Seattle near Des Moines with her husband John Potter and their two small girls, Kay and Helen. John was a welder; Ruth had formerly been a country school-teacher and later would start a ceramics shop.

Issaquah therefore seemed a good destination for the worn-out farmer cashing his greatest asset, his farm, to support himself in his later years; two of his three children lived within range, and there'd be grandchildren and family gatherings and mutual support. Another attraction was the work available. Fred Newman was a farmer but also a skilled painter. He soon began working at the Todd Shipyards in Seattle, painting Liberty ships for the war. The pay was good for an old workman, and certainly more dependable than a farmer's income.

~

To describe my life during the later war years I need to take a very short detour into genealogy to identify my grandmother Nellie. Her mother was Sarah E. Melugin (1850-1911), and from the Scots-Irish Melugins I could, if I wished, claim European American ancestry from the early eighteenth century. There was John Melugin (1754-1835), a Revolutionary War soldier, and then later Zachariah Melugin who in 1834 founded Melugin's Grove, Illinois, on the stagecoach route between Chicago and Galena. Then still later came his great-niece Sarah (above), who in Spruce Hill, Minnesota, met Thomas J. Gordon (1843-1897), a sawyer-farmer, married him in 1873, and soon set out for the golden West to catch up with him after he'd found a place to raise a family.

Sarah Melugin Gordon with Daughters
Georgie and Nellie

Thomas J. Gordon, born in Indiana, was of Scots ancestry and descended from the Highland clan. He was the son of a prosperous miller and farmer with the same name. With his broth-ers and cousins, all armed men, he headed west in the mid 1870s, ultimately to the Kittitas Valley, where, as I explained earlier, the Native Americans were just then being subdued and driven into the Yakima Reservation. I've read some of the letters that Sarah, 26, wrote him from Minnesota before they were reunited in Thorp. Amid her accounts of the weather, crops, and family health, her longing for him is quite plain and endearing. Here's an excerpt that typifies many pioneers' letters:

Glenwood, Sept. 8, 1876

Dear Thomas, There is a lecture up to the school house tonight but I am not going. I went last night but got disgusted and came home before it was out. I think Glenwood is pleasantly situated. I like the Institute real well. The best I ever attended, and I would enjoy myself first rate if you were here my happiness would be complete. I know now from experience what I was perfectly satisfied of before that there is not much enjoyment for me that is not shared by you. Grandma says come with both teams to carry home the plums. She was out today and found some splendid ones. I am eating plums while I am writing. By the way if you can't read this just keep it until I come and I'll read it for you. I ought to be ashamed of myself to scribble so. Wouldn't some of professors hold up their hand only if they could see it but they won't. . . For now goodbye darling my darling from yours always. Sarah E Melugin P.S. September 9 it is raining this morning but the tent does not leak. Try and start as soon as you get this. Sade

I don't know many details of Sarah's journey, but it's a fact that she gave birth to my grandma Nellie in North Dakota, in 1879, before arriving in the Thorp area.

So now at last, leaving behind the Melugins and Gordons who produced her, we come to the dear woman I got to know so well when I reached Issaquah with my mom. Nellie was, as I noted, born in 1879, a year before Fred Newman, my granddad. In tiny Thorp they must have known each other well and been schoolmates before tying the knot. According to the U.S. census of 1900, Fred was then 19, living at Newman Island with his parents and younger brothers, and working as a farm laborer. He didn't own any property yet. Apart from farm work, he was painting houses and barns, and doing repair work. Probably he'd already begun courting Nellie, and it's likely that she attended the weekly reading and debating society that he'd helped to start.

Her father died in 1897, causes unknown. This was a very sad blow, but her mother had made many friends in Thorp, which had grown rapidly after JMN founded the town only three years earlier. Sarah in the 1900 census is listed as a widowed, self-employed head of household, working as

Thorp's postmistress—such a job was often given to a widow who'd lost most of her income. The Northern Pacific Railroad reached the area in 1887, and one of her postal duties was to hang sacks of outgoing mail near the tracks so that speeding trains could snatch them off without stopping. For a 19-year-old boy like my grandfather, watching his girlfriend's mom hang those mail sacks, then watching them fly away, must have provided alternative thrills, a change from all the cow-tipping and outhouse-boobytrapping. Also watching from nearby, and maybe watching Fred too, was Sarah's daughter Nellie, with a ribbon in her hair. She'd started her own small shop that sold school supplies, small toys, ribbons, candy, apples, packets of this and that.

They were in their mid 20s when they married in 1904. In their wedding photo they both look splendid. Nellie Gordon sits in a beautiful lace-topped satin dress, its collar tightly wrapped around her neck in the fashion of the day, her cuffs in lace, an elaborate corsage of baby roses above her left breast, her glossy black hair in a bouffant arrangement topped by a frilly little white lace cap. Her expression is intense: her sharp eyes seem to pierce the camera's lens straight through to its silvered photographic plate. But her lips, thin and tight, suggest dry amusement.

Fred Newman, handsomely dressed, stands beside his bride in a trim and well-tailored single-breasted worsted suit, complete with buttoned vest, a white high-collared dress shirt with white tie, a dangling gold watch fob, and a white orchid boutonniere. His glossy dark hair has been cut and perhaps dressed with pomade. His expression is unreadable. He looks straight ahead but not directly into the camera. Like his bride, he smiles very faintly. He looks poised and confident—and why shouldn't he? He's got his girl, and looks ready to take on the world.

Flash forward 40 years to the early 1940s when I first met these good folks. Here's the mental picture, here's how I remember them. Fred's large face and mobile features are now craggy with wrinkles, sunshine and age, his hair has thinned, his fingernails are caked with paint, he wears an old plaid shirt, his pants are held up by suspenders, his feet are in battered high-top shoes, he smells pleasantly of tobacco, he smokes a pipe; I watch him inject a diabetic's dose of insulin slowly into his own right thigh; he gives me the same unreadable look.

And there's grandma Nellie: her once glossy black hair, now gray, is pulled severely back and knotted at the back of her head in a bun, her ears lie flat against her head, there are wire-rimmed glasses on her nose, she is dressed in old-lady clothes—a dark dress with a thin apron on top—and old-lady shoes, scuffed and re-soled with neoprene. She sits with an old black cat, Smoky, in her lap, and with thin fingers she ceaselessly works, making a beautiful laced cloth that inches bigger and longer by the hour. She crochets, the crochet hook moving in and out, forming stitches in the yarn, chain stitches, double crochet stitches, treble crochet stitches. She looks up, she looks at me, I see those same piercing eyes, a watery blue, and the same half-smile.

For three years, 1943-46, we lived together, the four of us. Except when I was at school, going to first and second grade, I stayed at home with my grandma Nellie, who occupied herself with cooking, cleaning, ironing, gardening, berry-picking, canning, and, always, crocheting. She'd crocheted since she was a child, and I must have spent a hundred hours watching her slowly creating the most gorgeous webs of lacy tablecloths and bedspreads—all her family received them as presents. We'd chat as she worked; she told me about the Valley, things my dad had done as a kid, her dead sister Georgie, her parents and Gordon kin. All the while, her fingers worked that small silver hook through that sturdy white thread, leaving lace behind.

She loved cats, and like Gramlin spoiled them rotten. It was a family tradition to buy Dungeness crabs at Christmastime, one for each person. She'd crack and painstakingly clean hers, and then, ignoring wisecracks, feed it all to Smoky, or Grey, or whichever cat was sitting big-eyed and expectant at her feet. When she was preparing other delicacies, however, we all watched her. She was a fine cook—nothing fancy, of course, just the meat-and-potatoes stuff that farmers liked. But her biscuits were awesome, and that brown gravy she made from pan scrapings, milk, flour, and seasonings was miraculous. That gravy, if bottled and sold as, let's say, "Newman's Own," could have made us rich.

Grandma Nellie with my dad

I recall another way she made a sensation in the kitchen. My mother observed that "she could use a dish towel like a whip, snapping it at you. Sometimes if she wet the end of it she'd actually lift a chunk of hide off of you! She never did it to me, but she did it to her grandkids!" Yes, I remember how, in the kitchen, she could snap a dish towel at me, but it was usually with an impish look on her face, a little game of dodge-'em as I skipped out of reach. Towel-snapping, I suppose, must have been some weird ancient Scots art form like caber tossing.

The other thing we did together was pick blackberries. Those Himalayan blackberry vines that sprawl everywhere in western Washington are sometimes big as a house and full of nasty briars, but we'd head into them with buckets and not stop till dark. Berry-picking, like fishing, is one of our tribe's oldest pastimes. It's very absorbing, it's something that draws you in and makes you ignore everything else. It's as though you were thinking . . . "Hmmm. . . First this berry, then that one, then that one over there—such a nice big one! Now, where's another? Oh, *there!* . . ." In my mind's eye there forms a vision of the Scottish Highlands at the height of berry season. There on a hillside are my Gordon ancestors, engrossed in berry-picking, their kilts filthy and stained. They look up with annoyance at that rackety Battle of Culloden going on over yonder. The noise, those blood-curdling yells and clangs of metal, are such a distraction from the business at hand. "Shut up over there! Can't you see we're picking berries?"

My grandfather Fred worked in Seattle, painting warships at what was called the Port of Embarkation, a complex of shipbuilding operations, warehouses and docks. My mother was a secretary for the Port's fire department, so every morning they got into that old black Ford and drove to Mercer Island, then across the floating bridge spanning Lake Washington, then along Rainier and Jackson Avenues down to the Seattle waterfront. They got along splendidly; my mother loved in him the same boyish openness and humor she'd found in my dad. Sometimes on hot days when they drove home after work they'd stop off for a cold beer, "and then," remembered my mother, "we'd chew sen-sen like crazy on the way home because Mother deeply disapproved of all alcohol! And Dad—darn his hide!—would open the door, put his lunch bucket on the counter, say 'I'm home, Mother!' then head off to the boathouse to get the boat ready so we could go fishing! But I would have to go in and change my clothes, have to be around Mother Newman. I *knew* she could smell the beer!"

I remember his fingernails, caked with gray paint. He worked all day with a giant eight-inch brush full of heavy oil paint. (Latex paint wasn't invented till later, and wouldn't have protected ships anyway.) Gray paint, even though he cleaned his hands with turpentine at the end of the day, had built up under each fingernail, layer by layer, till it was maybe an eighth of an inch thick. Sometimes I'd watch him scraping it out with his pocketknife, but that was hard to do completely if you'd labored all day with paint drying on your hands, soaking your fingers—I don't think painters used gloves, because they'd have needed a new pair every day.

He was amazingly deft with a paint brush. During lunch-time he'd offer to paint the fingernails of pretty secretaries. "With what?" they'd ask. Drawing forth his huge paintbrush, he'd say, "With this!" Sometimes the girls, on a dare, would let him do it. My mother witnessed how perfectly he could do the job. He was a perfectionist, and this typified it. But it also revealed the joker in him. This was the teasing grandpa who played with five-year-old me the silly game of "smash the finger," daring me to bash his pinkie before he could whip it off the table's edge. This was the same character who had sneaked red pepper into his homemade blackberry wine,

then generously offered it to his four brothers when they popped by to visit. An old guy told me that "your grandfather was the joker of the clan, the one who you knew must have put the burr in your saddle-blanket or the dead skunk in your bed-roll. Used to write his brother Jess love letters and sign the names of the ugliest girls in Thorp."

I said he was precise and good with his hands, and I noted earlier his skill at displaying fruits and vegetables at the county fair. He also pursued a metalworking hobby, picked up as a blacksmith's son. He fashioned letter openers, brooches, and rings out of various metals, then gave them away. I remember him making me a very nice little ring, fashioned from silver and formed to resemble a small belt with a copper buckle. He also taught me how to garden, grow beans, tomatoes, and squash—there are pictures of me standing beside him in the garden, holding up vegetables. He took time with me, showing me how to do things, just working away and expecting me to remember what I saw.

My most important lesson, though, was how to fish. Sometimes I'd go down to the lake by myself with worms from the garden, and fish for perch and sunfish. Still better was going out with him in the rowboat to fish for rainbow trout. We didn't have an engine; we rowed the boat, trolling glittering lures called "Jackaloids." We rowed slowly, each of us pulling a weighted lure with a worm on a hook at the trailing end of the line. We'd wait, and we'd wait. My grandfather would smoke his pipe and watch his pole tip, and we'd chat, or, more often, not; sometimes we just sat still, listening to water lapping on the hull. My mother often came along, too. "'Bout time to catch a fish," she'd say. "Sure is," was the response. We all three loved fishing and nearly always caught a few trout. My grandmother Nellie only came out fishing once, I think. If she'd caught anything, it would have gone to Smoky.

My main support through the war was my mom. She was at the center of my universe. In fact I now see that Loree—she was then less than 30 years old—was at the center of several universes revolving around her—her mother's, and my dad's, and mine. We were all in her spell, relying on her strength and capacity. When she was very old, I urged her to write her memoirs. Here's how she remembered our relationship during those war years:

Jerry was a great kid. He was absolutely truthful, he would never lie to me. He was loving, thoughtful, but much less capable than he later turned out to be—I never dreamed that he would turn out to be a miniature of his father and grandfather. For fun, we skated, we swam, we fished, we went to movies. I would read him lots of stories. We'd read Pooh, and the House at Pooh Corner, and Charlotte's Web; and we got into cowboy books. We would go on weekends to Vassa Park, rent skates, just skate around and around in the rink for about three hours. At that time he was my only child, but it wasn't the sort of relationship I'd had as an only child with Mom; my relationship with Mom wasn't as close.

Seeing her reference to Winnie-the-Pooh reminds me of how, changing her voice into a high squeak, she *inhabited my Pooh Bear*, asking me pooh-like questions, giving me pooh-like advice, making me laugh. I still have that bear right here on my desk. He's survived all these years. I've never given him up despite everything else, the moving-about, the changes in life. It's a strange thing, a sudden plunge into mystery and wonder, to look now, after thinking these thoughts, at his face, gently smiling, buttons sewed on for eyes. I stare at him and he stares right back, smiling. That little Pooh still has my mother in him. With love we exchange a nod.

Maybe, other than Pooh, the memory that best symbolizes for me that special closeness is the recollection of a car trip over Snoqualmie Pass one winter, to go see Gramlin in Spokane. Very distinctly I remember how frightening that journey was for me. It was snowing very hard, and it was at night. I don't remember other cars on the road, just us. My mother was driving slowly, and yet the road ahead was barely visible through the blinding snow dashing against our small windshield. The road itself was deep in drifting and blowing snow, its shoulders were piled high with snow-banks. I was very cold despite the car's  primitive heater. We were in that ancient rattletrap of a Ford, so old that its accelerator was a hand-operated lever under the steering wheel near the "spark" lever. The thin windshield wipers were beating hard at every second, trying to clear the snowflakes swarming against the windshield. I can still hear the beat of those wipers now, and through the blizzard I can even see the tiny abandoned roadhouse on the left side of the road after we'd gone well past the Summit. I was scared, she must have been scared. There were no weather reports, so my mother likely had no idea, when we left Issaquah, that we were heading into such a terrible blizzard. On that trip over the Summit her nerves and steady hands were our only protection. That experience, I suppose, helped in its own little way to cement the lifetime indebtedness I feel toward her.

Something we always did together as a family was listen to the radio. We'd listen, all four of us, to that big, upright, polished wooden Zenith radio with its semicircular dial. We listened to thrillers like "The Inner Sanctum," with its eerily squeaking door, and "The Green Hornet," about a crime-fighter in green overcoat and mask. We couldn't *see* the action, so we *imagined* it—rather a good thing, no? On Saturday mornings I always got myself ready for "Let's Pretend," a fairytale kiddie show with a lilting musical signature introduction. But, best of all, after dinner we'd listen to an episode of "The Lone Ranger." How did the introduction go? Aha! There it is, complete with sound! I find it online, and listen. There in the background at breathtaking tempo is the 'William Tell Overture,' and then amid trumpets comes the wild sound of a horse's galloping hooves, and then comes the famous call to arms in that announcer's unforgettable baritone voice:

A fiery horse with the speed of light, a cloud of dust and a hearty Hi-Yo Silver! The Lone Ranger! ... With his faithful Indian companion Tonto, the daring and resourceful masked rider of the plains led the fight for law and order in the early western United States! Nowhere in the pages of history can one find a greater champion of justice! Return with us now to those thrilling days of yesteryear, when from out of the past come the thundering hoof beats of the great horse Silver! The Lone Ranger rides again! "Come on, Silver! Let's go, big fellah! Hi-Yo, Silver, Away!!!"

It carries me away again just to think of it, just to hear it all again. Such a long time ago. My dear old granddad and grandma and mom, all gone. I'm surprised as tears come to my eyes. I sniffle. I think myself a sentimental old fool.

Speaking of which, the first time I *failed to fix stupid* and made an epic fool of myself was at our family Thanksgiving in 1945, when I was six. The cooks had prepared the feast and we were just about ready to sit down to it. There were twelve of us. The countertop was covered with food, and "resting" in its broiler pan was a huge baked turkey, so huge that the pan had been placed across the seats of two wooden dining chairs in the kitchen; sitting there beside it was the pot of hot gravy. At last it was time to place all the chairs around the dining table. Jerry, the little helper, assisted. Unthinkingly he pulled a chair from under the turkey pan, which fell to the floor, clattering loudly and spilling the bird and giblet gravy all over the place. At which, considering it prudent to absent himself from dining activities, he bolted out the front door and into the woods. Cold, hungry, and drenched with rain, he stayed there till well past dark. At last he crawled back to face the odium and horror of his act—that, and the charitable amusement of his elders who'd wisely chosen to let him punish myself. He'd been an idiot, and it was good to let the lesson sink in. I think I cried into my pie.

The other people at that dinner included my Uncle Rowland and Aunt Hope, who lived across Lake Sammamish from us. Rowland, my dad's older brother, was nice but somehow faded and wistful. He'd left college when only a few credits short of graduation, leaving my grandparents unhappy. I remember his wan smile and thinning hair. His wife, Hope—everybody called her "Hopie"—was very pretty and very nice to me. I think I developed a little crush on her, though I was barely six. I've always liked older women. Younger ones, too.

Hopie had two sons, adopted by Rowland—Claire, the older one, was calm and humorous, Bill was a little menacing. But they were nice to me, their young cousin. Anyway, one time, in her kitchen, I watched Hopie churning butter, making butter from cream in a churn, and smiling at me. I didn't know she was going to discard those smiling teeth, but false teeth were extremely common and she wanted some. She told me she'd consulted a dentist about false teeth, so, later, I brashly announced the fact to a rather large band of elders—we were on my first elk hunting trip in the Cascade mountains. It was evening and everybody was standing around the campfire. I said, "Aunt Hopie is gonna get falsies." Everybody laughed, even Hopie, who was there too, because "falsies" was the word for those rubber things that ladies stuck into their bras. I pretended not to know that, but I did. I pretended to look surprised at everybody laughing. That was my first joke, or at least the first I remember. Now I see, lit by that campfire, a cloven hoof, a sign of future mischiefs.

～

We were in wartime, of course, so I had to have model fighter planes, a dirigible for observation, a decoder ring for top-secret spy stuff, some kind of a bayonet in a scabbard. I didn't share my equipment with other kids because there weren't any near where we lived. I did attend grade school in Issaquah, going through the first and second grades, but don't remember a thing about it. That suggests that I experienced no connection with other children. I suppose it's partly because I lived out in the timbered boondocks, away from playmates, but I also think Issaquah was somewhat resistant to newcomers. Unlike Coffeyville, there was no swirl of soldiers and military people moving in and out. Anyway, I lived there near Lake Sammamish for such a short time that I didn't have much opportunity to break into the pattern of established friendships. I was a newbie, and to make friends would take more time than I had.

Maybe that's why my only school memory is one of flinging bark at other boys during recess. The school area was forested, and lying around on the dark forest floor beneath the evergreens were heavily rotted cedar logs. Those logs were so spongy that you could dig your hands into one and pull off great clods of wet, rotting red cedar bark. These, it seemed obvious, were meant to throw at someone. And that's what we did. We threw clods of bark at each other. That was our extracurricular activity. Do I seem regretful about the absence of something like soccer? Yes, of course. But oldsters in every era are envious of things they came too early to enjoy. I'm envious when I see the travels, the opportunities, the sports activities and learning possibilities, the myriad options for having fun that today's kids can enjoy. My mind boggles at its own undernourishment! And yet, never knowing what we were missing, we cared nothing about the future and probably were better for it. Envy eats up contentment. And so, all by myself, I've worked it out that ignorance is bliss.

Living in the boondocks, I rode a yellow school bus. On one occasion I got off it with another kid who lived in what I remember as a sort of grotty place under overhanging trees—I think there was a kind of trailer park there. We were going to play, but I remember that he first went into an outhouse and came out with a gob of his own feces on some toilet paper. Suddenly, before I could stop him, he rubbed it onto my nose! Charming. I can't remember whether he laughed or thought this some rich joke, but I failed to see the humor and declined later invitations.

Another experience was worse. There was a big kid on the bus, maybe five years older than I, named Whitey. He invited me to play, so we got off the bus near his place; I was going to walk home afterwards. But we didn't play. Instead he led me into the woods, let down his pants, and commanded me to suck his penis. I was terrified. I touched it with my lips, then spun and ran away to the road and back to my own house. He didn't follow me. Naturally I told my mother and she was fit to be tied. Enraged, she stormed up the road toward Whitey's house. I can't remember what happened then, but I do know she raised hell with the sheriff and that Whitey was made to pay for that wretched act. Probably he rotted away in jail long ago for something worse.

So, what was the fruit of my delightful early school experiences? Not much. I learned to read, calculate, and be wary of other kids. As I said earlier, I think I was damaged a little by having no siblings, no good friends, no lasting classmates. The war, while it lasted, left many children rootless. I certainly didn't suffer as much as millions of others did. But child psychologists say that as a kid develops from ages two to six, it's important to learn to cooperate with other kids; that's the period at which one learns basic "people skills." I didn't interact much with other kids during that period, and suspect this helps explain why, later, I tended to be either a loner or a director, a go-it-alone guy or a supervisor. Later I did learn to cooperate and be a team member, but the early bouncing-around left me unpracticed at it.

Anyway, to sum up, in those three years I learned a lot, mostly from my relatives, while we dwelt there by the lake. I also learned something about the war and the big, wide world. By 1945 I knew that the Italians were beaten, the Germans defeated, the Japanese bombed to smithereens. I must have learned something too about the American political system, if only because I remember Franklin Delano Roosevelt's death in the spring of 1945 and the way my mother and grandparents were devastated by it. We learned of it by a phone call somebody made to Bill Lewis, the gas station guy next door.

That year, 1945, was the last year of the war, and I will never forget the very last day of that year, New Year's Eve. That was the day of my father's homecoming. Home from the war! Home from the Far East came my conquering soldier dad!

～

What was he like now? What was I missing? I'd lost touch with him, but my mother did her best to keep his image alive. I think she sensed that things might be difficult when he came home, and that, while he wouldn't ignore me, he would most likely plunge into making up for lost time, building a new career. I watched her write him nearly every day, and she read out his letters to the three of us.

Those letters are now lost, but I did find the big packet of letters he wrote to Gramlin. They begin in November 1944, after he arrived by ship in New Guinea, and they describe the devastation he'd witnessed already. He was 32, a captain in the army, chosen to lead the Civil Affairs Detachment because of his prior experience with oriental peoples and languages. Later he was assigned to the Base Surgeon's Office, to work with other veterinarians. There he cared for military animals, especially horses, and helped control livestock diseases in areas occupied by American forces, but his main work was as a meat inspector, checking all fresh meat, eggs, dairy products, and frozen and canned foods brought in by ship—all the food, in other words, that was destined for consumption by American soldiers. He mentioned examples of his work: he condemned rice that had been spoiled by tropical rains, and outlawed the eating of chicken that had thawed too long before being cooked—it was heavily peppered, so no one could tell by smell whether it had turned bad. To be on the safe side, he ordered it thrown out.

Nearly 30 letters survive from 1945 alone. In them I encounter a meditative dimension I didn't often see later. Something that absorbed him was the issue of leadership in war, and leadership in general. Leadership, in his mind, meant training, and performance with very few mistakes. This led him to several reflections on the relationship between morale and work:

Morale is one of the greatest factors in war and morale is impossible to maintain if even forgivable mistakes are made. When things are moving, morale always goes up. Stagnation is hard on morale. Have a job or make one, even if it means cutting the buttons off your shirt and sewing them on again for 3 or 12 times. You're busy then, even if it doesn't get you any place.

Work is valuable even if it's meaningless—he taught me that, and I believe it. I also heard him jokingly commend "sewing buttons on a broom handle" as preferable to idleness, and I believe that too. Writing Gramlin, he tried to make his letters amusing:

> There is Spam in the States for I saw it, otherwise I would swear it was all in New Guinea. Sometimes we think we are getting a nice breaded pork chop but when they toss it on the mess kit it always turns out to be camouflaged Spam. . . We live in tents and have cots with mosquito net suspended over the top. I'll be stoop shouldered if I am not careful! . . . I'm plenty fed up with washing clothes. I told Punk [a pet name for Loree] that I'd resign immediately when I get home. We use our helmets for a wash basin.

From New Guinea he went to Guadalcanal and viewed battlegrounds of some of the bloodiest struggles of the war. Then he went to the Philippines, recently retaken by the U.S., where he visited a cemetery full of American graves.

> I felt miserable that our boys had to fight and die there. I am glad to have seen those places for it makes one realize what has taken place in the past. News reels can only show the half of it. . . . . It made my heart grow very heavy to see the rows of white crosses and a name—some unknown. Just to chase these yellow —[word omitted]—out of here. A lost finger alone would be too much and yet there has to be prices paid as great as lives. Best I not get started.

I see he declined to use what probably was the expression "yellow bastards," but he was never one of those blowhard patriots who run down foreigners and trumpet American greatness. He did see enough of the world, though, to appreciate our country as one of unusual freedom and opportunity, where the little guy had a chance to build a happy life. To him one proof of this lay in the successful struggle of his own forebears, the Newman family. They'd been authentic American pioneers. "Hardship and pioneering made America as great as it is because it was not easy," he remarked; and he added more generally, "Some of our greatest people have become great because of hardships."

Time passed, and the war progressed: "The war news the last few days sounds very good, both on the European fronts and here. It is a slow costly process regardless." As he contemplated the war's end, he began thinking of what to bring my mother as a gift. There were few attractive options, as shops were closed and destruction lay everywhere. Then he came up with the idea of bringing her something improvised from the military supplies available to him. It made me smile to discover this:

> While I think of it I'd like to have Loree's measurements on the q.t. [i.e., on the quiet, without her knowing about it]. I think I remember them correctly but I don't want to take any chances. Mayhap I may get hold of an equipment parachute and I'd like to have it made into a dressing gown. Think it would be nice? I'd keep it until I came home and surprise her. I may not be able to get hold of one but I have seen the material and it is very nice. It's just an idee [idea].

That inspiration to *make a silk gown from a parachute* is so very typical of the man I later knew as my dad. He was a brilliant improviser. In another letter he tells about how he abandoned the discomfort of his regulation military cot by building a bed-frame from 2x4's, then cutting into strips the blown inner-tube of a large vehicle, then weaving them crossways together into a dandy mattress to stretch over the frame! So comfy! And so very like him.

The war against Japan ended on September 2, 1945, when General MacArthur received Japan's surrender aboard the USS Missouri in Tokyo Bay. Eight days later my dad suggested that he might be re-stationed: "Maybe I will be going to Japan shortly. I would sure like to go." In fact he left Manila late that month, heading toward Japan, his ship dodging typhoons and accompanied by destroyers to clear the mines that were thick in Japanese waters. On the way he contemplated what he would do as soon as he was discharged: "I'm thinking that a person had better make hay while the sun shines. I'd give a lot to have a going business to go back to or at least have the money to start one."

Arriving in Yokohama harbor in early October, he described the desolation wrought by American bombing. He was astonished at how precisely some city blocks had been obliterated, while others—those with warehouses which he thought the Americans had preserved for their own use after a Japanese surrender—still stood whole and well-preserved. He traveled to look at the Imperial Palace: the areas around it were totally destroyed, but the palace and grounds were undamaged. "Bet the Emperor shook in his boots when he saw how close our bombers would come and how accurately they could bomb what they wanted to."

His duties were fewer in Japan, and he even found himself eligible for a week's vacation. A luxury hotel on the shoulder of Mt. Fuji was taken over by American forces and then used by army officers for a week of rest and recuperation. My father was able to go, and in late October he described his 40-mile drive with into the mountains. "Really, Mom, this is a beautiful country." He thought sadly of my mother: "I've missed her so much up here. In fact it has made me extremely lonely being up here and not having her. Things are so beautiful that it seems a shame that I should be here without her being able to enjoy them too."

By December he was anxiously forecasting his discharge. Already his mind was racing about his return to civilian life. He wanted a newer car, and my mother had recently written about buying one when he got home: "Cars, from what I hear, are plenty high yet and that sounds like a good buy at 800 or even $900. Punky says she might be able to get $400 for our old crate."

My parents' relationship changed because of the war. She'd grown up strong and independent, working in high school and earning her way in college, but then after marriage she'd become more reliant on him. She really grew up fully during those 30 months near Lake Sammamish, raising me, driving back and forth every day to work in Seattle, corresponding with my father and her own mother, and handling the family business, which now included scouting for a car. She was 29 when the war ended.

My dad, seeing all this, was discovering her maturity, loyalty and dependability. Noting how capably she was running things in his absence, he sat there on his bunk in Japan and commented to Gramlin: "Just between us," he wrote, "I had no idea how competent she is—sounds kinda funny but it's the truth. She has handled everything & I mean everything in the same way I would have. I liked being depended upon but it was by no means essential. I told her, too, that she could keep the books and earn the money for the family & I'd do the housework and cooking when I get back. I explained however that that didn't mean I could have the babies too!"

By early December 1945 he'd already received, via ship, his Christmas presents. "Received my Xmas box from Punkins yesterday. It was a grand box of eatments, socks from Jerry all wrapped fancy by him and a little booklet of pictures of Loree and Jerry and the folks!" I smile as read this, reminded of another of his charming characteristics. At birthday and Christmas gatherings, when opening his gifts, no matter what they were or who they came from, he was always delighted! He'd laugh, he'd rave, he'd hold the thing up for all to see. He sensed how important it is to make a happy fuss, and this made him just about everybody's favorite birthday boy.

Dr. Major Leonard L. Newman was discharged much earlier than he'd hoped. The last thing I remember about that period of my life came on New Year's Eve, the last day of 1945, when he came home to us. It was at night. I'd just turned seven. I remember him entering the front door of that little house, squatting down and holding out his arms, and me running to fold myself into them. My dad was home, and the war was over! And that's not all! Look, he'd brought postage stamps for me from the Philippines, and funny round coins with square holes in them from China, and that fantastic big officer's sword from Imperial Tokyo itself! Bliss! Absolute bliss! The war was over and MY DAD WAS HOME!

But there'd be a different sleeping arrangement in the trailer that night. I'd spent half my life sleeping near my mother; I can't remember what I made of my banishment, but, knowing my mother's ways, I know she coached me to accept it. Both parents, throughout their lives, could see around corners, they were excellent planners and near-perfectionists in the execution of their plans. They were a great working pair, wonderfully matched. In spite of that dreadful war I was a very lucky little boy.

3

Maverick Tendencies

CHEHALIS, 1946-1950

In early 1946 my mom and dad and I moved to Chehalis, about 80 miles south of Seattle. It's a small town, about midway on the road between Seattle and Portland; on its east side it stands at the base of low, forested hills. The Chehalis River runs nearby; the Cowlitz River is just south. It's a pretty area. My dad was anxious to begin a veterinary practice, and found one for sale there. He was 34 years old, and felt he needed to make up for lost time. We moved to a small house in an old residential area just a block from the schools.

My parents immediately began remodeling the garage, to make a small operating theater for spaying dogs and cats. But although they built a little clinic, most of my dad's calls came from out-of-town farmers, wanting him to cure their sick cows, horses, and sheep. I remember accompanying him on some of these doctoring calls, watching him work. Sometimes after examining a cow's eyes and tongue he'd ask the farmer to help him prop it up it from a "foundered" or lying-down position to rest on its "brisket"— new words for me then. I'd watch him treat cows for "milk fever," a common ailment. He cured sicknesses like "mastitis," an udder infection, and "leptospirosis," a bacterial disease. He would surgically repair prolapsed uteruses, deliver calves, and perform rumenotomies in which he'd have to cut into the cow's abdominal wall to remove pieces of ingested wire or other foreign materials. Much of this was life-or-death stuff, and he was good at it. I quickly came to understand that a veterinarian is certainly a real full-fledged doctor, having to know all about anatomy and symptoms and diseases, but with the additional disadvantage of treating patients who couldn't tell him how they felt.

I went along sometimes when he was testing cattle for Bangs disease, drawing blood from their neck veins into a test tube. Often they objected to this, so it required courage and strength to complete it. A cow is a big, heavy animal that can crush a man against a stanchion or break his skull, snap his bones, with a quick kick or a jerk of the head. I have a very scary memory of how, at my father's sudden command, I rapidly scrambled high up a ladder to escape the enraged bull that had broken loose and was charging him below.

I admired everything he did. He was good with both head and hands, and, it seemed, could solve any problem. He was respected, he was very serious about his work, he was extremely concerned not only for an animal's health but also for its comfort and freedom from pain. When, many years later, he died, clients who had known him for years praised him to the skies for his skills, friendliness, honesty and reliability.

Maybe the most important part of his support for me lay in the fact that he was, after all, a medical doctor. When necessary, he'd practice his medicine on family members, removing splinters, swabbing our sore throats with some ghastly purple stuff he used on dogs, dressing our scrapes and wounds, checking our ears with his otoscope. But that does remind me of his "joker" strain.

One day, having nothing better to do, I lay face-up on my bed, being the typical seven-year-old idiot, flipping a dime into the air and trying to catch it in my mouth. Of course that was a silly thing to do, but consider my age! At seven you reach the silliest age before hitting eight. So there I was, flipping the dime into the air and trying to catch it in my mouth, flipping and missing, flipping and missing, till I actually *did* catch the dime and *accidentally swallowed it!* Choking, I couldn't get it back up again; it went all the way down. Alarmed, I ran to the doctor—Doctor Newman. What would the dime do to me?

Very grave he looked. This was a serious situation. Foreign bodies could be toxic. Coinage was never meant to be swallowed. Dimes, though not in all cases fatal, had to exit the system. A dime could be especially tricky because of the intestinal cavities where it might get trapped. Surgery, a grisly procedure, would be required unless by a lucky chance I'd discover it in my stool. Looking worried, he disappeared into his surgery and came out with a new pair of rubber gloves and a bottle of a bathroom deodorant, "Sweet-Aire." He presented these to me with all the solemnity of a physician handing over a radiology report. Slowly and with emphasis he instructed me to inspect, minutely, every hour and every day, any and all deposits. That dime must be found.

I was only seven! Feverishly with my rubber gloves and Sweet-Aire I searched for days but never found that dime. Is it still in me? Will it, before I die, come out my elbow or neck, like one of those lost sewing needles in "Ripley's Believe It Or Not"? Is it trapped in one of those three sharp turns we see in diagrams of the colon? Immersed in my labors, I looked long and hard but never found that dime. In my imagination, however, I can hear my father's muffled chortling behind a closed door. When I listen harder, I hear my grandfather joining in.

~

My mother continued to be the most important person in my life. We shared, only with each other, little things like a taste for salt on watermelon, and a love of black licorice—I still remember how she'd gleefully stick out her blackened tongue after she'd eaten some. She tried to promote my development, signed me up for piano lessons, which I failed at, and for cornet lessons, ditto, and became a Cub Scout den mother for me. But she was busy, too. She was my dad's right-hand helper, she was dispatching him here and there as he traveled about, she was assisting with the small-animal surgeries in the evenings, doing the bookkeeping and secretarial work. She was also keeping house and attending to my grandmother, Gramlin, who, now divorced again and moving to Chehalis to be with us, needed help finding a house to rent and a job. She had to take care of me, to buy my school clothes and shepherd me into the third grade, and, last but not least, she had to prepare for the arrival of my baby sister, Lynn.

They didn't lose a minute in finding me a playmate. Lynn was born on 22 September 1946, almost exactly nine months after my dad's return. The family story is that at her arrival I suggested she be carried back to the hospital, but that's a joke. I'm sure my folks did all the right stuff to enlist my readiness to share the nest. They were no fools, they knew the facts of sibling rivalry and understood that Lynn's birth might be destabilizing for me. I, the crown prince of the household, was only rebuilding my fealty to the king when out popped this princess! And such a sweet, small, and helpless little thing she was, too.

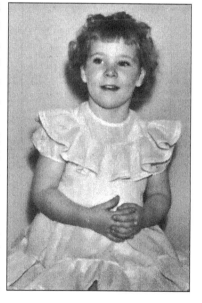

I was nearly eight years older than Lynn. Certainly the early photos of us show me happily participating in her care, and smiling broadly through the big gap in my front teeth. I didn't see her as a gate-crasher. My ruling attitude toward her combined amusement with affection. I felt protective toward her and liked being her big brother. When she was a tiny tot I shared in the glee over her mangled pro-nunciation of her first words—"showsie," for example, was her word for "flower." I indulged her mistakes and tantrums, and when she was older I most generously shared thousands of valuable suggestions for arranging her life. She was my first student, so with her I began training to fix stupid!

Gramlin took up residence just a few blocks away. She'd come to din-ner, enjoying her grandchildren, and she often invited me to visit her af-ter school, even trying to teach me how to play the piano—I remember

.learning the 1946 Hoagy Carmichael hit "Buttermilk Sky," though I could sing it a lot better than play it. So there we were in Chehalis, a family of five, and we continued our friendly relations with all the rest in the clan. In 1947, when I was eight, I went back to Lake Sammamish to spend the summer with my Uncle Rowland and Aunt Hope, and my cousins Bill and Claire. I was being trained for work. Here's me in the first non-Santa Claus letter I ever wrote:

> Dear Mom, Pop, and Lynn, . . . <u>Working</u> <u>in</u> <u>the</u> <u>woods</u>, cutting, sawing, chopping trees, & hauling wood, <u>I've earned $5.00</u>. I feed the chickens, pigs, goat, cats, dog, cow, calf, turkeys, & myself. . . I didn't write because I've been busy from 9-5 in the woods. After that we eat then do chores. By then I'm tired out. Today I'm going to pick blueberries if it doesn't rain. I've went to my first merchandise auction. We go swimming about twice a week, sometimes 3 or 4. I am getting homesick. Please write. Yours, truly, Love, devotedly Yours, Yours, Sincerely Yours, Jerry. P.S. I'm growing mucles cutting wood.

I see my youthful self was a decent speller and punctuator. Even the misspelled 'mucles' suggests familiarity with the right word. I also like the stab at humor, though it looks desperate. And what about the rest of my family—my grandparents, and my Aunt Ruth and her husband and kids? They were now all living together. With the war over, Fred and Nellie had decided to move to Des Moines, south of Seattle, where my Aunt Ruth and Uncle John lived with their two daughters. My cousin Kay was about my age, cousin Helen a couple years younger. Kay was flirtatious, highly gregarious, a risk-taker; Helen was more cautious, reserved, a calming influence. Their mother, Ruth, had bequeathed good looks to both daughters—in her youth she'd been, I think, a Rodeo Princess at the Ellensburg Rodeo. Uncle John came from back east and I liked him a lot. He had a square face and short hair, which he wore in a crew cut. He smelled a little of burnt metal because he was a welder. He was a master at grilling salmon, the main delicacy of the Pacific Northwest—I can see his outdoor grill and the lemon butter sizzling on a fileted king salmon. Both girls shared the same distinctive and unforgettable laugh they inherited from him, a kind of long, descending whinny—I chuckled when hearing all three of them laughing, it was like a chorus of horses.

I suppose a sociologist would say our whole family was, technically, very lower-middle-class—in fact you'd call it working-class, if middle-class status implies higher education, urban living, and mercantile or professional pursuits. The whole clan contained no wealthy sophisticates, literati, high-toned urban professionals. The only two people in it with college degrees were Aunt Ruth, who'd made it through Ellensburg's Normal School, and my father, who went through WSU and became a board-certified veterinarian with a teaching post. (My mother later finished her B.A.) All the rest, including my grandparents, would be classified as workers engaged in farming, industrial painting, metalworking, sales, or housekeeping. Certainly this isn't to suggest they were unintelligent. They rarely sat around talking about books, music, or foreign languages, but they were all sensible and discerning. With each other's help they managed to live decent and productive lives, put away some money, and enjoy their time on earth. That's a testament to the reality in those days of the American Dream.

Living in Chehalis, I sadly missed the grandparents who'd been so important to me, but Fred and Nellie would occasionally drive south from Des Moines and stay a week or so. Fred decided that our house needed painting, so in July 1948 he packed up his brushes and buckets, and, with Nellie, headed down to Chehalis. He'd see that we'd get a good paint job, and maybe thought he and my mom, and maybe his son too, could sneak out for a beer without Nellie taking notice of it.

There was a shed in our back yard where he stored his house paint. That shed became the seat of a searing childhood memory. One hot July afternoon, watching him clean his brushes, I sat down on a bench for perhaps ten minutes before experiencing a slightly tingling sensation on my fanny. I got up, looked at myself, looked at the bench I'd been sitting on, and discovered that I'd been sitting in a pie pan full of turpentine! Turpentine, if you've sat in it, is something you'll never sit in again. The burn literally sneaks up on you, then sets you on fire! There are, um, sensitive tissues in that area. I've never figured out whether Grandpa knew I was sitting in that turpentine—he claimed he didn't, but I don't know. Remembering that red pepper he'd snuck into his brothers' wine, I'm wondering still.

Unfortunately I never had time to quiz him more because a few days later he died. Dead at 68. My mother told the sad story in her memoirs. He'd finished painting the house, and afterwards wanted to celebrate by going out to a movie and eating some ice cream. My mother went with him—they went alone, renewing the bond they'd established during the war years. After the movie she remonstrated, though unsuccessfully, about the ice cream, as he was diabetic. That might have been what killed him:

> Mother Newman in the middle of the night called Leonard into the bedroom. She said, "Leonard, your dad is having a heart attack!" Poor Len was in the position of giving artificial respiration until Dad died. The doctor came right away. He saw that Len had done about all he could do, even though Dad had not died quite yet. It was very hard on Len.

Indeed it was very hard on us all. Fred Newman was the only Valley Patriarch I ever knew. His sudden death came like a tree falling on me. He was buried under a modest stone in the Thorp cemetery alongside his father and four brothers. Nellie joined him 18 years later, in 1966. I remember the occasion very well. I remember the wind loudly whipping the lone evergreens up there on that knobby hill. The sun was bright, the sky cloudless. There was a big turnout of mourners from the area, ordinary folk wearing dark suits and dresses, looking stolid, looking sad. Now, in my old age, I go to that cemetery every Memorial Day to tend the graves of the Newmans. There are a lot of them, and each spring the job seems a little harder. I walk uncertainly as I carry big buckets of water from the nearby irrigation ditch. With clippers in hand, and bunches of cut flowers, I pause, I linger at the gravestone of Nellie and Fred Newman, remembering that old brown house by Lake Sammamish, her dish towel snapping at me, his paint-caked fingernail vanishing from the table's edge before I can hit it. And I kneel at the grave of Leonard and Loree Newman, feeling a little closer to them, but also feeling helpless. In that cemetery I always feel profound helplessness.

~

Chehalis put me on track toward a normal childhood. So far, I'd lived almost entirely in a world of seniors more or less unconsciously shaping my morality toward helpfulness, respect, tolerance, and self-restraint. Though Christianity was the family religion, it was rarely mentioned in polite company and I'm glad of that; I later discovered how ruinous some Christian educations can be. Look at T. H. Huxley, Darwin's "bulldog" propagandist. His evangelical youth nearly wrecked him and he hated it afterwards. He was, of course, the inventor of the word "agnosticism."

In Chehalis I suddenly acquired a world of peers, other kids my age, and began to learn from them. There were my immediate neighborhood friends—Jerry Nichols next door, and Dean Hackett on the corner beyond, and Buster Sommers on the same block. There were the other boys in my third-grade class, and in my fourth, fifth, and sixth: Robin Kennicott, Burdett Skinner, Gerald Hobson, Tommy Severns, Chuck Downey, Ronald Harper, Orville Something, Harold Something. Those were important characters who'd assist my development.

Play, of course, is a boy's main way of learning life's lessons at that age. I would play with the neighbor kids in my own backyard, or climb the apple tree over at Hackett's, or ride my bike with the others around the odd-shaped block we lived on, or even, on a dare, coast all the way down the hill from the top of First Street, where there was that Ghirardelli poster on a wall, down past my own house without ever slowing down or applying the brakes.

Other games were safer—marbles, for example. Lots of kids played marbles in that age before TV, smartphones and Xboxes. We'd meet on an empty lot and draw a large circular "pot" in the dust, then we'd take out our bags of marbles. There'd be a big "shooter" (mine was amber and very scuffed-up), and then the smaller marbles, made of glass or agate, some in a single color, others, called "cat's eyes," very pretty with swirls running through them. The whole point of the game was to win other kids' marbles. In fact the general term "playing for keeps" derives from marble-playing: when you kept your winnings, you were playing for keeps, and when it was understood that you'd return others' marbles after the game, you were "playing for fair."

In winter, I'd go sledding with other kids on that big hill above the town. I had a wonderful time racing downhill on my small and very speedy Radio Flyer sled, my mittened hands gripping the steering handles in front of me, handles that slightly tilted the runners right and left while my feet trailed off behind to help guide my course. The scariest and most exhilarating experiences came from ripping at breakneck speed down the narrow, winding, sharply descending trails we made through the frozen thickets of blackberry brush. Getting a running start, I'd throw myself onto my sled and enter that thicketed run by leaning right, then quickly left, then sharply right again as my runners scraped through snow and rocks; and then with growing speed I'd desperately steer beside boulders and through the murderous overhang of frozen bushes. My sled was like a greased luge, and it's a wonder I didn't kill myself on that hill! If you missed a turn you were sure to end up with scratches from the frozen vines, or worse. One kid actually broke bones, and another's parents had to be summoned to take him to the hospital. Sledding on that hill, performing with other boys, tested my "guts" and helped to "make a man of me."

~

The elementary school, Cascade School, was just a block or so away from our home. I must have learned something during the four years I went there, but I can't remember what. Gramlin, bless her heart, saved every scrap of paper from my childhood, and in that trove I found the first document I produced. At its top is the word "Penmanship," and beneath is "Cascade School. Chehalis. Washington. Jerry Newman. Grade 3-2. Mrs. Stroud." Then in childish scrawl: "When a snowflake leaves the sky/ It turns and turns to say good-bye/ 'Good-bye dear clouds so cool and gray'/ Then turns and hurries on its way." At the top is a big sticker, red, white, and blue: "GOOD WRITING." I'm saving it for the Smithsonian.

I recall certain noteworthy characteristics of my classmates. Gerald Hobson always had a horrible green stuff on his teeth and liked to copy off my papers. Or maybe I copied his? Orville Something was an ostrich, all tiny head and Adam's apple. Burdett Skinner had that pointed shock of greasy dark hair jutting down over one eye. Come to think of it, he was my first really memorable character!

Burdett never paid any attention in class, he just sat there at the back, making the most elaborate stick-figure drawings with his fat lead pencil. Every page of his coarse, lined, Indian-Head paper tablet was covered with those stick-figures, each with just a circle for a head, and a single straight line for the trunk; the same for each limb, with five tiny lines for each hand and foot. Sometimes he'd draw distinctive differences between these ant-like figures. One might have a fedora or ball cap, another he'd fit with scraggly women's curls or a sawed-off crew cut, another would have no head at all, just a neck spouting blood. Most amazing were these figures' actions—there'd be squadrons of airplanes flying upside-down through snow storms, and steamships being dragged by ant-people over mountain tops, and stick-figure cowboys careening down icebergs on horseback with six-guns blazing. Sometimes you'd find more than one of these activities on the same page! My guess is that Burdett, later, if he didn't end up a graphic artist, ended up on a funny farm. His stuff was much like that done later by the wild-and-crazy radical pornographic cartoonist Robert Crumb, famous for a dark comic-book style and gigantic speech balloons full of nutty manifestos. Maybe Crumb, too, began with ant-people?

I retain a surprisingly detailed memory of the exterior layout of the school grounds, and now I remember with special vividness the outdoor place where "the bars" were. That place saw the dawn of my interest in the female sex. The bars were smooth polished horizontal steel bars, held up at both ends by steel uprights. The ground there was covered in deep sand, to cushion falls from the bars. Concentrating hard, I can faintly remember a typical school recess, with the little kids running about, yelling and laughing. During school recesses, while the boys were running this way and that, or kicking footballs, the little girls would heft themselves up to one of these bars and then, hooking one or both knees over it, begin rotating like propellers, rotating their bodies around and around.

Now, it must be pointed out that little girls in those days wore short dresses. They didn't wear pants or jeans, so this healthy outdoor activity meant that school recesses were, among other things, a time for the full and unimpeded study of their underpants. In that I was by no means the only male scholar. As we boys zoomed around running this way and that, we found occasion to venture into the zone of the whirling underpants. The little girls, of course, paid us no mind—already they'd learned to ignore us. But I do most vividly, most distinctly, remember a little girl, it was probably in the third grade, hanging there motionless upside-down by her knees—maybe she was taking a break from whirling?—and Robin Kennicot, a very cute little blond-haired boy who already was becoming a tease, darted over to kiss her face, her defenseless little face, he kissed her on the lips! Poor, shy, backward little me, I wouldn't have dared it, though I was greatly impressed by Robin's speed and resourcefulness. Promptly I marked him as a rising star of my generation. Which demonstrates, I suppose, that I was making the healthy transition towards adolescence. If I weren't terrified of mixing metaphors I'd call those whirling underpants a milestone.

Third Grade: Sandra Creech at 2nd Row, center; at her right, Robin Kennicott; then, me; then behind me in black, Burdett Skinner; top row with bucked teeth, Paul Solberg

So that was the beginning. The next stage, the following year, was falling in love, or at least succumbing to a mad crush. My target was an ineffably cute creature named Sandra Creech. Sandra can be seen in a class picture from 1948, when I was in the fifth grade. She has a small face with a big smile, her hair is parted straight down the middle. She was lithe and limber, and the reason for that was that she was the star student at "Mrs. Hilton's School of Dance" over in Centralia, a few miles from Chehalis. Sandra would go there every week and practice acrobatics. She was a marvel. She could slither all over a big mat on the floor, twisting her body snake-like this way and that. Most amazingly, she could lie face-down on the mat, elevate herself with her forearms flat beneath her, then slowly, with her spine arching into a perfect "C" back-bend, bring her legs and feet up and over her head, and then, in the same continuous slow motion, lower them in front of her, together and straight out in front of her nose with her toes pointing ahead like an arrow! In that position, resting on her elbows, she looked almost like the Sphinx—except, of course, for her feet seeming to jut from her forehead.

The first time I witnessed her doing these contortionist acrobatics was at a school assembly. I simply had to get closer to that marvelous creature! And so to my thunderstruck parents I announced my new interest in dancing as an art form. My mother thought this rather sudden, but willingly signed me up at Mrs. Hilton's. Remembering my failure at piano and trumpet, maybe she thought I'd find myself in tap-dancing. I began riding back and forth on a local bus to Centralia, and the rest is history. Well, actually, not. It's true that I was overcome with a brain-numbing crush on Sandra and used tap-dancing as an excuse to get near her, to chat her up, to win her affection. I even learned to dance an entire routine of slap-rattle-hop-step-step and, with it, to sing a catchy song, "Dinah," for some sort of school assembly. I worked so hard, I tapped so feverishly, I sang so loudly and confidently, that even today I could do it with two or three pretty nurses holding me. In retrospect the whole experience reminds me of the absurd bobbing displays, the mating dances, of exotic male birds seeking friendship.

What I remember with a vividness extraordinary for memories laid down so long ago was a special talent show in the high school gym. Sandra was the only performer—at least in my tunnel memory. There, in the middle of the basketball floor, was her mat. Someone turned the lights down low, a spotlight fell onto the mat, a phonograph began slowly playing "Somewhere Over the Rainbow," that magical song with its rainbow dreams rising to the place where bluebirds fly, and "why, oh why can't I?" Then Sandra appeared, or rather materialized, in a skin-tight maroon body suit spangled with sequins that flashed the reflected light. Slowly she turned this way and that, she writhed, she was magical, she was cat-like. She did handstands and headstands, backsprings, rolls, the splits; and then in one long slow sequence she did the signature Sphinx-like backbend, the move with her trunk coiled up into a C behind her, her legs poised over and in front of her head. She finished by gently touching her toes to the mat and then effortlessly rolling forward to a standing position, her feet together and pointed, gracefully bowing to the audience; and then, with the lights coming on, she danced out of the gym with all the lightness of a ballerina glissading offstage at the Met.

To me Sandra Creech was a divine being, a miraculous, disembodied emanation from above. She really had no earthly parts, she was not like all the rest of us. She didn't sweat, she didn't pee, there were no boogers in that divine turned-up nose, farting was an impossibility, she didn't do any merely mortal things. She was a dream that walked. In fact, she didn't walk. She glided. On air, she glided. So I determined to arrange things so that in my classroom, my desk would be next to her, just across the little aisle that separated one column of desks from another. I would chat and laugh with her, we'd snigger at lesser beings, I would jolly her up, I would pass notes back and forth with her, I would make her mine.

I was progressing well with all this, I had actually managed to seize and hold the beachhead near her, the desk beside her, changing places with some blind unfeeling chucklehead. Occasionally she'd even smile at me. Then one day Sandra grew very ill. Naturally I was the first to note this because I stared at her all day long. (This may be why I remember nothing of my fifth-grade lessons.) And as I watched her growing ill, I saw her bend her head halfway toward me, put her small hand over her mouth, and then begin to vomit copiously through her fingers, vomit copiously onto the floor in my direction. The mess was all reddish and clotted with greenish particles. Tableau and fade to black.

As I review my passionate admiration and love for Sandra Creech I discover that scene, the scene in that classroom, to be the end of it all. There's Sandra vomiting through her fingers, then a blank screen. Finis. No more Sandra. No more angel in human form. Just a sick, vomiting little girl. Later I was to discover that it wasn't such a bad thing that girls weren't disembodied spirits, that they peed and had boogers and moved around on solid body parts. But that was well after my years in elementary school.

～

There was a reform school, a boys' reformatory, somewhere outside Chehalis, and my sixth-grade teacher, Mr. Drake, taught there for ten years or so before taking a job at my own school. Looking back, I can see my sixth-grade classroom quite vividly, and there, coming into view, is Mr. Drake. He is middle-aged and balding, he carries himself stiffly. He's got a military sort of bearing. He struts with a book in his hand. He's dressed in dark green and tan. The tan blur becomes his trousers; the green, his jacket. I see that it's a sport jacket.

Mr. Drake had brought with him the teaching methods, if you can call them that, that prevailed in the reformatory. In particular, he enforced discipline by sneaking up behind unwary mischief-makers and smashing them on the head with a book. It was not always a heavy geography book. To be fair, sometimes he chose an arithmetic book. Arithmetic, in those days before quadratic equations, was somewhat lighter. Most often, however, the disciplinary lesson was delivered with a spelling book, which was still thinner and required less wrist-action. Quickness was essential. And now, focusing my memory, I summon up the vision of that sixth-grade spelling book. It's blue, and thin, and has some kind of cheerful cartoon on the cover. I remember that it makes, instead of the geography book's watermelon-like thump on the skull, something more like a smart "whap," a cracking noise like that of a small-caliber gunshot, resounding but less likely to produce concussion.

Our class included lengthy periods of quiet homework as we sat at our desks. We were given assignments in reading, writing, and arithmetic which we were to perform quietly while Mr. Drake sat up front, grading papers. But, inevitably, various kids were, from time to time, tempted to pass notes, or whisper, or make each other laugh by making faces or inventing ridiculous hand signals. That's when Mr. Drake would quietly rise from his seat, pick up one of the books on his desk, and walk over to the windows along one side of the classroom—I can still see those windows, and, through them, the high school at the top of the hill. He'd stare nonchalantly at whatever was going on out there, then he'd amble slowly toward the back of the room, pretending to look over kids' shoulders to inspect their work.

At the back of the room he'd move quietly and unseen till he reached the aisle of desks where he'd spotted an offender. Then he'd creep forward, his victim in his sights, then instantly "WHAP!" the miscreant with the book. No explanation was asked for, and none was given. The kid would certainly stop doing whatever he'd been doing, and not repeat it for weeks. Everybody knew what had happened, and "back-talk" was strictly forbidden; Mr. Drake taught by example. Before many days passed we all grew wary when seeing him rise from his desk with a book.

Nonetheless, kids sometimes forgot themselves. That generally happened if there had been a long lag between whaps. One day, poor Paul Solberg forgot the most important lesson in Mr. Drake's class and paid for it. I remember Paul as fiercely buck-toothed. This was laughable because he also played the flute. Above the moving silver flash of his flute appeared the unmoving enamel gleam of his tusks, suspended over the metal instrument. He did keep them clean, licking and occasionally polishing them with his sleeve for fear of lettuce or spinach. But watching him play that flute was like watching a beaver gnawing a water pipe.

The sight of Paul playing wasn't the only thing that made us giggle. He was notorious as a momma's boy, and everybody thought momma's boys ridiculous. But really he was likeable enough, I suppose. Paul's teeth made him seem friendly or at least pitiful. I knew him personally a little bit. I'd visited him at his house. Their front door was recessed under a tiny peaked porch. I met his Mom. They were decent people. She made excellent cookies.

Anyway, one time, Paul was furtively passing notes back and forth with a classmate sitting near him. Mr. Drake snuck up behind him and smashed him hard with the spelling book. I think it was the spelling book, but the sound was loud, and Paul didn't take to it at all. In fact he abruptly left the room without permission, crying, which was something we boys wouldn't get caught dead doing in public. I believe the whapping event must have occurred toward the end of the day, or else there would have been a bigger general sensation. As it was, we just looked down and finished up our work, then went home.

Next day, at about the same time in the same classroom, Paul started passing notes again to the same kid. I didn't see him do it because I was reading a book and farther forward in the classroom, but I learned about it afterwards. He was baiting Mr. Drake, and the other kid was in on it. Mr. Drake, ever watchful behind the books and papers he was pretending to read, got the spelling book and began his stalking moves, walking toward the rear of the room and then up Paul's aisle. Suddenly Mr. Scroop, the Principal, opened the classroom door and said, chillingly, "Mr. Drake, a word, please," and summoned Mr. Drake into the hall.

Paul had ratted out Mr. Drake to his mother, his enraged mother had set up this ambush the next day, and Mr. Drake never again taught us spelling in the same way, or arithmetic, or geography. Our new-found respect for Paul Solberg, for his courage in setting that trap, made him zoom in popularity. In our eyes he was transformed. If poor Burdett Skinner hadn't flunked out already, he might have rendered Paul's teeth as the bared incisors of an enraged wolverine.

~

I guess it might have seeped through that I didn't like Mr. Drake. And since I'm now about to end this chapter, I see that it may be time to fess up to the fact that Mr. Drake perceived my attitude and repaid it with interest, inventing some ridiculous infraction that probably never even happened—I certainly don't remember anything of an infractious nature—and, worse, he reported it to Mr. Scroop, who, by the primitive code then employed, was legally empowered to inflict corporal punishment on persons such as myself.

It might help my case to point out that I was, in the spring of 1950, 11 years old and about to finish grade school. Sixth-graders like me were the most senior kids in grade school, the ones most likely to, let's say, act up, annoy teachers, show disrespect, and exhibit what were described as uncooperative behaviors. I certainly did none of those things! But love for the truth may require me to add, simply as a sort of bookkeeping fact, that for three years running I had earned what were termed "D's" in what our unfair report cards called "Citizenship." Apart from that, there's little hard evidence that I was any sort of disciplinary problem. To be ignored is the testimony my mother gave in her memoir, which I'm about to quote. And doesn't she qualify her words? Doesn't she smooth the whole thing over? I quote her:

By the sixth grade he had begun to show his maverick tendencies. I think that's a typical boy tendency, insistence on being your own person and breaking loose, showing your individuality. I think most boys do that. Jerry did. The school principal gave him a licking for something, so Len gave him one to match it!

Obviously my crime, the "something" she couldn't remember—I can't remember it either—was so insignificant that it hardly bore mention in her memoirs. My crime was so unmentionable, in fact, that I only touch on it here because otherwise someone might compare her account with mine and draw undesirable conclusions. But note how laudatory is her artless term "maverick," how un-judgmental the passage about breaking loose to become one's own person.

I will not say that Mr. Scroop was the worst and definitely the most ho-
micidally violent principal that Chehalis ever had. I will not suggest that he
was an antediluvian brute with no recognition of excellence even when its
backside was, so to speak, staring him in the face. I will leave it for others
to point out that while he flogged me, he flouted what were to become, in
a later era, mandates against punishing America's youth on some of their
most tender and impressionable areas.

As for the flogging my father gave me immediately after he learned that
the Principal had done so?—that is, after paddling me in precisely the same
area targeted earlier by Mr. Scroop? Well, I like to think that that was just
to make sure I'd doubly remember what my perceptive mother had termed
my "individuality." Egad, I'd soon be in my teens.

4

Mr. Howard's Beastly Island

ELLENSBURG, 1950-1953

Moving Time! For the sixth time since I was a baby we moved again, this time over the Cascades to the ancestral Kittitas Valley. That was in the summer of 1950. Ellensburg, near tiny Thorp, now became my home town. Settled like Thorp in the 1870s, it became the Kittitas County seat in 1883, then the regional center of higher education, and grew rapidly. We moved there because my dad wanted to build a larger practice and was encouraged by the fact that the Newman name might ensure more clientele. He bought a 17-acre parcel a mile south of Ellensburg on Canyon Road with nothing but grassland between it and the city. Today that mile of road is crossed by I-90 and cluttered with gas stations and fast-food restaurants.

A View of Ellensburg in the Kittitas Valley; I-90 and the Yakima River run across the scene; the city water tank tops Craig's Hill; Central Washington University buildings at upper left]

The plan was to build a long, single-storied structure that would contain an animal hospital at one end, and a home for us at the other, all under one roof. My dad paid a man with an earth-mover to scrape the parcel and level it. He and I then laid out the footprint of the entire building, using pegs and string. We began work on the Fourth of July, 1950, in broiling heat. First we dug the footers, channels in the dirt where the walls would be erected. We, or rather I, then mixed great quantities of concrete, and with his help wheeled the stuff to the right place and dumped it into the footers, where he worked it with a shovel, leveled it with a trowel, and inserted upright rods of rebar.

That was very hot and heavy work, but I was my dad's only helper. I was 11 and knew how to work, though I'd never worked with him. His philosophy was that you didn't work till the hands on a clock reach a certain position; you work till the job is done. He wasn't the sort to relax or take a break. On hot days our shirts became sopping wet with sweat but we paid no attention. Ditto our faces, our hair, our whole bodies. We went for long periods without stopping to drink water: we would have fallen over laughing at today's crusade to "hydrate." Working with him was not like working in a barbershop or garage with other men, chattering about sports, or hunting, or school, or memories of military service, or anything else. He didn't care about that stuff. We didn't even talk about the day's work plan—he had it in his head, and that was sufficient. We worked in silence, so I often didn't understand what we were doing, or why we were doing it this way rather than that. The result is that I learned little about construction, and at some point stopped caring. But the work routine itself became engrained in me.

After the footers came the pouring of the concrete floor, then we built the walls from cinder blocks and glass blocks, then came the roof, and then, in the hospital end of the building, a floor of beautiful square green vinyl tiles. Above that we finished the ceiling with perforated 12" x 12" white acoustic squares. I can still see, by a late night's glowing light bulb, my dad, his shirt drenched with sweat, standing on a platform in what would become the main hall of the hospital, grunting with his hands up over his head as he fits another square into the vile-smelling mastic glue he has just troweled up there to hold it. I, meanwhile, stand watching, wordless, hungry for a dinner long postponed, holding more squares, ready to hand him the next and the next and the next. It's important to finish the job. We work in silence.

~

It was brilliant to plan the whole north end of the building as a residence, the south as the animal hospital. My dad's daily commute, and those of his receptionist (my mother) and helper (me), would amount simply to opening two doors and walking from one end into the other. The whole set-up saved time and money, and it meant, to clients, peace of mind in the knowledge that if they came there, they'd certainly find someone to help them. That's important to people with sick animals.

The half where we lived was small and compact but I wasn't bothered, at first, about dwelling in a place with a sign out front, "Ellensburg Animal Hospital," because at age 11 I'd reached my insensitive clod stage. The other end held the animal hospital, which smelled pleasantly of antiseptic. There was a pretty reception room, an examination room, a pharmacy, and an immaculate surgery with a surgical table, bright overhead light, cautery, trays of surgical instruments. Across the central hallway were more rooms to hold dogs and cats in kennels.

Essentially what we ran was a three-person operation. My dad spent most of the day zipping around the Valley in a Volkswagen bus, taking care of sick large animals. My mom dispatched him by radio from home, received patients, did the books, and helped him perform small animal surgeries at night. My job was to be caretaker for the whole place, feeding and watering the dogs and cats twice a day, cleaning their kennels and the dog runs, mowing the lawns, and cleaning and waxing the hospital floors. I did the floors on Sundays, which were boring anyway. I never went into town for church till later, to attend Methodist Youth Fellowship—not to worship God but to chase girls. There was a popular song, "Teen Angel." I wanted to find one.

My mother, in her memoirs, commented on my very time-consuming work routine. "It wasn't fair to Jerry, and kids at school made fun of him, made cracks about cleaning the kennels. He didn't like doing it. And kids were mean. But we really didn't have much choice. We were trying to make a go of the practice, and we had to watch our corners and save our money. And we did. Jerry was part of the casualty of that."

"Casualty" is too strong, but once I became my dad's laborer but not his buddy, the distance between us grew greater. However, I did get paid for my work. My folks, good Republicans, believed in the trickle-down theory.

I can't remember how much my allowance was, but it was enough. They were always generous about money, and all my life stood ready to help me if I needed some. That was a comfort not many kids have.

The Ellensburg Animal Hospital opened with much fanfare on March 3, 1951. It looked shiny and beautiful, and my parents' friends helped out by conducting tours for townsfolk who came to look around. The opening was a sensation because attendees found, in the reception room, a big, framed portrait of the most famous dog in town, a reminder of a dramatic event that had occurred a few weeks earlier. Two of the best-known townspeople, bachelors named Branner and Sutton, ran a bookstore on Pearl Street where the signature Bull statue now stands. Their big, handsome Doberman Pinscher "Boots" was the town favorite. She'd trot around in the store, rolling over to be given a tummy scratch. But one day she swallowed a rock as big as a walnut. Her owners were wild with worry. They brought her to my dad, who hadn't even opened yet. Dropping his construction work, he plugged in his brand-new X-ray machine to locate the rock, then surgically extracted it. The bookstore guys were ecstatic and henceforth kept that rock in their cash register, showing it to customers and lauding Dr. Newman. They'd commissioned that portrait for the hospital's reception room; it proudly signaled promising outcomes to future patients.

~

The Kittitas Valley is a beautiful agricultural plain between high ridges that run southeasterly out of the snowy Cascade Mountains. The Yakima River, originating in mountain snow-melt, flows through it toward the mighty Columbia. Viewed from a hilltop, with the hills and snowy peaks of the Stuart Range at its back, the scene is one of the prettiest on Earth.

But the wind could knock you down. There are jokes about it. The Safeway store used to have a "wind gauge" facing the northwesterly blast. From its top there hung a mighty logging chain, each link big as a kielbasa—as if our legendary wind could budge

Mom in our yard, the wind blowing her hair

that monster chain! That wind wasn't such a great bother to my pioneering ancestors because it also left absolutely blue and cloudless skies, and dazzling sunlight for crops. Folks got used to it, and I did too. I liked the way the trees thrash around in the wind, the loud bashing-and-crashing racket of buffeting trees, the wild gusty pandemonium, and I loved the way I could become wrapped in its noise, solitary in it, unable to see or hear or sense anything else but its racket and pressure and raw force. Ellensburg had a natural "surround sound" long before audio inventions. Walking through woods in the Kittitas Valley during heavy winds gives me a sensation similar to snorkeling all alone in choppy water, lost and absorbed in another world's mystery and noise.

What was Ellensburg like? Neither the wind nor the town have changed much since I first arrived. The entire city of about 8,000 souls lived within a square mile of land dominated by a single large hill, Craig's Hill, where the Yakima Tribe once camped and traded—the young braves competing in horse-races and the oldsters engaging each other with that noisy gambling "stick game" where two teams, pounding boards with sticks, sat facing each other, hiding bones and distracting each other with singing and noise. Fascinated, I eagerly watched that game as a kid when the Yakimas came to help open the rodeo. Wearing buckskins, bead dresses, feathers and bells, they'd ceremoniously ride their ponies down Craig's Hill, then perform war-dances in the arena.

By the 1880s, rich white people had displaced the native folk and taken over that hill. Middling and poorer people lived in old but often pretty homes around the downtown core, which really was just four blocks of businesses and shops. The state college, "Central," with its leafy campus, was a part of the town. Ellensburg prospered as the last significant way-station on "the East Side" before the winding two-lane Highway 10 climbed the mountains to drop down toward Seattle a hundred miles away.

The local population was a mix between rancher-cowboys and college professors, buckaroos and eggheads. The richest person in town was a potato farmer living on Craig's Hill, but the smartest lived on Ninth Street a stone's throw from Barge Hall, teaching English or Physics. There was friction sometimes between the two leading social sets, but also tolerance and good will. Rancher-cowboys went to campus concerts and gawked at the ivy, professors got used to horse parades dirtying the streets, and both chomped corn dogs at the annual Labor Day rodeo. At the County Fair just next to the rodeo arena you could view giant bulls huffing and bellowing, and you could do the same at large lecture halls just three blocks away where many professors showed why they were called "Full." The town's real power center lay not in City Hall but 15 minutes away at the Ellensburg Golf and Country Club, where ranchers and bankers and merchants teed off in foursomes and graciously called each other's ten-foot putts "gimme's."

It wasn't till many years later that I understood the special spirit of that town, its extraordinary blend of voluntarism and democracy. There's a general spirit of self-help throughout the American West, but the impulse was stronger in Ellensburg because of geography. I see a certain similarity to Athens, the birthplace of democracy. Ellensburg, like Athens, was extremely isolated, shut away from other communities by miles of forbidding hills that inured its inhabitants to cooperative defense and civic participation. Ellensburg when I arrived in 1950 (freeways weren't built yet) was surrounded by barren hills that receded into deep forests to the west, and uninhabited deserts to the east. It was connected only by a few winding two-lane roads, lifelines to all the rest of America—you had to drive three hours to reach anything resembling civilization. And so, living there, if you wanted to buy something, you had to find it downtown. Our people had to make do for themselves; they couldn't trot off to a mall in some town nearby. That made for a rare spirit of cooperation, participation, and volunteerism.

Things have changed since those days, newcomers have arrived, fast cars and freeways have revolutionized commerce and recreation and the entire spectrum of choice. But little Ellensburg was my home town, and I think I was lucky to have grown up there.

∽

Jerry Newman, a total newcomer, went for the first time to Morgan Junior High in early September, 1950. 160 kids entered seventh grade that year. Assigned to my home room, I nominated myself to be home room president! I put myself up, on that very first day, to be the leader and big cheese.

An old friend recently told me that "everybody remembers that about you." Like neglected food on my shirt, I suppose, it sticks to me. So why did I do it? I think I was trying to establish my identity. Imagine my insecurity that day! Eleven-year-olds feel awkward even when not plunging into a new town, so what better time to assert myself than the first day of the rest of my life? Memory fails, but since amour-propre doesn't, I'm sure I got at least one enthusiastic vote. But nobody knew me from Adam. The other kids had been playmates since youth, and there was I, an ugly new duck in their big old pond, splashing noisily forward to become their leader! What an ass. If there's a Jackass Regiment in the great army of stupid people, I signed up that day for a six-year tour of duty.

But something good that happened to me that week was meeting the guy who'd become my best friend for life. Unfortunately he died in 2019, and I miss our bantering conversations terribly, the old warmth of each other, the familiar recollection of just stuff. His name was Lannes Spencer Purnell, "Lanny" for short. He was intelligent and geeky. He looked the nerd with his glasses and chipped front tooth. He already seemed destined for a career in science or engineering, and in fact later left high school as co-valedictorian with a four-year scholarship to Cal Tech.

Back there in 1950 he invited me to his house, and in his room I saw model airplanes made of balsa wood, musical instruments he was building, stuff like that. But although we were very different, we seemed to complement each other. I was the joker, he the clever straight man; I'd come up with something crazy, he'd elaborate it with something even more ludicrous. All our lives it was that way. How I miss his voice now on the phone, even though in recent years it was all complaints. I'd cheer him up, and before long, laughing, he'd lose track of being old and pissed-off. I had no idea he was so close to the end when in Portland, where he wound up living, we went out together and drank beer at a brewery, sitting at a bar, staring pleasantly over our pizza at the fanny of our young waitress.

His father was the Junior High principal. Mr. Purnell was always polite and somewhat hesitant with me, and very sober—the Purnells didn't drink, and it showed in their appraising looks and dry speech. Mr. Purnell was quiet, thoughtful, very deliberate in what he said, and often quite humorously wry—Lanny inherited his ironic humor. I'd never heard people express themselves the way they did, by inversions. For example, if his dad thought something despicable, he might describe it as "leaving something to be desired"; if a fire were to break out in a crowded theatre, Lanny might suggest that "it might be desirable to vacate the premises." I also remember being struck by how Mr. Purnell would sit by the fire in the evenings, the clock over the mantle slowly ticking, reading a story to his growing houseful of children. He was a different sort of dad, a contrast to my own. Lanny's mom was a very sweet woman with a crooked grin that she bequeathed to him. Unfortunately she died of breast cancer when still fairly young. It was a great loss for her family.

Lanny liked camping and I did too, so once I borrowed a horse for him so he could accompany me on a pack trip with my own mare, Babe—she was an awful horse, would always bite me on the leg, and when we gave up on her and passed her to my cousin Helen, she bit her too. Anyway, we took horses for an overnight expedition to one of the high mountain lakes in the Cascades. Our intention was to fish, but after I borrowed Lanny's new reel to try it out, I fouled it up so badly that we had little time for fishing. He had to spend hours swearing and unsnarling the mess of monofilament, and all I could do was stand ashamed nearby, silently looking on, trying to radiate sympathy. And then I suddenly had to deal with something even worse, I had to find our horses! They'd bolted when maddened by a swarm of yellow jackets. Truly, that whole trip was such a fiasco that I wouldn't mention it here except for the happy ending. Descending the trail, we ran into other adventurers on their way to the same miserable hornet-infested lake. They asked how the fishing was. "Terrific," I exclaimed, but said I was hopeful they'd brought *some periwinkles*: "Periwinkles are the only thing they're biting on!" Naturally their faces fell. It was a mountain lake, and you couldn't have found a periwinkle for 30 miles. No disapproval, please: I *said* I was becoming an ass!

In high school we often drank beer socially, or you might say medicinally. We'd drive out behind the I.O.O.F. cemetery on Saturday nights while all the other guys were probably "making out like a bandit," and even, we imagined, "getting to third base" or possibly even "home." We'd languish there, each sitting on his wallet holding his ancient unused condom, splitting a six-pack of beer and commiserating on how unloved we were. We'd turn the problem this way and that, looking at it from multiple directions till it got blurry. Then we'd go home.

We also made a habit of giving each other ridiculous Christmas and birthday presents. We'd buy the stupidest things we could find—car compasses that didn't work, toilet-shaped air sweeteners, Annie Oakley action figures, zombie sleep masks, canned gravy fountains—then wrap them up and present them as solemnly as principals handing out diplomas. That was all part of our friendship, the silliness of it. Something we did when older was telephoning each other and, in disguised voices, informing the other one that he now had a serious problem with the IRS or the Draft Board, or a Paternity Court, or the Center for Disease Control. He'd need an appointment immediately to explain some very grave discrepancies in his records. Pinching my nose to disguise my voice, and stifling my laughter, I'd attempt to arrange an appointment date for an official interview on the payment of back taxes, or a re-check of that unreported case of herpes.

Me (14)—and others mentioned in text, Butch Sterling (4), Johnny Moser (13), Lanny Purnell (1), Steve Moe (back row, 3rd from left.

Remembering Lanny reminds me of a story that includes another friend from that era, Johnny Moser. Johnny was a very good-humored fellow, a lovable puppy-dog sort of guy. He had a round face and smiled a lot, and was well liked. Everybody knew him because his dad owned a men's shop in town. Johnny worked there, and after his dad died, he took it over and had to watch it die too. That took three decades, so he scraped out a meager living till chain stores wiped out all the town's private shops.

Though he operated a cash register all his life, Johnny was no genius at higher mathematics. Our ninth-grade algebra teacher, however, was a tough and pitiless old coot named Paul Nelson. He was the track coach as well as the math teacher, so he was accustomed to driving young men to put their best onto the field. His disgusted phrase, contemptuously employed, was, "If you can't tell 'em, they'll never learn!!!" He was a martinet. His algebra students lived in terror of public humiliation, for he'd drop crushing put-downs onto anyone who couldn't answer his math questions.

Now, Lanny and I, in that algebra class, sat side-by-side in the front row of the room, just feet away from Nelson, who'd sit on the front edge of his desk, swinging his feet back and forth, staring belligerently at all of us. Johnny sat in the back row, trying to be invisible. Nelson would ask a math question, and members of the class, after they'd figured out the answer, were expected to put their hands up in the air to be called upon and then to spit it out.

I soon learned how to avoid embarrassment by waiting till Lanny, who was the acknowledged math genius, would put his hand into the air, and then I too, with a languid expression on my face, would do the same, even though I usually had no clue what the answer might be. I was fixing my own stupid!—not the thing itself, but the appearance of it. And that was the safest course of action because Nelson would invariably pick on one of the dimmer lights first, and then maybe another one second, by which time, employing a law of averages based on the wrong answers, and utilizing the extra eighty seconds, I might have worked out the answer or at least a less mortifying mistake than the first two wild guesses.

But poor Johnny Moser was nearly always Nelson's first victim. I remember, as clearly as if it were happening right now, Paul Nelson sitting there, swinging his legs and feet, aggressively sucking air through his teeth and making that annoying sound he always made, then asking his question—say, "What's the square root of 73?" There would be a very long pause; and then the word, or rather question—or was it an accusation?—would come out slowly: "MOSER?" Johnny had been invited to solve the problem.

Slowly at the back of the room the round face of Johnny Moser, at first crouching so low he couldn't even be seen behind his desk, would appear, and he would open his mouth, and . . . nothing would come out! Then, after another long pause, the zinger: "NEXT TIME, MOSER, BETTER BRING YOUR TEDDY BEAR!" By that time, looking bored, and with my arm modestly half-lowered after working to hold it up over my head alongside Lanny's, I'd be ready with the answer if Mr. Nelson was ready to turn to us smart kids up front. The truth is (and even Lanny didn't fully know this), I hated algebra so much and was so bad at it that it took all my energy that year to conceal my bottomless ignorance. Even when I studied hard, I couldn't understand those x's and y's, or why you had to put them above or below those stupid lines divided by an equals sign. And my geometry wasn't much better. It wasn't till I was in my 20s and visiting a zoo that it became entirely clear that a hypotenuse is not a baby hippopotamus.

Another good friend was Pete Cunningham. Pete was short and even more pie-faced than Johnny, with lots of freckles and a big smile, a very sunny guy who always brought out the best in people. In sports he was an excellent second baseman. Something I vividly remember from my long friendship with Pete is a car ride I took with him and his dad. Virgil Cunningham was the sports writer for the *Daily Record*. Pete invited me to accompany them to Yakima, to attend a semi-pro baseball game so his dad could write it up in the paper. I don't remember anything about the game, but I do remember that Pete's dad, on the way home, asked him what he thought of it. *His dad asked him what he thought about the game and then said nothing, waiting to hear Pete's opinion.* I was flabbergasted. He was talking to his kid as though he might have something interesting to say! "O brave new world, that has such people in 't!" Here was another segment to add to my learning curve.

~

My oldest surviving document from the seventh grade is an assignment I presented to Mr. Howard, my science teacher. That document, "Air Pressure Demonstrations," begins with 24 pictures laboriously hand-drawn with ruler, compass and protractor. They, and the five pages explaining them, must have cost me many hours of labor. My endeavor astounded Mr. Howard, who gave it a big fat red "A" and wrote, in red, "Very good work!" with three underlines. Obviously I went overboard, but evidently was determined to do the job as perfectly as an insecure seventh-grader could.

Mr. Howard was an odd duck, a talkative show-off and a ham. He could use his suspenders to shoot pieces of blackboard chalk at us. That was funny and made us like him, but there was something very disagreeable about him too. He made everybody take out a piece of paper and put down the name of the person they'd most like to spend time with on a desert island; then he collected the papers and read out the tallies. Now, popularity, as everyone knows, is critically important for kids at that age, so conformist and fearful of exclusion. Naturally those students whose names ranked high were elated to hear the results. Marilyn Meyer told me that she and Patty Lindsey had gone to see Mr. Howard after class and luxuriated in the knowledge that other kids pined to be near them. Do I need to say I wasn't high on the list? Here was another experience that helped to build my lifelong critical view of authority figures.

I was, however, always willing to follow a *good* leader. Which reminds me that I did make one nice splash that first year. I turned out for the Morgan Junior High School Tigers football team. The coach was Pat Martin, also a math teacher. When the season ended I found, to my surprise, that I was the only seventh-grader to get a varsity letter, an "E" with a little orange football sewed to it for my new letterman's sweater. My achievement was faute de mieux. Larry Miller, a ninth-grader, the team's starting right guard, had broken his arm just before the first game of the season. It was as the team's least terrible bench-sitter that I walked off with his glory.

I should mention that in those autumn months after the annual Labor Day rodeo, our only venue for football games was the rodeo arena. It contained no grass; it was, and still is, just a dirt field used for barrel races, bull-riding, calf roping, steer wrestling. This meant that it was, and still is, half dirt and half horse turds, with generous helpings of cow pies and bull pies. It was called The Ellensburg Football Field, but we players who often had our faces pushed into it called it the "Dung Bowl." Opposing teams didn't like playing there either, but they only had to do it once a season. Fortunately there's little rain there after Labor Day, so the dung was usually dry, but to a lineman who had to go down in a three-point squat before every ball was hiked, and fall into the stuff with every tackle, that dry dung could be tiresome. After games I looked like a party-goer in Calcutta where pulverized dung is flung around as a blessing. I complained less than the others, though, because I was home-schooled in dog-do.

We had some pretty tough competitors; we played schools with very big and aggressive teams. Kickoffs were the scariest thing. Our guy would kick off, and then an opposing runner would catch the ball and come barreling straight ahead, his knees churning—straight, it often seemed, at *me!* My assignment was to stop that locomotive bearing down at about 30 miles an hour, cleats flying. Let me note that ordinary tackles performed at the line of scrimmage are different from open-field tackles, which can produce concussions. I managed some but missed others. I never did what's called a "flop," but was mainly dissuaded by fear of shaming myself with Coach Martin if he saw me do it. Even so, I cracked a tooth in one open-field tackle; it's a front tooth, and the crack is still visible today. In another open-field tackle I broke the pinky on my left hand. Football teaches courage.

⌣

My interests were expanding, and I began showing dramatic talent. At the beginning of my eighth-grade year I turned out for an operetta called "Ask the Professor." Prophetically, I was given the lead. The newspaper wrote that "Jerry Newman as the professor gave a very amusing and convincing account of himself." A year later I played the Royal Wizard in a production of James Thurber's "Many Moons." The *Daily Record* commented: "Come and observe the Royal Wizard as he conjures spells, creates potions of wolf-bane, nightshade, and eagle's claws to ward off heartbreak, witches, demons and things that go 'bump' in the night." That prose was better than my performance, although as part of my wizardry I extracted from my left ear a three-foot sausage.

Me at center right; other friends mentioned in text are Beth Knudsen & Art Reitsch (far left), Roy Pinney (crown), Kay Kendall (lorgnette).

The most promising part of my eighth-grade education was creative writing. I took a course in it from Rodney Weeks, the first of four teachers to attract me into the teaching profession. He was also the first person in the world, apart from doting Gramlin, to treat me as "gifted," and in fact has the distinction of being the only one. Six of my stories, all written for his class, remain in my memorabilia. They all have "Excellent! A" on them in red pencil. On my essay "My Dog Duke," he wrote "very very good, A," and followed this with a note: "Jerry—Save this paper and read it over later. I think you have real writing ability." Here's a tiny excerpt, written when I was 13. The essay brings back memories of my wonderful first pet.

Duke is a two-year-old, lovable, frequently-embarrassed, affectionate, devoted, intelligent dog. His eyebrows are of a brownish-tan color, as is the inside of his ears, and the hair which borders an embarrassing spot to the south end of him. He has shifty brown eyes, at least I think they're shifty, and if he had a cigarette in his mouth and a hat pulled down over his floppy ears, I'd think him some sort of dogster. He has four aims in life: eating, sleeping, irrigating, and eradicating moles. He is a wonderful advertisement for the hospital. He has a habit of sleeping on his back with all four feet straight up in the air. Well, he was indulging in this pastime, as usual, when an alarmed motorist drove in and informed us of the dead dog lying in our driveway. We chased his carcass to the garage.

It's nothing great, but I was trying, at least, to write clearly and amusingly. And I was maturing in other ways, passing into the age of puberty, experiencing strange new sensations, groping my way toward more advanced groping. Forgetting my earlier experience with the vomiting Sandra Creech, I began plotting to take somebody out on a date. That, more than anything else, helped me summon the courage to ask Blatty Hommilton, not her real name, to accompany me to the movies. The destination was the Pix Theater. Every Saturday there'd be double-features with all our cowboy heroes in them—Roy Rogers, Tom Mix, Hopalong Cassidy. You'd stay most of the afternoon, watching those cowboys riding the purple sage, chasing bank robbers with six-guns blazing, crooning love songs to their girlfriends and horses.

Blatty was chunky and covered with freckles, she resembled a spattered sofa. She was, however, available. Hoping she'd be thirsty for love, I took her to the movies. She was my first date! I remember us sitting side-by-side through the whole first movie of the double-bill, exchanging not a word. After the intermission, after we bought popcorn, we resumed our seats and sat there masticating thoughtfully for nearly the entirety of the second movie. I completely lost track of the film, instead nervously calculating what to do next. I was frozen by indecision. I wanted to grab her hand, which lay temptingly in her lap beside me. I wanted to hold hands! But I was afraid she didn't! I was afraid she'd snatch hers away and that the whole afternoon would be a waste, except for the popcorn.

So, just as the movie ended and the lights came on, maybe even as we were standing up and leaving, I grabbed her hand. I was surprised, then overjoyed, to find her responding warmly. In fact her left hand was even clammier and more eager than my right! It was like a hot poker! And so, almost in spite of myself, I passed another milestone on the road to maturity. And, of course, cashed the fifteen cents I'd spent on her ticket.

There was other stuff going on in the early 1950s. Of course I had no political consciousness yet, and even if I had, I probably would have "liked Ike" and not been "madly for Adlai" in the 1952 presidential elections. Ellensburg was a predominantly Republican town and my folks were moderate Republicans. They were professional business people, after all. Democrats, associated with labor unions, strikes, deficit spending and softness on Communism, were foreign to their interests and experience. Later, reacting to Republican outrages, my mother would veer Democratic.

With Gramlin and Lynn

There were some big movies coming out at about that time in what was called "the wonder of Cinemascope"—"Quo Vadis" (1951) for example, a big extravaganza with a cast of thousands. My mother took my sister to Seattle to see "The Robe" in 1953. Lynn was about six, I think. There are several pictures of Lynn at that age, and, strangely, she looks serious in all of them. She wasn't a particularly serious child; I think she just adopted that expression when posing with me, to make me look frivolous and scatter-brained.

She did have one reason, though, to look serious, and that's because we all kept trying to drown or stab her. She'd almost drowned a couple times in Chehalis, once because Mom was bathing her but not paying attention, the other because she wandered into that miniature fish pond in the back yard—I was the hero of the day because I saved her, and maybe hadn't even pushed her first. She'd also escaped stabbing twice, once by Mom carelessly leaving a pair of shears that fell off a railing nearby, the second time because I was furious at her and threw a fork at a corner of the building where she'd just disappeared—she abruptly reappeared and took the fork in her forehead! I was panicked that I'd badly hurt her! Now she's gotten used to the fork and we tease her about it. With tinsel, it's stunning at Christmas.

That was after we came to Ellensburg. She had by that time already befriended Tish Young, who was to remain her pal ever afterwards. She and Tish played and rode horses together, developing dazzling equestrian showmanship and rarely falling off. She was also learning, in the family tradition, to tickle the keys. As to our relationship, Lynn was my dad's favorite but I took that in stride, organizing her under the heading, "Cute and Lovable Younger Child." We were eight years apart and got along reasonably well, though sometimes she was more blister than sister. I mostly ignored her because really, how could I have paid attention to our relationship? My starved ego, limited friendships, fluctuating "huskiness" and teen pimples were enough worry without concerning myself with excrescences in the household.

Unlike, say, Italian or Polish families, ours had few traditions apart from the celebration of birthdays, Christmases, Easters, and Kwanzaa which we'd never heard of. We did, however, listen to the World Series every fall on the radio—every year it was the Yankees, Dodgers, and Giants, all teams in the East. Everything was in the East; the East was so far away; I'd never been there. But we followed those games avidly. My dad would return from calls and want to know right away what was the inning, what the score. My mother set up radios so we could move around without missing an at-bat. Instant replay would have been highly welcome, but as yet we didn't even know what a cathode ray was, and in fact some of us still don't.

By comparison with cozy family life in today's America, we simply didn't do much of it. We had no TV till the mid-1950s, my parents were too busy to attend my football games. As to other things we didn't do together, the world was full of them: my folks had played tennis in Singapore but no longer did; they liked to go salmon fishing every year but did it with neighbors; Mom didn't swim much anymore, and my dad with his fair skin wouldn't swim at all; my mother had read to me when I was three but that would have been embarrassing at 13, even though I didn't know the entire alphabet till after I'd begun shaving.

We did, however, drive into the hills occasionally, and took a ghastly camping vacation once to the Olympic Peninsula. We pitched our tent near

Olympic Hot Springs. The weather was dismal and rainy, no good for fishing. One morning, Lynn, who was just six or seven, wished passionately for just one little fish. Never one to disappoint her, my dad strung up his pole, donned his heavy jacket, and set off through the brush. He came back three hours later, his coat soaked with rain, his boots full of water, but in one pocket he carried a slimy four-inch minnow. It had only one eye. My sister loved it—the eye, not the fish.

I know the details of that trip because I wrote them up afterwards in a short story. What I left out was the moment when, sitting at a picnic bench with my family as we prepared to eat hot dogs, I came up with the genius idea of using a hammer to loosen the top of a new ketchup bottle. That bottle was defective. With the others eyeing my every move, I tapped it ever so gently and broke the glass. I then received multiple kicks to the backside as I scrambled around the campground! Ketchup happened to be my dad's favorite food.

I'd appointed him to fix my stupid until I was fully able to take over the job myself. He wasn't the perfect dad, and I wasn't, um, the perfect son. I was insecure, sometimes I was moody, and, like other kids at that age, I tested the rules. In a ten-page essay, "A Portrait of My Old Man," I talked admiringly about him at length, but revealed that "Dad and I have not always understood each other like a father and son should." I respected him tremendously but also, over the years, had become wary of him. I was becoming a horse of a different color.

Well, then, what sort of horse? Earlier I spoke of Mr. Howard's science class in 1950, when I was just entering seventh grade. I have no memory of how I scored in his nasty popularity contest, but my lingering indignation suggests that I didn't score well and that my sense of justice was injured. Anyway, my point is that when I first entered junior high, nobody knew me at all.

So had I, three years later, by the end of ninth grade in 1953, made any headway on Mr. Howard's scale of belonging? Would anybody have voted to be my island chum? Let's see. On the negative side, there was a student newspaper produced that spring, an eight-page rag called "Tiger's Growl," done in our two Journalism classes. Examining a copy, I see that the kids who produced it generously praised themselves but also published sundry notes about many others. The fact that Jerry Newman got only one mention doesn't speak well for his belongingness.

On the positive side, I think I do detect some progress. First, there was the fact that I was a football letterman and had proven myself an athlete. That would have been worth one point on Mr. Howard's stinking island. Second, my grades were superior in every class except Shop (in which Mr. Barnhill gave me a C from pity). I starred in English and was a solid "B" or better student in everything else—a fact confirmed when I was inducted into the Honor Society, whose membership was based on grades, leadership, cooperativeness, and so on. That was a giant step up from the "D in Citizenship" perpetually awarded me in Chehalis's totally unfair grade school.

So I'd swum toward Mr. Howard's horrid island on two fronts, athletics and scholastics. Maybe it was also a plus that I was becoming an entertainer? I'm not sure when that began. It might have started in seventh grade on that memorable first day when I nominated myself for big cheese, or in the eighth grade, when, obviously writing for laughs, I composed that account of "My Dog Duke," or in the ninth grade, when I entered an all-school talent show with a comedy script I wrote and performed with Art Reitsch.

The premise of that script was that we were goofy radio announcers. Sitting behind a desk on the big stage of Morgan Junior High, wearing fedoras, chomping fake cigars and holding fake microphones, we delivered our patter: "Good evening, ladies and gentlemen. This is station K-O-R-N-PLASTER, the voice of Washington. When we're on the air, people want to stop breathing it. First we have a few news flashes from our yokel [not local] correspondent, 'Woman gives birth to triplets in plane. Father counts three and jumps.'" We included fake commercials: "Remember, we work hand in pocket with Morty's Mortuary, where there's never a cough in a carload. Morty's guarantees satisfaction or your mummy back. In 35 years they've never had a customer complain." The script was appallingly corny, the jokes stolen from joke books, but my comic appearance in that all-school talent show indicates my growing ambition to shine as a creative ham. Later that year I played the wizard, a comic part, in that school play I mentioned earlier, "Many Moons."

Still later, in the spring, there was a big school dance, a "Freshman Frolic" held in the cafeteria, where, providing the principal entertainment, I delivered what was billed in the program as "a humorous monologue, 'My Life,' by Jerry Newman." I'd forgotten all about that till I unearthed a photo and then the program. But really, that was the event of the year. The girls wore formals, the boys sport jackets; there were extravagant decorations, live music, student royalty with crowns and robes, and, as chaperones, a dozen members of the Junior High faculty. There's a photo of me in the middle of that large room, entertaining everybody. I wore nice clothes for the occasion—a black bowler hat, black pleated trousers, a striped necktie, a cane, and a gorgeous gold-figured dark shirt. On my youthful face I see a very contented smile—evidently I was performing well enough, and I certainly do look confident; and on faces in the background I detect smiles, too. The whole thing must have added something to my image as a comic writer and entertainer.

Acting out *My Life*

And there was one more thing. In that same spring of 1953 I was finishing up a year of Latin under our teacher, Maxwell Gates. Gates was a small, wiry man with a thin moustache, smoke-stained teeth, a shrewdly penetrating gaze, and an exceedingly dry humor. He was very well educated—I think he'd graduated from Columbia University. In addition to teaching Latin he also was the school's best drama coach. In fact he himself was a man of immense thespian talents. I wonder now why he'd chosen our little burg to teach in. He could have made even the sourest Shakespearean critic roll on the floor with laughter. I saw him once enact ALL the "rude mechanicals" in the play-within-the-play contained in Shakespeare's "Midsummer Night's Dream." In a barrel behind him he had wigs, a lantern, and lots of other props: he would recite the lines of one character, using a distinctive voice, then quickly turn his back and snatch the wig or prop of another character, then spin around and enact that character's lines in a different voice, then do the same again and again, impersonating Snug the Joiner, Flute the Bellows-Mender, Quince the Carpenter, Snout the Tinker, and Bottom the Weaver as they ridiculously vie for speaking parts ("Let ME play the lion too," declares Bottom), and then perform their absurd but hilarious tragedy of Pyramus and Thisbe, the star-crossed lovers who wind up dead by mistake.

Now, in Mr. Gates's Latin class I had become something of a personality. I liked Latin, and Mr. Gates liked me. He'd humor me when I asked crazy questions about the Romans, and he gave me decent grades on my papers. I still have my book of Latin assignments: "Amare, amabo, amabis, amabit, amabimus, amabitis, amabunt." See what a good learner I was? I even memorized the first canto of the *Aeneid*, and can still recite much of it today. "Arma virumque cano Trojae qui primus ab oris." I can go on for another 20 seconds, singing about "arms and the man."

But before continuing this story I should mention that by the ninth grade I was going by the moniker "Big Jer." I've forgotten how that started. Probably it originated in some silliness between me and some other kids, calling each other "big this" or "big that." Anyway, the "BIG JER" stuck. Now, it so happened that in junior high we moved from one classroom to another at the ringing of a central bell. The bell would sound and the kids in their classrooms would pick up their things and go to their next class. There'd be a ten-minute interval.

Since I was often the first kid into Mr. Gates's Latin classroom, I started going up to the blackboard and writing there, in chalk, in big letters, "BIG JER." It's stupid, but there you are: the would-be class clown announcing himself. Other kids would drift into the classroom, see the "BIG

JER," and greet me with gibes and good-natured insults. On most days when Mr. Gates came into the classroom he'd smile thinly at the "BIG JER" on his blackboard, pull an "I'm tired of this" expression, walk over to the "BIG JER" with an eraser, and briskly rub it away. He'd erase it in order to start the session with a clean blackboard.

But on that one laughable day I still remember, he walked in, pulled an exaggeratedly sour expression, and, walking over to the "BIG JER" with chalk in hand, didn't erase it but instead just added an even bigger "K" to end the word. Everybody broke out laughing, and I was the biggest laugher of all. He'd cut down the cut-up.

Last year, having a beer with Johnny Moser, he reminded me of the day when he and I and his dad were lounging outside the Mosers' downtown store, and a local sheriff's deputy, a Barney Fife kind of goofball, came walking up the sidewalk. Johnny remembered how I, for a joke, suddenly faced the deputy, dropped into a crouch position, and "slapped leather" as though drawing six-guns, crying "Hands up!" with my index fingers pointed at him. For a split-second he recoiled, but then laughed, and Mr. Moser laughed, and Johnny laughed, and I laughed. I blew the smoke from my two barrels and tucked my six-guns into my pockets. Looking back and changing the metaphor, it seems clear that at 14, unconscious of other destinations, I was dog-paddling toward Mr. Howard's beastly island, trying to earn belongingness as a free-spirited joker.

5

Yrrej Namwen

ELLENSBURG, 1953-1956

I think today's teenagers are more politically conscious than kids in my own era. Today's kids care who's handling the country and where it's going. When, in 1953, at age 14, I entered high school, I certainly knew our President was Dwight Eisenhower and that we were in a "Cold War" with "International Communism." Communists were terrible, they'd fluoridate our water and make us live in underground bomb shelters, but I didn't know much more than that, and nobody else in my classes did either.

Our naiveté came partly from living in a western backwater, but the 1950s was a decade of unthinking complacency in general. We knew all about Communism from Senator McCarthy but were pretty blind to everything else. We didn't see the seeds of the turbulent 1960s being sown in such things as the refusal of Rosa Parks, in Birmingham, to give up her seat to a white passenger on a bus, or the abrogation by South Vietnamese President Diem of the Geneva Accords' promise to hold a nationwide election in Vietnam. The turmoil of the decade ahead was worsened by our indifference to what was happening under our noses.

But although I was clueless about all that, high school changed me quite a bit. I remained socially uncertain but developed intellectually. Under a famously good teacher I wrote some very mature stuff. I reinforced my brand as class comedian and socially branched out to make many new friends. I gave up some sports and tried others. I learned how to drive, got a car, and expanded my world. With potential girlfriends I was a pathet-

ic loser; with guys I made some enemies and had one memorable fist-fight. I continued defining myself, and experienced certain groups I wanted no part of. I ran for Student Body President and nearly won. I began thinking about career options and dimly sensed that they'd combine writing, arguing, and entertaining.

One notable change was my turning away from football, where I'd cracked a tooth and broken a finger. Golf looked interesting, and since my folks had played it without losing teeth, I began frequenting the Ellensburg Golf Course out on the old Thorp Highway. That course is not very difficult, but the irrigation canal along the first hole is a menace, and, worse, you also have to drive across it when teeing off on the second. The good news was that that canal held probably a thousand golf balls. So, for supplies, that's where I went, with a simple kitchen sieve secured to a long stick. I spent hours fishing for balls. They were like rocks, but that didn't matter because I'd soon lose them again anyway.

Do I need to say my drives were erratic? I wrote earlier about the Kittitas Valley wind. It blows so hard that local golfers learn to compensate for it. For many holes you've got to perfect a hook, a drive that curves to the left, if you want to stay on the fairway; otherwise it's out into somebody's hay field. I got so I could negotiate the course, on a good day, with something like a 55. That's a shameful score, but it was good enough to make me the second-best golfer on our pathetic golf team. And so, when the state golf tournament was held at Port Angeles in 1955, I got to go. I was tickled pink!

Just imagine my arrival at the tournament with my mismatched clubs and the best of my waterlogged balls (though I'd bought three new ones for the event). The other players were dazzling—some were the sons of golf pros. They sparkled with all the latest clothes and equipment, the most beautiful wing-tipped golf shoes with little spikes in the soles, leather bags full of the latest woods and irons, those snappy little golf gloves peeking from their back pockets. There, on the other hand, nervously gawking at them, was I with my crappy mismatched clubs and neoprene golf bag, its pockets filled with ugly balls plus the three shiny new ones I'd soon lose.

Imagine how nervous I was when teeing off the first time. Dozens of foursomes, bright in their gaiters and fancy togs, were standing around, watching. They lounged there, with nothing better to do while waiting to tee off than stare at me. And of course Fate made me the first up in my own foursome. I took a few practice swings with my driver, sending clods flying into the gallery. More people, hearing muffled laughter, ambled over to watch. With great deliberation masking my inner trembling I teed up my ball, swung wildly at it, and shanked it through some nearby poplars into a parking lot. There was a metallic sound as it hit somebody's hubcap. Murmurs rose from the crowd, and louder laughter.

That was just the beginning of my agony on that miserable first hole. I never totally whiffed on any of my four attempted drives, but I did begin by losing all three of my shiny brand-new balls, hitting them one by one into the overflow parking lot. At last, my presence of mind returning, I knocked the best of the ugly ones about twenty yards down the fairway. The crowd didn't know whether to clap or guffaw, so mercifully decided against both. The silence was palpable. Walking down the fairway with my foursome I tried to explain the special aerodynamics of golf in Ellensburg, but they were uninterested.

After two days of mortification, there on the leader board appeared a final tally of players with their total strokes. Again the whole crowd of players stood around watching. I saw my own name appear at the bottom of the list of 42 names. Sniggering occurred. I thought I heard a groan mentioning my name—"NOOman . . . Who's NOOman?" I looked around, pretending to search for the individual in question, then slunk home and prayed Mr. Cunningham wouldn't write up the state golf tournament.

I had more fun playing on the tennis team. Our racquets were primitive, they were homemade from cake pans. We were always laughing, and one major subject of mirth was our coach, the Home Ec teacher, Gladys Baker, an old lady with a pug nose and dense facial hair. Gladys is pronounced "Gladiss" but we turned it into "Glades," and, borrowing a slogan from Burma Shave, greeted each other with the question, "Howya fixed for blades, Glades?" Miss Baker's driving was even worse than her coaching, and nobody wanted to be with her when the team car-pooled to matches down south. The curving two-lane road to Yakima followed high cliffs above the river.

My best tennis pal was Jim Gosney, a year older than I. He was thin, wiry and dark, with hooded eyes. He smoked Camels, had a brooding expression, and so accurately channeled Humphry Bogart that he even looked like him. He'd get that tough-guy Bogart look in his eyes and say "A hot dog at the game beats roast beef at the Ritz," or "The only point in making money is, you can tell some big shot where to go." Apart from tennis, we spent time just bullshitting and laughing about this and that. Unfortunately I began smoking Camels the way he did, and continued to smoke for decades afterwards. Stupid, but there you are. It was high school, and, up to that point, the only thing I could even think about fixing was my baby sister. But my smoke rings were amazing.

I also began learning to ski. A few of us went to the Swauk area near Blewett Pass, where, deep in the forest, there was a crude rope tow. Lanny, Art Reitsch, Johnny and I must have gone up there a dozen times. Again there's a giant contrast between then and now: the Swauk's ski conditions were, by today's standards, Stone Age. Given any alternative whatsoever, no self-respecting kid today would ever ski in the Swauk. You had to trudge through a quarter-mile of forest *in deep snow* to get to the ski hill, there was no equipment for grooming the slope, we began a skiing session by lining up and physically tramping the sidehill snowdrifts from top to bottom of the run, there was no warming hut, we were freezing cold after only an hour of skiing (though we would continue all day), our equipment was pathetic and dangerous (wooden skis, cable bindings, laughably wobbly leather boots), and we were such terrible skiers that often our main method of stopping was to grab a lone fir tree near the bottom of the hill! When our aim was off, or our timing poor, we'd hit the tree or each other. Today's parents fret about concussions, but heck, I had four or five every day at the Swauk. Anybody who'd worn a helmet would have been scorned as a pantywaist.

By our senior year in 1956 we'd begun driving to Stevens Pass, Snoqualmie Pass, and White Pass, all offering much better skiing. My favorite run was "Cascade" at White Pass, quite long and broad, challenging but hardly death-defying. I became more proficient but have always skied too fast. I love the sport's speed and danger, the sense of transport that comes from velocity, skill, risk, rhythmic body movement, and total concentration. Skiing well is like playing professional hockey at high speed, which explains why I've also injured myself about six times, tearing my rotator cuff and triple-fracturing my pelvis. Of course that last injury came seven years ago when I was hot-dogging for my grandkids. What an idiot, still not totally fixed.

When describing my earlier years I mentioned a few brushes with the opposite sex. There were Sandra Creech, and Blatty Hommilton, and several others who don't count because they were good friends who just happened to be girls—Kay Kendall with her curling red forelock, and sunny blond Marilyn Meyer. But by 1953, when I was 14, I was somewhere in the vicinity of puberty. Today I have to look up "hormones" for reference, but at that time I suppose mine were, as they say, "raging." I know I was taking a more serious interest in girls because, looking back, I see that an Ice Age of lonely crushes and objectless pining was about to begin.

To pursue full-blown romance it was essential to possess a motorized love-nest. I turned 16 halfway through my junior year, and my parents, unaware of my plot, gave me a car, a 1948 Chevrolet coupe. We didn't have "driver training," but I did practice how not to hit rural mailboxes as I drove around country roads before going to the State Patrol Office for my driver's test. It was my birthday, and I was ready to roll!

I passed the written exam, climbed into my car with the testing officer in the passenger's seat, started the engine, and drove exactly as he told me to. It was a snap! I stopped smartly at corners, looked both ways with gusto, alertly signaled right and left for turns, prudently stopped for pedestrians more than a block away, and then at last, at the officer's request, pulled up beside a high curb where he told me to execute the standard "parallel parking" maneuver between two parked cars. Smartly peering forward over the dashboard, then back through the mirror, I carefully edged forward, then back, then forward, then back again, then forward. Great! I'd parked next to the curb, on the street, between two cars! And hadn't hit anything!

After I finished, the cop gave me a look, then asked, "Are you done?" I considered my answer. "Yes," I decided. He instructed me to exit the car and come around to the curb side. I saw that I had parked *the entire right half of the car on the sidewalk!* It listed like a beached sailboat. "Come back next week," he growled. "Next week?" I quailed. "One week from today." Afterwards I found the cause of my difficulty. There were no curbs on country roads. Why hadn't somebody prepared me for that? The entire fiasco was somebody else's fault.

Next week, I parked nearly in the middle of the street and, after discussions, got my license. I then swung into action. For my hormones' sake I made a list of the prescribed changes for an up-to-date young man's love chariot. I had to turn my Chevy into a "hot rod," I needed to make it a "chick magnet," then I'd get me some "poontang." First it had to be fitted with twin "pipes"—the old single tail-pipe would never do—the car had to purr. Then too, its Chevrolet hood ornament had to be removed: the rounded nose of the hood had to be "leaded," that is, filled in with solder and sanded smooth to make its whole front look more like a man bomb. Moreover, the entire car had to be "lowered"—that was indispensable; no one but a "dweeb" drove around without his car hugging the ground. At last, as the finishing touch, the car had to be re-painted—I painted mine an irresistible metallic blue. Finally, I was supposed to get a bunch of mesmerizing doodads to hang from the mirror—I balked at that, but anyway, I was now driving my Fräulein Fishing Lure, it was gorgeous. "Where's the women at? Any pigs want a ride? Howza bouta game of back-seat bingo?"

With Deathmobile

As transportation, that blue 1948 Chevy coupe served me well for years, even though, with its vacuum shift and sometimes inexplicable horn-honkings, it earned its nickname, "Deathmobile." But unhappily it remained my Garden of Innocence; I was still a blushing virgin when I graduated. I did manage a little kissing. The first girl I ever kissed was Suzanne Drake, when I was 15 or so. Gosh, that was wonderful! She was beautiful, she had a heart-shaped face and extremely full, luscious, lips, and she actually kissed me back! I don't recall what became of our short romance, or even if there was one.

I had other dates, but mostly there were just boy-girl occasions like the sock hops at the YMCA. In the gym's dimmed amber light the girls would line up on one side, the boys on the other, then we'd choose partners with the canned rock 'n' roll blaring, and we'd jitterbug. Yes, that's the word, jitterbug. Silly, isn't it? But I've seen people of my generation STILL jitterbugging even today—the ancient shapeless woman spinning under the ancient crooked guy's upstretched arm, the two antediluvian partners "bopping" back and forth. It's like a window into the Mesozoic Era, watching mating triceratopses.

I remember another girl I kissed, or rather found myself nearly chokingly kissed by, Junie Biggalater. She not only kissed me but thrust her entire tongue up to its roots into my startled maw. That "French" kiss, a suffocating attack on my tonsils—where the hell had she learned *that?*—was my first and last. Junie was bad news but her enthusiasm, at least, was commendable and left me hoping for what might come next. Nothing did, and my future was saved because she was the class dummy.

Principal "Warden Willie," Suzanne Drake, Bill Bieloh

And then, *Wham!* came my crush on Beth Knudsen. In Junior High I'd had my eye on her but had been too terrified to make a move. However, in high school I was getting older and, uh, more mature. And so at some point I decided I loved her, wanted her, needed her. Being impulsive and half-convinced that whatever came out of my mouth would be received with, at least, politeness, I more or less told her so.

She recoiled in horror. Looking back, I'm not surprised. With the wisdom that comes with age I honestly believe that recoiling in horror is the first thing mothers teach their daughters. Along with milk at the nipple they take it in. "Spring back, dear, and bug out your eyes." So with no further ado Beth let me know she wasn't interested. I could tell it from her expression. It's as though she'd found a beetle in her sandwich. It's obvious *now* that rejecting me was the biggest mistake of her life, but she was so young. Youth is blindness, and almost the entire generation of girls in that era were stone blind to the thrills and surprises that awaited passengers in the Deathmobile.

Unfortunately she attended a lot of my own classes, so I had to be around her a lot. It's too bad I don't have pictures of her, I shredded them to stuff a pillow (but see p. 77). Anyway, she dressed demurely in white blouses with collars, blue cardigans over them, like an English girl at a prep school. She had sexy high cheekbones, and I was magnetized even by the slightly wicked effect her irregular canines, her "eye teeth," gave to her killer smile. Everything about her was cool and subdued, so of course her reserve constituted an additional challenge. She was a cheerleader like other popular girls, but she was also a good student, performing well in what would have been Honors classes if we'd had any. Naturally this made me like her even more. Even an ugly smart guy can coax a dumb girl into his arms, but a smart girl is a challenge. That's why girls that are both smart and pretty are so highly prized. When tracking the species, they're the trophy prey.

So I plotted, and tried to act normal when my heart was beating wildly, even though I foolishly lunged at her once when she unwisely consented to go out with me. I think the expression that would rise to the lips of a young lady today would be "Eeuw." But at last I came up with the right strategy. Looking at it now, I see that it was very like the strategy I'd used so successfully in grade school to woo my first love, the unforgettable contortionist Sandra Creech of dance lessons memory, before she threw up. Beth worked at Jerroll's Café as a waitress. To be near her, to jolly her up while working alongside her, I interviewed for the new job there as soda jerk, and was given a trial run for a day. I had to wear the uniform, a white shirt and white pants.

I must mention that Cherry Cokes were all the rage in 1955. I'd been given full instructions on how to make one. You put ice into the glass, then you squirt into it some of the specially flavored cherry syrup, then you fill the glass to the top with Coke from the fountain. Easy. Well, receiving an order for a Cherry Coke, I performed the first part of this procedure magnificently. With steel nerves and lightning footwork I got the glass and added the ice. And then, glancing sideways at Beth to make sure she was admiring my performance, I squirted the cherry syrup all over my white shirt and pants! Actually, in sports terminology you'd say the ice got the assist: I squirted the syrup so clumsily that it bounced off the ice to spatter me! I wasn't fired at the end of the day, but that's only because I hadn't been hired yet. Let's just say it was decided by management that soda at Jerroll's should be jerked by a steadier hand.

I carried a torch of misery for Beth for years. For me, she was the main subject of those beery meditations with Purnell behind the I.O.O.F. cemetery. At last, at the end, she married the podiatrist David Kitts. She could have landed me like an exhausted trout, but chose somebody else. I think it best to look at the whole matter philosophically. Young podiatrists are entitled to their share of the world's happiness too. And probably she would have thrown me out at some point anyway.

~

As to other work, well, of course I continued to keep my hand in as Dog-Do Associate of the Ellensburg Animal Hospital. But in the summers I took up working on a hay ranch owned, coincidentally, by two brothers named Hay—Jim and Don Hay. That work was hard, but it was good for me. Larry Chamness and Gerry Platt and I worked as a crew. We'd arrive in overalls, grab our hay hooks, and take off in the big flat-bed truck, heading into the hay fields where already the Hay brothers, driving baling equipment, had left behind long rows of baled hay, 80 pounds to the bale. (Today's bales are much bigger.) With one guy driving and the other two on the truck's bed, we'd drive alongside the rows, guiding the hay-loading apparatus through the bales, which it speared and dragged upwards, one by one, to the bed of the truck. There we'd grab it, stack it neatly, grab the next one and stack it too, until the truck would be so fully loaded that it'd look like a haystack on wheels. Then we'd head slowly back to the ranch, start the powered lift, and unload all the bales into the barn, stacking them neatly all the way up to the roof. All day long we did this, sweating hard with the sun beating down on us. Often the wind blasted so sharply that it drove chaff into our faces, ears and noses.

And now autobiographical truth, which frequently means confession, obliges me to say we did something bad. We picked our noses. Or rather more than that, what we did was pick our noses and add what we'd re-trieved, with many "oohs" and "aaahs," to the enormous colorful display of dried snots, we called them "loogies," on the inside of that poor truck's windshield. After only an hour's work in the wind, our noses, doing their God-given job of filtration, would be so full of dust, chaff, and dirt that we could barely breathe, and I think it was Chamness who came up with the idea of creating this "Living Gallery of Flagrant Snots," as we called it.

So, adding to the Gallery every day, we made a gigantic collection, accompanying each colorful installation with appreciative remarks and critical reflections. We actually had some glorious loogies there. But then one day Don Hay asked us what the hell was that stuff that had dried all over the inside window of his hay truck? We didn't have a good answer. We looked at our shoes. Talking about our "Gallery" was out of the question. Don being a serious-minded individual of bourgeois tastes with no flair for cubist modernism, we thought it best not to roil his mind with the current concepts.

So we just stood there in silent contemplation, as though dumbfounded. As though we had no idea. Don Hay, staring at our Gallery, told us to get it the hell off the windshield. That really was a loss, and I wish I'd been able to take a picture before Platt chipped it away.

~

Composing this memoir reminds me that teenage boys can be pretty immature, filthy, stupid and crazy. I don't mean Platt and Chamness. They were indeed good friends, guys I got to know well by working with them. Chamness was really a fine young man; poor fellow, he died young a couple decades ago in California. I remember when he was Master of Ceremonies at a class reunion in the 1980s. I'd come all the way from Ohio to attend it, so he presented me a gag gift for my long journey back, a roll of toilet paper with, for privacy, a huge tumbleweed. But now, thinking of him, I'm reminded of another story, a pretty horrid one, a pretty shameful one too.

Chamness and another friend of mine, Tony Chase, and still another, Butch Sterling, took me with them over to Seattle on one occasion. Chase, the son of a prominent Ellensburg banker, knew Seattle well because for a time he attended Lakeside School, a prep school for rich boys. Tony thought I was a funny guy, he liked me, we'd sometimes go to the Ellensburg drive-in movie in a car-load of guys and yuck it up; I admired him as very cool. We stayed in Seattle a few days—I can't remember where. The four of us went to Playland, the amusement park that used to be there, and we had other adventures. But one night we got very drunk and decided, I don't know how this happened, that we'd go into the poor part of town and "find some whores." In a broken-down tenement house we found two women, prostitutes, one older, the other younger and very fat, who asked us, four drunken high schoolers from out of town, who was to be first, who was to be next; and then they proceeded, in that dim room lit by a single hanging light bulb, to flop back onto a moth-eaten bed and throw up their skirts—I was shocked to see they had no underwear on!

Me first? Not me! I was so wasted and drunk and shocked and scared that I burst out of the room, down the fire escape, and threw up in the alley! I know, the whole sordid episode is disgusting. But I didn't forget it, and later, in college, I wrote it up as a supposedly fictional story. The writing professor gave me an A and commented favorably on its "many vivid passages," but observed that because its characters weren't clearly defined, a reader couldn't sympathize with any of them or care much about what happened in that godforsaken tenement building. The criticism was just. But I now see the story's significance in a way that neither I nor the professor did when I wrote it. In reality the story presents a window into the minds of respectable but drunken teenagers hunting sex but appalled to find what it looks like in that sad world so far beyond their understanding.

There's one more rough story to tell. Just as I made new friends in high school, I also made some enemies. The era of rock 'n' roll was beginning, and that was the era also of what were called "greasers." Greasers cared less about school than about pomading "duck tails" into their hair and rolling their T-shirt sleeves above the shoulder and perching a "pack of smokes" up there. They'd ride around in their hot rods with the radios blasting, leaning out the window, "cruising Main" and "dragging Water" while trying to look cool. I didn't like them. They weren't my sort of people—which, I perceive, also signifies that I was beginning to figure out what sort of people WERE my sort.

I come now to the Pinney brothers. Roy Pinney was a classmate. He was a big guy with glasses, a flat-topped haircut and a piercing stare. He played football and often turned out for school plays. His older brother, Ralph, was a mechanic in a gas station just beside Jerroll's. This story is about me and Ralph, the older brother. Now, I was in a more elite social set, and something of a popular class cut-up; and I'd decided that greasers were beneath me, I wanted nothing to do with them. I guess I was becoming a bit of a snob. And Ralph knew it. So one day when I was going into Jerroll's, Ralph hollered at me from outside his gas station, "Hey Noooman! Hey Noooman! C'mere." He had three or four fellow greasers around him. I couldn't refuse without looking like a coward, so I went over to him. The fellow greasers looked on with anticipation. Mr. Anti-Greaser Smart-Guy was going to get his gizzard handed to him!

Ralph Pinney weighed about 40 pounds more than I. He was two years older, and one mean SOB. I knew this was going to be a difficult situation. "Yeah?" I asked. "What?" He simply balled up his fist and said something insulting. I cold-cocked him. Before he could say another word I hauled off and slugged him in the face as hard as I possibly could! Why? It's simple. I knew a fight was coming and that he was going to beat the stuffing out of me, but I wouldn't let him or his friends have the satisfaction of making me a coward too. So I hit him first. There was no other choice.

He thrashed me within an inch of my life. He beat me up while bending me painfully backward over that metal tire-changing gizmo with the metal peg in the middle of it, you know the thing, it's in every gas station. But, nursing my wounds on the way home, I had a young man's satisfaction of knowing that I'd not chickened out. Seeing him several days later, I noted that he had a discolored, swollen place on his cheek near his nose. And whenever I saw him again after that fight, we'd just look at each other. He never said another word to me and never insulted me again.

～

Figuring out what I wasn't—a greaser—must have connected up somehow with figuring out what I was. Does a social winnowing occur in high school? I think it did in ours, and that it expressed itself most clearly in classes chosen, and in after-class activities. My own preferences, apart from sports, had to do with intellectual stuff, creative writing and entertaining. I'll admit right away that I was no bookworm, I had little interest in outside reading even if I'd had time for it. But I loved Radio Production, a class which, I now perceive, was a launching pad for the school's eggheads. My friend Art Reitsch, with whom I'd written and performed that comedy script in the ninth-grade talent show (he too later became a professor, by the way), and Pete Cunningham, the sports journalist's son, and Kay Kendall, and Beth Knudsen, they were all in it. The class taught creative dramatic writing, acting, sound-effect technology, and production for radio, which of course in the early 1950s was still the *via media*, the main national medium of communication. (Black and white network TV was just getting off the ground: in 1950, only six million sets were sold nationwide.)

Our teacher was Ruth Argall, an old, thin, shrewd and very experienced spinster who had seen (and put up with) a lot in her time. She was dry, humorous and tolerant. One of the memorable things about her, besides her explosive laugh, was her graceful but very arthritic fingers, somehow stuck together like two pretty little pink wedges that she waved in front of her face to emphasize a point. She gave us a lot of freedom, but we were self-starters. She handed us the reins and we rode away, creating all kinds of clever stuff without much supervision. In the technical sphere, we learned how to revolve a wooden wheel in a barrel of canvas to make the sound of wind, we learned how to clap coconuts to simulate the sound of horses, we played with bells and ringers of all kinds, we created thunderstorms by slapping and wiggling large sheets of aluminum.

More important to me was the fact that we wrote, and adapted, radio scripts, which, in turn, we performed as actors. We practiced them at school, and then, at station KXLE on Radio Hill (managed by Kay's dad), we acted and transmitted them to the entire local radio-listening community. Our Radio Production class gave us great experience in what was, in that day, one of the country's most demanding and creative professions.

To give examples of what I did, I wrote a humorous parody of "Dragnet," a popular national radio show featuring a lead detective, Sergeant Joe Friday, and his clueless sidekick, Officer Frank Smith: together they'd track down some Los Angeles criminal by driving from one shady dive to another, interviewing low-lifes. It was fun parodying the latter—delusional eccentrics, crazily loquacious, talking 'way off the point or taking the question-and-answer format down some absurd rabbit-hole. I made the famous audible signature, "Dum da-Dum Dum," punctuate the action after every little encounter.

Another project was my adaptation of the 1952 short story by Roald Dahl, "Dip in the Pool," which is all about a fateful event in the life of a fearful and too-jumpy American man named William Botibol—too jumpy because he foolishly jumps overboard and drowns himself in the Atlantic, thinking he'd be safe and win a fat bet. In radio-listening Ellensburg my adaptation was received as one of our class's best productions.

A different project was my tribute to Irving Berlin, the great composer who wrote such timeless hits as "God Bless America," "White Christmas," "Always," "Alexander's Ragtime Band," "Heat Wave," and "A Pretty Girl is Like a Melody." I wrote the script, narrated it, and cued the music, managing the whole thing. That was a great learning experience which also initiated my life-long admiration for Irving Berlin, originally a poor immigrant from Belarus, America's greatest all-time song-writer.

But acting in school plays continued to be my favorite extracurricular activity. Our school yearbook, the *"Klahiam,"* pictures me in nearly every dramatic production of my high school years. My favorite was the abbreviated "Midsummer Night's Dream," directed by Max Gates, our drama coach and Latin teacher. I still have my copy of the script: it's an excerpt, from the Shakespeare play itself, of the whole little "play within a play" performed by the "rude mechanicals," the rustic workmen who enact its performance for the entertainment of the "gentles" (the Duke and Duchess of Athens and their court). The play's climax comes in a mock-tragic rendezvous that occurs at night in a dark cemetery between two lovers fatefully separated (like Romeo and Juliet) by an ancient family dispute—between Pyramus, the bumbling ill-fated suitor, and Thisbe, his equally ill-fated and bumbling inamorata. I mentioned earlier that Max Gates, our director, could, just as a parlor trick, perform all the play's action and dialogue just by himself, assuming all the roles in sequence while snatching disguises one after another out of a barrel.

The golden part in this play, the screamingly funniest role in it, was given to me. Max Gates knew his man, the "BIG JER+K" from his Latin class. I can still recite most of my lines from that play, especially that last graveyard scene, in which I, playing Pyramus, appalled at my (erroneous) discovery that a lion has eaten Thisbe, stab myself to death with my sword, upon which Thisbe makes her appearance and collapses in grief over my body. Of course I didn't just recite my lines, I most hammily *acted* them, lisping, bugging out my eyes, pretending to jab them to make tears flow, hauling out my SWWWORD (pronouncing the W) with both hands to hara-kiri myself at the end, expiring while still speechifying.

We performed the play three times for large and delighted audiences, all on the venerable stage of the Junior High auditorium. Roy Pinney, the younger brother of the bully, played Thisbe in drag, wearing a dress and a ridiculous veil. Roy was very big, a tackle on the football team, so the effect of him playing my love-struck girlfriend was even more absurd. In the final scene his voice wavered as he sobbed out his love for me over my dead body. Holding my corpse he yelled out his grief in a screeching voice that made him sound like an Italian castrato. The whole scene was too ridiculous for words, which is just as well, because whatever Roy yelled was drowned out by the audience's roar.

~

In 1950 I'd been a complete stranger to my classmates. By 1956, after six years, I was well known throughout the entire school. But who, or what, was I? Well, for starters, I was *Big Jer*. *Big Jer* was that pudgy kid whose dad was a veterinarian and who carried with him some taint of living in dog-shit but who also played some football and golf and tennis and had a decent-looking car and knew how to jitterbug and also a guy who'd fight you if he had to, if you insulted him, but otherwise give you a smile or more likely a wisecrack in the school hallways, and who was top of his class in English and Radio Production and Latin, and who was still remembered for putting himself forward on a certain first day of school, and who, often a show-off, came up sometimes with funny public stunts and was a sort of hammy and jackassy kind of guy who, romance-wise, was infatuated with a girl who thought he was amusing but, up close, creepy.

That was the guy. A pretty ordinary high school kid, rough around the edges but not totally without potential, a bit conspicuous and needy but basically just doing his own thing, unconsciously preparing, as we all were, for an unknown future. Jerry Newman was socially insecure but intellectually confident when he wasn't feeling socially confident but intellectually insecure. Oh yes, one more thing, pretty much in character too—That *was the noisy screwball who decided to run for the highest student office in the school, Associated Student Body President.*

I still have no idea why I did that. I think Jim Gosney talked me into it, and that the more he talked, the more I liked the idea. It's only now, in retrospect, that I perceive the obvious match between this event and that other one my first day in junior high, when I proposed myself for home room president! In 60 years that parallel never occurred to me. What was it that made me push myself forward in that way? Honestly, I have no idea. Brashness? A death wish? A degree of social courage that I certainly don't possess today?

Anyway, I threw my hat into the ring. Why not? What did I have to lose? But my decision upset the applecart of Steve Moe (pictured on p. 73), the fair-haired son of the richest family in town, the star quarterback of the football team, a forward on the basketball team, the only guy in school with a swimming pool *inside his house* to which he would invite the other golden people; and, of course, to add to his credits, I have to admit now that Steve Moe was also the Number One Golfer in high school, the guy who *accompanied me to that tournament in Port Angeles and witnessed my shame there!* He was slobbered over by everybody. Everybody but me. Well, maybe a did slobber a little. I started wearing argyle socks after admiring his.

Well, actually, like everybody else I liked and envied and admired him. And despite being on top of the pack, he was really a pretty modest fellow. He even signed my *Klahiam* backwards (see below). Anyway, Steve, if I hadn't entered the race, would have won it hands-down. We were the only two candidates. Gosney and I, planning my role as plucky underdog, set about putting together my campaign. It was fun to work on, but also very unorthodox and visibly disrespectful of school electoral traditions. Most high school electoral races, no matter where they occur, are simple popularity contests. Most candidates cover this up, though, by modestly listing their own good grades, honors, responsibilities, public activities, and so on. It's also a good idea to mention helping an underprivileged family, but in rural areas where there might be only one or two, candidates wage fist-fights to claim one. But the main way to seem worthy of the heavy responsibilities of office is to brown-nose the Principal, brown-nose the Vice Principal, and stand around ornamentally at boring events.

My approach disregarded all this. My approach was to treat the whole election as a farce, something I didn't seriously care about, something simply to get a laugh out of. My campaign slogans made this clear. "Newman Kisses Babies!" "Go Average With Big Jer!" "One Vote, One Free Car Wash!" "Cheapen Standards, Vote Newman!" "Get Nutty with Big Jer!" My election publicity had nothing to do with making the school better—in fact it almost promised to make it worse, especially with that slogan about installing prophylactic dispensers in the library. But it was iconoclastic and funny, which meant it attracted the lazier and more frivolous students, and that was more than half the student body right there. And then maybe I could also count my friends, who'd vote for me simply because they liked me. I'd shake things up; my presidency would amuse; and if I screwed the pooch, what did it matter to anyone except the Principal?

The day of the election came. Unselfishly with only the good of the school in mind I voted for myself. The ballots were tallied in the office of the Principal, William Brown. I wondered about that. Did he fool with them? Mr. Brown was a very sober character, stiff as a board, always calm;

he'd have looked calm even with a cat in his trousers. We called him "Warden Willie." He always looked grim. When he smiled, *if* that was a smile, we thought he was just clenching his teeth. I've seen babies loading their diapers with more convincing smiles on their faces. Anyway, I never wanted to be near him: he always stared at me in an unmistakably menacing way.

And in fact, if I have to tell the truth, I *never did* see him smile, even once. That stuff that I just wrote, about him smiling? I made it up. He never, ever, smiled. Instead, Warden Willie maintained the frozen look of an animal tamer determined to break a cage of laughing hyenas—which in fact he was, sort of. His job was to break and tame our animal spirits, make us grim and dull and law-abiding like himself. You can imagine what he thought of my candidacy.

Did he juggle the vote-count? Even now, I'm simply too pure of heart to imagine that he let his, uh, ambiguous feelings about me affect how faithfully he counted the votes. But at the end of election day he called Steve and me into his office to announce a tie between us. A dead heat. There'd been, he said, equal numbers of votes between us. A run-off would be required.

So again came another election day, but with a difference: Art Reitsch had decided to enter the race. What kind of friend was that?!? Anyway, the result? Art split Steve's vote, he split my vote, and he wound up winning the ASB Presidency! I was pretty unhappy about that. True, I'd gone into the whole race in a very light-hearted way, but I took news of the tie very badly, smelling a rat, and then the news of the loss with sharp disappointment. Looking back, I remember that after the first go-round I was distressed to learn that some of my best friends hadn't voted at all. My old friend Marilyn Meyer was one. To my face she confessed that she'd missed the voting, saying she'd been too busy that day in Mr. Kibbe's photo darkroom and had forgotten the election. *How could she?!?* Merle Kibbe's darkroom, by the way, was legendary as a filthy den in which teen cuties like Marilyn got groped.

I now think it possible that Marilyn, being one of the divinely golden people herself, really voted for Steve Moe. The other possibility is that, as she said, she really didn't vote at all—not because she was too busy getting groped in that darkroom but because she found herself unable to choose between her two very different friends, the handsome homecoming king and the slap-happy court jester and tennis buddy.

Though disappointed by the result, I kept up a brave front, treating it as a lark. A few months later, when everybody in my class was asked to produce a "Senior Will" bequeathing this or that to upcoming kids in the lower grades, I found something funny to say about that lost election: "I, Jerry Newman, hero amongst the feeble-minded and champion of the oppressed, hereby will and bequeath 14 bales of punctured balloons and used campaign posters to Adlai Stevenson, because I don't want him to win, either."

~

Somehow, despite all the moving-around since my high school days, some three dozen literary efforts have survived the years and the dump. This pile of stuff must represent weeks of adolescent concentration and literary workmanship. Though some of the paper has yellowed, everything remains quite legible, whether typed or written in longhand. There are stray ideas, short essays on various themes, biographical sketches, pieces of fiction, poems of varying lengths, and, as if pointing to later years, serious discussions of historical, literary, and psychological subjects.

Sifting through this stuff and attempting to evaluate the mind that produced it is an unusual experience. I think I can judge that I was getting a little smarter and more creative. Is that what happens with all misfits? Probably. Here's a spiral-bound commonplace booklet that I made, not as any class assignment but simply for myself as a notepad. It contains lists of words ("vapid—dull, spiritless, inane"; "timorous—afraid"; "tantamount—equivalent in value"), and odd snatches of descriptive prose,

as if I were trying my hand at creating atmosphere: "At the first crack of thunder in the bleak skies overhead, the mouse spun on his heels and scrambled for his favorite pine tree, pausing only to glance reluctantly back at the partly-eaten remains of a fish head he had discovered on the beach." It also contains odd sequences of words with no explanation: "Glide lunge stroke steal slash/ Hide plunge choke reel smash/ Kill free throat fleet sought/ Swill flee smote beat caught."

Further on, it contains jottings about poetic feet (anapest = - -*, iamb = -*, dactyl = *- -), playful efforts to write limericks

("There once was a pointer named Sturdley/ Who claimed he would never hunt birdley," etc.), and bits of doggerel: "While fishing for crab, I was hit by a cab / I'm now on a slab with a terrible scab." Or: "Little Mary, Little Mary, with her chubby legs so hairy, / Dug a pit and sat in it and played a game of solitary." Other poetic musings were longer, like my heavy-hearted composition in an Irishman's voice, "Knockadoon," about a shipwreck in Dungaruvan Bay, and a funny one in the persona of a roughneck cowboy in a tavern's bowling competition.

I was beginning to love the ring of words, and to rearrange them the way young artists might combine colors, or young musicians plunk out musical phrases. I was also beginning to record my own daily experiences. I'd not yet begun a diary, but the germ was there in sketches describing friends. As I think about all these doodlings it occurs to me that this is rather unusual, isn't it? Is this the sort of thing the typical high school boy does in his spare time, fill up a homemade commonplace book with snatches of doggerel, definitions, notes on poetic feet, descriptions of scared mice, sketches of friends? It's as though I'd built a little shop just like my forebears, but substituted wordsmithing for blacksmithing.

Looking at more formal academic papers, I reflect that whatever quality they exhibit was owed to my passion to impress the best teacher I had in high school, Marian Klobucher. She was a wonderfully intelligent woman who taught writing, the proper appreciation of great literature, a love of the ancient Greek writers, and Shakespeare. She was sweet, gentle, humorous and wise. She lived on Radio Hill with another teacher slightly prettier and younger; there were rumors that they were lovers. All the good students wanted to get into Miss Klobucher's classes. I took every subject I could from her and became her favorite. I admired her tremendously just as I'd admired Rodney Weeks, and, as with him, wanted to win her praise for everything I wrote. Again I'm reminded of how magically formative is the influence of an adored teacher. Few professions leave behind more lasting feelings of debt and gratitude.

What sorts of work did I present to the idolized Miss Klobucher? Well, I was continuing to write comedy. There was, for example, "How to Make Most People Feel Stupid," five pages long. (Klobucher's pleasant note at the end: "A. This sounds straight from the mouth of a professional.") Another, pretending to be an overheard conversation between "two females loitering on the corner," was packed with tip-off phrases (such as "Certainly a nice coat you got there, Hildegarde," and "I ain't got no bones to pick with you")—packed with tip-off phrases that point to the comic revelation, at the end, that the whole conversation had been between "two dogs meandering down the street, occasionally stopping for a breather at a convenient fire plug." (Klobucher's chuckling comment: "Pretty doggy writing.") Philosophically more engaging were pieces in which I addressed the human condition. One, a short story, captured a moment in the evolving roles of father and son, the former losing strength, the latter gaining it; another, an essay, was, though humorously presented, a serious inquiry surveying arguments on whether or not earlier humans experienced happier lives than those living in my own day.

What this shows is a developing interest in abstract thought and a curiosity about historical ways-of-thinking. Both are evident in a dense five-page psychological analysis of Macbeth, tracking his reactions to supernatural influences, and in a study of Greek morality in which like a scholar I grasped the importance of historical contexts: "There were always squabbles between political factions, not to mention revolutions, trade disagreements, and the ever-present plunderers intent on sacking a city; thus loyalty became almost the most important quality a man could possess." Another essay analyzed Homer's writing style: "Homer never wasted a word. All descriptions are concise, artistic, and accurate. The succinctness of Homer's descriptions provides a writing axiom usually forgotten by most prominent writers." Obviously I was thinking a lot about writing itself, the craft of it.

I was just a slightly precocious kid in the boondocks, so how to account for the unexpected qualities in these writings? The answer dawns on me. It's actually quite simple. The answer is that while other high school kids like Roy Doak were learning to raise heifers, Roy Pinney to fix faulty carburetors, and Lanny Purnell to balance binomial equations, the 17-year-old whose literary remains I'm looking at was tinkering away with words, phrases, sounds, images, propositions, arguments. Nor was he aiming only at competence; like those other boys he dimly hoped for mastery. Just as they polished their heifers, carburetors, and equations, he polished his syllables, images, and phrases. All to impress Miss Klobucher, but also, increasingly, himself.

∿

I'd begun to think about my future. A letter of January 1956 from my mother to my grandmother, who then lived in Seattle, laid out the terrain as we saw it then:

> At my suggestion Jerry went to talk with Miss Klobucher yesterday about his future. He says he would like to teach; that he loves history above all else, but is considering law or writing as well as teaching. Her suggestion to him was that he teach English, since in the teaching profession he would have time for travel, living and writing too. He isn't keen on teaching academic English, but might find his spot in literature, creative writing or drama coaching—even, perhaps a combination of them. I want him to go see our top lawyers in town and investigate law as a profession, and also to go see the dean of the history dept at Central while he is in the process of deciding his future. He would be good at any of these things, but I'm in hopes that a little investigation and thought can channel him in the right direction. He has been exceptionally fortunate to have Miss Klobucher this year, for she has a rare gift of bringing out the best in her students and helping them to distinguish the shoddy from the worth-while.

I don't remember talking to the dean or any lawyers, though with my mother pushing the idea I probably did. Maybe I'd begun thinking about becoming a lawyer; I knew only that the profession employed words, persuasion, argument. Anyway, with my future quite unsettled I plodded on to the end of my senior year and graduated on June 3, 1956. Our graduation ceremonies were held in the spacious gym of the new High School. Lanny and my friend Nadine Smith were co-valedictorians. There was so much hoopla connected with graduation that it took several days to get through it all; leaving our nest to fly out into the world was a big deal. Every graduation becomes hoary with school traditions, but the one that mattered most was the one where as individuals we received our yearbook, the *Klahiam*, and then spent an entire morning passing it around to be signed by others whom we might never see again.

I have my 1956 *Klahiam* at hand but must explain why it bears, on its front, my name backwards—"Yrrej Namwen." I'd asked to have it printed that way. By the spring of 1956, while some friends were still calling me "Big Jer," others, especially those who knew me well, were calling me "Yrrej"—Yrrej Namwen. (It sounds like "Yur-REDGE NAM-wen.") This, like so much else I did, had a stupid joke in it. And also, let's observe, it was all about words.

I'd just taken a typing class and become fascinated by the finger-by-finger search for the right letters on a standard keyboard—I even went to sleep at night half-consciously typing words, moving my fingers as I reached for each letter, tapping spaces and punctuation marks as well. Does anybody else do that when learning to type? Anyway, the fixation didn't end there. Instead I went on, whether awake or asleep, to start typing words *backwards* in my mind, and I made such progress that before long I could spell out, backwards, with almost blazing speed, almost any word that anybody tossed at me. Then, the next step, I began *pronouncing* those words backwards, for if I could spell them, it was no trouble pronouncing them. The fixation became a game, then a gift that others marveled and laughed at: Yrrej Namwen could *pronounce any word backwards, in two seconds flat!* Crazy, for sure! *Yzarc, rof erus!* And the funny thing, the *ynnuf gniht* ("yun-NOOF gu-NITT"), is that I can *still* visualize and pronounce words backwards, though with much less speed than in those days when practicing the trick was habitual. *gnizamA!*

Anyway, back to my *Klahiam* with "Yrrej Namwen" on its nameplate. I mentioned that the high point of graduation week was to pass one's yearbook around for other kids to write in. For its biographical value I'm going to copy out a few comments by my classmates. The compliments should be discounted as simple good spirits and goodwill, but the contexts reveal something of what other kids thought of me as my youth came to a close.

-Hi Jer! Have fun buckin bales. Be good & good luck. I know you'll go a long ways. Gerry Nielsen

-Dear Jerry, To a pal I really think has a terrific future. I've always had a lot of respect and admiration for your many talents, Jerry. I hope we'll always be close friends. Love, Kay

-Newman for Pres. Maybe some day you will win plenty Glory. Until then you will have to content yourself with having a Hero as a friend—Good Luck—take it easy on the U. Lannes Purnell (Hero)

-Dear Yrrej, Hey You—I think that you'd better come up and play tennis with me this summer cause I need some laughs once in a while—I think you're lots of fun Jer—and you make me laugh—Be good next year and think of me—Marilyn

-I've sure enjoyed being in your class this year. You've got a tremendous ability in writing. Loads of luck to you. Your friend Fred Johnson

-Jerry—I can't think of a nicer, friendlier kid that I would like to be in a class with. You may not know it but you've added a lot of hilarity & fun to my classes—Pete Cunningham

-Yrrej, er'uoy etiuq a dik. I hsiw uoy eht tseb fo kcul dna evah nuf ta eht "U" txen raey—Evets Eom

So there, somewhere, was what I was, the inner tadpole that later, after years of hopping around and roaming the ecosystem, became the Kermit dissected in these pages. We high school seniors were now liberated, freed from our little world. Soon we'd leave our out-of-the-way hamlet that was, as I said earlier, connected only by narrow roads and many miles to the centers of American life. We were now to find our separate ways in worlds far apart. Some of us were happy, some scared. I was mostly happy, I think. And that was the right mood, for although I didn't know it, I was about to embark on the best four years of my life.

PART TWO

Learning Life Skills

6

Joe College?

UNIVERSITY OF WASHINGTON, 1956-1960

We thought "Central" in Ellensburg a very good school, but believed the University of Washington was the best in the state, so that's where I went. Seattle was a provincial city in the 1950s, though today it's arguably the shiniest, richest, and best-educated metropolis in the nation. The Emerald City has always benefited from its natural beauty and commercial importance as the major northwestern seaport, but it has also benefited from its pre-eminence as a center of new technologies and businesses, all of which have attracted vigorous, well-educated and well-paid younger Americans from other states.

The University of Washington campus has also changed a lot since I first arrived there, and the cost of tuition, too! In a 1959 letter I informed my parents that I'd written a $71 check for the next quarter's tuition—in total, I paid $213 that year in tuition and fees. Today an undergrad pays $11,400! The university's main buildings are still there, but what a clutter has been jammed around them! When I was there the campus was majestic. Its buildings, wonderfully imposing neo-Gothic structures beautifully faced and decorated, soared into space and stood among wide alleys of flowering trees and shaded walkways. Now, however, the university, always accommodating more people and agencies, is losing some of its grace to continuing construction. Time changes everything.

～

I said it was a "given" that I would attend the U, and the same held for pledging a fraternity and living my four years in a frat house. My father had been a Theta Chi at Washington State, and his experience indicated that for a student hailing from far away, a fraternity meant a ready-made group of comrades, plentiful advice and friendly supervision by older "brothers," and a full run of pre-planned extracurricular activities. The objections against fraternities that are heard today, the dislike of them on the grounds that they are little more than breeding-grounds of drunkenness, rape, brutality, and mindless Republican conformity, didn't exist at that time.

And so, arriving at the U in early September 1956 as a pre-law major, I went through "Rush" and at the end of a hectic week accepted the invitation of Delta Kappa Epsilon (D.K.E., abbreviated to "Deke") and moved into that grand old white mansion on 21st Street N.E. The Deke fraternity is one of the nation's oldest, with a distinguished list of members including Robert Peary, Howard Heinz, Robert Lehman, Cole Porter, and Presidents Hayes, both Roosevelts, Ford, and both Bushes. When I joined it the Deke house was known for its athletic strength in varsity golf and crew, its recruiting power among popular boys from the entire Lake Washington area, its admired parties, and its academic excellence, with the second-highest grade-point-average among all the frat houses. I met some very smart guys there, and I met others more content to coast along with "gentlemen's B's," still trying to find themselves, and always up for a good time. I was one of those.

The Deke House

Many of my new frat brothers had decent cars; my Deathmobile was an exception, and its brakes were death-defying on Seattle's steep downtown hills. But cool cars weren't the only reason the girls considered Dekes cool. They had manners. Good manners were drilled into every pledge and were strictly enforced. The Deke house was a sort of finishing school for me, where I learned many of the finer points of etiquette. Regarding table manners, for example, the first thing to remember was to wear a sport jacket and tie at every evening meal. I was taught how to sit properly at table, keep my arms, elbows, and cuffs away from its surface, and use the proper tableware. A soup spoon, I learned, was to be dipped away from the body when loading a mouthful of soup, not, as is more natural, forward towards the body. I learned the right way to pass food dishes up and down the table: it was a grave fault to receive a dish coming from the left with the left hand, or to pass it to the right with the right hand. I've never forgotten any of this. Even when camping I remain a stickler about correct placement of the butter knife.

My pledge class, "the class of 1960," was the largest in memory with 42 members—at 17 I was the youngest. They came from all over the state, and a few from elsewhere. All were white, with similar backgrounds. Typically their parents were moderately well-to-do people from the upper middle class, mostly professionals and business owners. In high school my pledge-mates had gotten decent grades, and as college freshmen we had no option to studying hard because the house officers were intent on competing scholastically with other frats, and were fully supported by the mass of senior Dekes. We had an extremely rigorous system of enforced study.

Our big white frat house was a handsome three-story mansion with lots of common areas in it. The living quarters, the rooms we studied and slept in, were some two dozen semi-private rooms where 60 or so young men lived. Over time those rooms, like almost everything else, had acquired funny names like "Fairyland," "Seraglio," and "the Hole." Typically, each housed an "active" (an upperclassman) and a pledge. With this living arrangement, each active was both the roommate and immediate supervisor of the pledge billeted with him. Often he also became one of his best friends.

Upkeep of this entire complex was the work of each year's pledge class. Every Saturday morning the full pledge class would assemble under the direction of the House Engineer, an upperclassman charged with keeping the house clean and shiny from top to bottom, as well as with general maintenance. Sloppy work by a pledge would result in a "ding" by the House Engineer.

The disciplinary system worked on these dings. You could get dinged for lots of infractions, but most serious were such things as lipping off to an active, or bringing shame upon the house. A ding meant the pledge was required to make an appearance at that week's "Senior Court," where the house officers informed him of his offense, listened to his reply, and then usually punished him with several severe "hacks" with a wooden paddle against his buttocks. The hacks, though often only three were prescribed, were *hard*. I know that because I was one of the most frequently dinged people in my entire pledge class! Yes, I took a lot of hacks. I was fairly popular, but, playing for laughs, I sometimes crossed the line with some grouchy upperclassman. My "Maverick" tendencies persisted.

Working together on Saturdays was one of many routines that made us a brotherhood. Group life was modeling us, making men of us, and also making us Dekes, which meant shaping us in a particular way. We had to learn about all the Deke chapters in the United States, we learned secret passwords and handshakes, insignias and coat of arms. We celebrated our fraternity's fellowship by singing its drinking songs and love songs and wistful songs of college days gone by. Today "The Halls of Ivy" still puts a catch in my throat and a tear in my eye. And, dear reader, can any hard heart resist "The Whiffenpoof Song"?

I loved our song-practice sessions, afterwards filing out into the chilly night to serenade somebody's sweetheart standing on the balcony of a sorority house. Our rich sound filled the night air. Especially on those cold Seattle winter nights, the serenading seemed magical. And then, sometimes on a sunny Saturday, we'd sing a Deke song as we paraded down to the stadium to watch the Huskies play. In my memory those football Saturdays were always sunny, with the autumn air sweet, the colors brilliant, and my spirits full of anticipation and a sense of *belonging* as we marched down the hill and over to the stadium, where we'd yell our lungs out for "the mighty men who wear the purple and the gold!"

Group singing, good cheer, jocularity and friendly ribbing were all regular parts of my new life. I met some pretty crazy jokers, too. I remember Roger Haapenan, a music major who entertained with strange duets, blowing a trumpet while blasting perfectly tuned farts. The most popular guys all had nicknames, many invented by another funny character, Rich

Holloway. A year older than I, he became my good friend, and we often drove together to Snoqualmie Pass for skiing. He was a bar-stool maestro at funny stories, and a master wordsmith at inventing ludicrous nicknames— Snoqualmie's ski area itself, Snoqualmie Basin, he dubbed "Snoquie Basseen" as though it were some fancy French resort in the Alps— and under his spell, Bruce Giedt became known as "Giedtus," Jay Winemuller (a tall crewcut guy with a faintly Asian look) became "Yosh," Tom Franklin was "Tommy Franks," and for a while I became "Alf" (in honor of the *Mad Magazine* character Alfred E. Neuman) but then later he dubbed me "Slewob" ("bowels" backwards in jocular recognition of my weird skill acquired in high school typing class). Finally, through some permutation, I got called "Beowulf," so that sometimes entering the house after morning classes I'd be greeted by a chorus calling me all three at once: "Hey, Alf," "Hey, Beowulf," "Hey Sleww-Wobb!"

We were a merry band of brothers, we loved a good laugh, and lots of mental energy was spent on concocting funny situations. For example, I had a pal named Bill Defoe. Like me, he loved to philosophize. Sometimes like all college kids we engaged in late-night skull sessions on the meaning of life, ethics, stuff like that. We were both smokers, so often lit up when wading into deep conversations. One night, late, I walked into Defoe's room, turned on the light, and woke him up. "Hey, Defoe." "Yeah?" Rubbing his eyes, he groggily sat up on the edge of his bed. "Here." I lit a cigarette and handed it to him. He took a deep drag, rubbed his eyes and looked at me, waiting for me to broach some big subject worth talking about at that hour. But already I'd walked out of his room, turning his light off, leaving him sitting there in darkness on the edge of his bed with the lit cigarette still in his hand.

Pranks were part of the whole happy-go-lucky experience. I remember the house's lunch-time phone calls. Those were the 1950s. Nobody had personal phones: instead we relied on the two or three "land-line" phones scattered in the house. If someone outside wanted to talk to any Deke, he or she would call the house number: a pledge was obliged to pick up the phone (actives never did so) and loudly page the recipient, calling out his name in every room. Inevitably this led to high jinks and ludicrous inventions. A phone would ring during lunch-time when there might be 30 or 40 people in the dining room, including various invitees, guests who weren't Dekes. An unsuspecting pledge would answer the call and be asked by a muffled voice (disguising some prankster calling from another room in the house) to page a certain individual. The unsuspecting pledge would then enter the dining room and, *because he had to*, loudly call out the name of the individual wanted on the phone—"Jack Goff," or "Willie Stroker," or "Mike Rotch," "Buster Cherry," "Mike Hunt," "Jack Schitt," "Mike Litorris"?—the raunchy variations were almost endless, and the result was always loud guffaws followed by gibes at the dim-wittedness of the pledge. But ultimately as our freshman year passed, even the lowliest pledges were joining the fun, making up ridiculous names to holler around at lunch time—"Seymour Snatch? Paging Seymour Snatch?" "Dixie Normous? Paging "Dixie Normous?"—to which there'd be another chorus of wisecracks.

Earlier I declared that those college years were my best on earth, my happiest. That, at least, is the way I remember them, though memory can play tricks. But if that was my happiest time on earth, a major reason for that was GIRLS! And the pastures were so rich! There were wonderful girls in my classes, in sororities next door and across the street and on the next block, they were *everywhere!*

Well, yes, I was still somewhat the tortured youth, still awkward and liable to put my foot in my mouth. But gradually, I don't know how, girls had stopped staring in shock and instead were starting to look interested. That was partly because in Seattle I was no longer seen as an alien crashing a small-town picnic, or a janitor hip-deep in dog-do. Comparatively speaking, I'd become god-like. I was a stallion.

You laugh. But at least I had no trouble getting dates. I met girls in classes and took them afterwards for coffee, I played bridge with others, my frat brothers set me up with others in double dates. I was a happy herbivore in sweet grass. I still have photos showing some of those happy times. And what parties! We had one nearly every Saturday night. My diary records nights like the one when I took one girl to a party, wildly flirted with two others, and took home a fourth. But, unlike the 1960s when birth-control pills became common, sexual promiscuity in the 50s was still off the cards. You could have melted iron in the desperate heat of the Deathmobile, but for me, despite my exertions, regular extracurricular entanglement still lay in the future, the free and bohemian decade ahead. However, I'm happy to report that in the spring of my freshman year I did lose my virginity. I offered it to a fantastic older girl, quite experienced and horny, that I met (where else?) in an English class.

Talking about girls brings back other memories. Nearly all the "necking" I enjoyed took place in the Deathmobile's cramped quarters, but there was one happy exception. There was one girl I dated for quite a while, a "townie" who actually stayed at her parents' house while enrolled in her campus sorority. This meant that after a date I got to take her home. We'd lie on the rug in her basement, supposedly watching TV while actually watching for her father with his blinding flashlight and death-camp hospitality.

With Emilie Duwe

I dated Emilie Duwe for many months. She was small and very slim, pixyish, with short dark hair, wide-set eyes, and a mischievous smile. We met when writing music and comedy for "Song and Stunt Night," a competitive all-campus variety show. I was head writer and co-chair of the junior class's show, and also I played the actor I ridiculously named "Lance Abscess." Emilie was "Mary Phrostikowski" and also the head song writer. I'd never before encountered any girl as laugh-out-loud funny. In a letter I described "her lightning-fast cleverness, her gentleness and friendliness." I recall a few things that were part of her regular funny-gal stock-in-trade. She was, as I said, very small and thin, and at her own expense, with that devilish smile on her face, she often made fun of her own flat little breasts, likening them to drink coasters or mini pizzas. It didn't matter if she was in a large group—she always drew a surprised laugh. Shortly after meeting her I described her in my diary: "A piquant and saucy humor. She is quite sexually broad-minded. When asked 'How are you?' by some friend, she replies, 'Oh—making expenses.'"

And then there was Diane Wood. I met Diane in a history class. She was smart, subtle, poetic, literary, and intellectually mature. She didn't quite meet my standard of beauty but we really enjoyed each other's company. I remember walking around downtown Seattle with her just before Christmas. Light snow was falling, there were bells and tinsel on the street lamps, music rang in the night air, we were laughing and looking at everything in the shop windows. I recall gazing into her smiling, rosy face and thinking what joy her companionship gave me. She told me she loved me.

Then we went home for Christmas break, she to Spokane and I to Ellensburg, and I never contacted her again! Such a fool. She had too much pride to contact me, so the whole thing ended without a word spoken. I was a terrible heel. I broke her heart, and I knew why. I was getting in too deep, I thought I might be falling for her—which, given my earlier experience with Beth, I believed, might ruin my happiness. But, worse, I knew *she* was falling really hard for *me*, which ultimately would result in even more terrible disappointment *for her*. I really cared for her, I cared for her, and even—what egotism!—*sympathized with her for losing me!*

And so, in my dim stupid consciousness I felt that it was better to stop the relationship abruptly with the Christmas break as an excuse; that this was the charitable thing to do, the right thing to do *as a favor to poor little her*. So that was the end of it. I'm glad to discover, in my diary, that I felt shame and acknowledged it two months later: "I've begun to feel quite guilty about my neglect of Diane. I hope that she does not still love me, for to lose at that game is the bitterest of defeats. Her announcement of her love seemed to extinguish the mystery about her, as well as my romantic affections."

So I forgot about her. That is, until I ran into her by accident five years later in downtown Seattle. *She was now stunning!* Gone was the body fat, she was heart-stoppingly beautiful. And that's not all. She'd gone to Yale, gotten a PhD in Literature, been married and divorced already, and was now teaching at Olympic College in Bremerton. I was totally smitten, but now the shoe was on the other foot. Trying to win her back again, I made an epic fool of myself, and she took pleasure in it; she hadn't forgotten how nastily I'd dumped her. So after that one late Saturday night when she kicked me out of her bay-view apartment in Bremerton, then mercifully let me into it to sleep over and wake up to sunlight glancing off the water, and scones and black coffee and Bach on her hi-fi, she kicked me out again. Filled with remorse, I took the morning ferry to Seattle and never heard a word from her later. I forgot her all over again.

Then, about five years ago, musing as we do about people we once knew, on a whim I idly googled her name. Wanna know what came up? *She had become an academic super-star!* There were many glowing articles about her. The first one, from the *Stanford University News*, December 15, 2007, ran the following headline: "Diane Middlebrook, professor emeritus and legendary biographer, dies at 68." This was certainly the same Diane; the pictures of her left no doubt. She'd taught at Stanford for forty years, was one of the founders of feminist studies there, had written biographies of Sylvia Plath, Billy Tipton, and Anne Sexton, and when she died of cancer was working on still another biography, of the Roman poet Ovid. Again the *Stanford News*: "When asked several years ago why she picked Ovid as her subject, she responded with characteristic breeziness, 'No estates, no psychotherapy, no interviews, no history—I just make it up.'" THAT was the woman, that was the luminous spirit who'd loved me but whom I'd considered myself too good for, back at Christmastime in 1959.

∽

Hell Week is the last stage in the life of a pledge. Ordinarily it occurs in the spring of his freshman year. The whole point of it is, or was, to crystallize the months of character-building already imposed and weld together under great pressure a band of young men who would trust each other and remember for life the unique bonds forged in their collegiate togetherness. For me, Hell Week was certainly very different from everything else in my college life. Today it's frowned upon, condemned as unhealthy, and in fact, under the title of "hazing," banned in most states because it imposes physical and psychological risks and may lead to moral degradation, injury and even death. We live now in a tenderer age, a mothering age.

All 42 pledges were made to bed down in sleeping bags on the basement floor for a week and to use the bathroom facilities nearby. We were to attend our classes as usual, but otherwise be at the beck and call of all the "active" Dekes; and every one of them had the right to impose any task whenever and however they saw fit. Acceptance into full Deke membership was the stated goal. We were sternly reminded that failure to perform any demanded action might jeopardize official acceptance into the brotherhood, and that our individual fates would be determined at the end of the week.

So we were, as you might expect, wakened at odd hours of the night and forced to perform calisthenics or do unusual tasks—crawl on the floor, crowd into closets, perform ring-around-the-rosies, descend stairs backwards. The actives, cruelly laughing—though, I must say, not without bits of friendly indulgence (for they too had undergone all this stuff as pledges)—treated us like slaves, demanding shoe-shines, recitations and songs, jokes, weather-reports, and the like. If an active wanted food brought to him, the pledge had to obtain and deliver it. A few of us were made to wear odd articles of clothing. I was specially ordered to don a green hood and "buzz like a bee" whenever prompted, and before long other actives, piling on, had me not only buzzing but flapping imaginary wings and running in tight circles with energetic butt-wagging. All this went on for a week.

Those, however, turned out to be only minor nuisances. We endured much more on two nights set aside for bigger trials. On Wednesday night there was a nightmarish scavenger hunt. On that dark night, which happened to be very cold and windy, we pledges were divided into teams of two, and given tasks that would take us out into the city and leave us operating there alone in darkness till well past daybreak the next morning. Each team was searched and divested of any money, then given one coin, a dime, and driven by an active to its destination.

I remember three of the specific tasks handed out. One pair of pledges was sent to Smith Tower to count all the windows and not return till the work was done—it was *at night*, and that alone, peering helplessly up into the gloom on all four sides of that tall building, was a challenge! Another pair was driven to the Lake Washington Floating Bridge, to count all the balusters along each side of it! And finally, I and my mate—it was Whit Smith—were driven to Washelli Cemetery, the biggest in Seattle (144 acres strung along both sides of Aurora Avenue!), and told to count the headstones! We weren't to use our dime (to telephone the house and ask for a ride home) till we had the exact number!

That was an absolutely terrible night. It was extremely cold and horrible, we weren't dressed for it, yet in the darkness we counted and walked through the endless maze of headstones. Even as it began raining we continued. The worst thing was that the headstones didn't run in rows but rather zigzagged crazily every-which-way, making their number impossible even to estimate, had we possessed night vision to see them better or strength to walk the whole acreage.

My mate and I had drunk the Kool-Aid, of course; we actually thought it possible that this was a real challenge to test character and see how worthy we were. In fact, our whole task was just tomfoolery, an elaborate prank like old-time "side-hill snipe hunts," but we didn't know that and were too intimidated to wonder. "Who knew?" we thought. Maybe somebody at the Deke house actually *had* the correct number of headstones!

So we counted and counted and counted. At last we were so cold and wet and miserable that, around 8 a.m., we used our dime to call the house. The actives, behind our back, had been rolling in laughter, but they never let on. With a frown, our driver, when at last he arrived, wrote down our headstone tally and took us home. Exhausted, we then dragged ourselves off to class.

But the worst was yet to come. Worst of all, without a doubt, was the *next* night, Thursday night. "Alumni Night" was the night we'd been primed for, scared about, for weeks ahead. And I went into it sleepless and exhausted from my all-night tour of the cemetery!

The Deke house was a forcing-house of lawyers. Many of its alumni were Seattle attorneys, and we knew that was true because on various occasions we'd met some. So the set-up for this terrifying Thursday night was that we would be led, one by one, blindfolded, by "Brother Pi" (an active wearing a hood), to appear in darkness before this distinguished body of lawyerly alumni to answer solemn questions probing our worthiness to be called Dekes. Only one pledge at a time would be in the darkened room surrounded by these alumni. We were repeatedly warned to be truthful because as lawyers they knew how to detect every lie!

So that was the set-up. But, like the scavenger hunt the night before, "Alumni Night" was an elaborate prank. The event had been embedded in ancient Deke traditions, then gleefully handed down for generations. It was a masquerade intended to turn each pledge inside-out for the actives' entertainment.

At the time, I knew nothing of that. There I was, 18 years old, blindfolded and alone, my mind a tangle from tiredness and sleeplessness, standing in darkness in the front hall, surrounded by nameless individuals—supposedly older men, many of them lawyers, all respectable Dekes. All those alums (I could hear them rustling in their places) were sitting around me in the dark, awaiting my interrogation. There seemed to be a lot of them. I could hear their whispers and their squeaking chairs. Then an unknown questioner broke the silence. In a loud voice he sternly inquired my name, age, place of birth, and other details. From the beginning, he aimed at tripping me up. Here's pretty much the gist of my interview:

STATE YOUR NAME, NEOPHYTE!
Jerry Newman, sir
DON'T YOU MEAN GERALD NEWMAN?
Well, yes. . .
STATE YOUR HOME RESIDENCE!
Ellensburg, Washington
DON'T YOU MEAN ROUTE TWO, *OUTSIDE OF* ELLENSBURG?!
Yes, sir.
ARE YOU EVADING MY QUESTIONS? ARE YOU TRUTHFUL, YES OR NO?
Well, sir, I try to be. . . .
TRY TO BE WHAT?
Truthful, sir.
TRYING WON'T DO! I SAID, *YES OR NO.*
Yes, sir.
WE'LL SEE.

Then he questioned me briefly about my studies, but that was just the warm-up to the main event.

DO YOU DATE GIRLS?
Yes, sir.
GIVE US THEIR NAMES, NEOPHYTE!
(I did so.)
ARE THEY LOOSE? (I could hear a slight rustling in the room around me.)
No, sir, I wouldn't say so. . . .
YOU *DON'T KNOW*?
I'd say they aren't, sir. . .
ARE YOU HAVING *SEXUAL RELATIONS* WITH THEM, NEOPHYTE?
No, sir, not exactly. . . Well, . . .

NOT EXACTLY? YOU DON'T _KNOW_ WHETHER YOU ARE HAVING SEXUAL RELATIONS? (More rustling.)

Well, yes, I mean . . .

ANSWER THE QUESTION!

Well, sir, it depends on . . .

DEPENDS ON WHAT, NEOPHYTE?

On what "sexual relations" means. . . .

*YOU **DON'T KNOW** WHAT SEXUAL RELATIONS ARE?* (Loud rustling.)

No, sir, I mean . . . .

DO YOU ***MASTURBATE,*** NEOPHYTE?

Well, I . . . .

GET TO THE POINT, NEOPHYTE!!!

Well, I, uh, . . .

YOU ARE LYING!!!

Uh, not very often . . .

NOT VERY OFTEN? ***CONSTANTLY, THEN?*** YOU MASTURBATE ***AT EVERY OPPORTUNITY?*** (Louder rustling with titters.)

No, sir, I don't . . . .

HOW OFTEN, NEOPHYTE?

Well, . . .

WHEN WAS THE LAST TIME YOU MASTURBATED? (Guffaws.)

Well, it was . . . I'm not sure . . .

YOU CAN'T REMEMBER? WHEN WAS IT?

Uh, . . .

BROTHER PI, REMOVE THIS MISERABLE NEOPHYTE!

My interview was ended and I left mortified. Later I learned, of course, that there were no lawyers in the room, only active members who'd congregated for laughs and the fun of witnessing our humiliation. But *they* had gone through the same exercise themselves and survived, and I would, too. I'd live to laugh at it. I'm laughing at it now.

By the last day of Hell Week we understood how it got its name. The class of 1960 had endured hardships and horrors, but also we'd helped each other along and gotten to know each other in novel ways. Increasingly we found ourselves laughing at the ridiculousness of everything instead of griping at the outrages against order and decency. I know I'd begun to laugh a lot, and to make others laugh with me as I buzzed around in my green hood—even though, as punishment for some infraction, I was, by the fifth night, being required to sleep in the fireplace! (I made jokes about that, too.)

I think we all knew by the last day that we'd all, every one of us, make it through to full acceptance as active members of the fraternity. We were happy about that, happy not just as 42 individuals but as a band of survivors. So the last night, "Fun Night," brought a perfect ending to the whole show with some really crazy games.

Take, first, "Bombardier," a game so harmless and outlandishly droll that we loved it. The venue was the central hallway of the house, at the bottom of the big three-story stairwell, where a pledge was required to lie on his back on the vinyl floor with his legs and arms splayed out and his mouth wide open. His open mouth was the target. The other venue was at the topmost railing of the third deck straight upstairs, where another pledge, the bombardier, got to crack eggs one by one, and then, carefully centering his aim, attempt to drop the contents, the gelatinous mass of yolk and egg-white, straight down into the open mouth three stories below! Each pledge got a half-dozen eggs for the fun, and by his fourth egg was starting to hit close to the target. Imagine how the target guy looked with his pants, shirt, arms, neck, ears, and forehead plastered with egg! We howled with laughter and clamored to be next!

The evening's finale was "the Olive Races." The actives brought out four big blocks of ice and a jar of green olives, then instructed us to pull all the curtains in the dining room and strip naked. Nervously we wondered what would come next as they divided us into two teams, lined us up, then told us the rules of the competition. We laughed out loud! It was a relay race. Each team member had to sit on an ice block, pick up an olive in his bare buttocks, transport it that way to his team's other ice block at the far end of the room, and deposit it there. No hands could be used by anyone, and should the olive be dropped, the racer would have to return to the first block and start over.

Just imagine how hilarious this looked! Picture a naked guy lowering his naked buttocks ever so carefully down onto a block of ice—the olive being utterly out of sight beneath him—and being guided every inch of the way by his teammates till he successfully squeezes and picks it up. Picture him then starting to crab-walk upside-down toward the other end of the room, then dropping the olive, then having to start over! Picture his buttocks growing so frozen that he can scarcely even *feel* the olive as he tries to grasp it! Picture the frustration of his naked teammates down on their hands and knees around him, squinting at the olive, trying to talk him into the correct position. "Up, now a little left, good, now slowly down, no, lift back up and more to the side . . . " He picks it up! He's actually carrying it now! Picture him awkwardly advancing, still backwards and upside-down, crab-walking toward the goal at the other end of the room, his buttocks clenched, his teeth clenched, his teammates at both ends of the room yelling encouragement and then watching, squinting, guiding—"easy, lower, more to the left, now straight down, now drop!" Oops, the olive falls off the ice block. Back for another.

Hell Week was a sort of coming-of-age in a funhouse. You see that even though it occurred more than 60 years ago I still recall a lot of it. That's partly because the pledges, at the end of the week, were asked to name in a secret ballot the comrade who had inspired them most. They named *me!* Yes, yours truly, Jerry Newman, former "Maverick," later "Big Jer," "Yr-rej Namwen" and "Slewob," received what was called "The Inspirational Award." That was one of the more memorable moments of my life as a Deke.

~

In my classes I took the usual meandering path from broad liberal-arts courses toward more specialized studies. As a pre-law major I had a good excuse to wander around, sniffing daisies. Pre-law students were rather privileged because unlike other majors they didn't have to buckle down till their fourth year, when they actually began legal studies. So I took lots of survey courses, enjoying many, but found most pleasure in studying literature, philosophy, and history.

In literature I read some of the greatest novels ever written—the longest was *War and Peace*, which I enjoyed so much that I read much of it twice! I liked Faulkner, Fitzgerald, Hardy, and Lawrence, I admired Mann and Dostoyevsky, Dickens was my favorite novelist. Kafka intrigued me so much that I wrote an ambitious 31-page essay, "An Analysis of the Kafkan Philosophy of Illusion, Struggle, and Despair," attempting to find system in his allusive and metaphorical works. Prof. Jones said he admired my essay's originality and called it "a well-executed piece of work—penetration is always pleasing."

As to *writing* literature, I took Advanced Creative Writing from an appreciative professor named Taylor. I think my best short story was the one about an eccentric geezer who, with pith helmet and butterfly net, goes out daily on imaginary safaris and unknowingly leaves a trail of disaster behind him; meanwhile his wife, equally eccentric, chops garlic in the basement and plays handball in the kitchen. One day when her bumbling explorer comes home, he finds that she's mistakenly ordered a truckload of concrete to be poured over the lawn, ruined the ship-in-a-bottle that he'd made from toothpicks, and squashed their pet frog. They solemnly conduct a post-mortem of the day's events, conversing awkwardly from either side of a hanging blowfish blocking their view. Prof. Taylor laughingly gave the story an A.

I guess I hadn't yet ruled out the idea of making a career from fiction-writing, for I find that I was making notes of real life-experiences to use later. Here from my diary is a Seattle strip club:

> Tonight attended my first strip show. It was at Benj. Franklin hotel, & lots of drunk & sober college guys there. 3 strippers, all young, 2 rather plump. Guys did the most shameless things, e.g. burying their faces in the strippers' crotches, holding dollar bills in their teeth for extrication . . . One stripper was making her first appearance & was embarrassed . . . I learned they were paid $35 apiece . . . But merely catalogue things here for future work by imagination.

I collected pictures like that, just as a geology major might collect rocks, an anthropology major, bones. Here's raw material for a different character study:

> On road I picked up hitchhiker, clad in faded blue cotton shirt, dark brown trousers with slits where once were pockets, bandanna clasped at neck with bicycle reflector, an old cowboy hat. One eye crossed inward. Informed me that he'd been employed in trash for 35 cents/hr. + rm. & board in New Jersey. Asked how he liked trash business. Enthusiastically said he liked it fine. Had lived in a converted garbage truck by himself, liked horseback riding, ranching, trash-collecting. Quit school at 7th grade level. Fiancée had reneged at last minute because discovered his infidelity.

Philosophy was by far the most explosive element in my undergrad education. I recall my excitement at being first introduced to it in a course on epistemology and ontology. Such stuff had never been mentioned in high school! I went 'round and 'round arguing with myself over Descartes' *Discourse on Method*, and went wild at Spinoza's *Ethics*. Evidently I revealed my excitement in a letter home because my mother wrote, "Spinoza sounds impossibly complex. I'm totally at sea just reading your description and shudder to think what it would be like to take your course. If you do get it—has it any value? Just wondering."

Ha! "Just wondering!" Her son is going loop-de-loop over some obscure philosopher and she "just wonders." She must have kept scratching her head while I studied all the ancient philosophers, then the British Empiricists, then was turned on by idealists like Bishop Berkeley (who posed the famous question, whether or not a tree falling in the woods makes a sound if there's no one to hear it). But that led me to more extreme German idealists like Hegel with his *Geistesgeschichte*—I recall writing a six-page analysis of a few pages of Hegel and getting nothing better than a "B," but I counted that a triumph because his ideas, though fascinating, were impenetrable.

All that heavy lifting was boggling my mind even before I encountered the philosophy of religion. Now, *that* is fascinating stuff! I plowed through Kierkegaard, Heidegger, Russell, Bergson, and Otto, and also much of both the Old and New Testaments when taking a wonderful "Bible as Literature" course. I admired Saint Paul, but certainly lost what little Christian faith I had left. When staying one weekend with Gramlin I remember receiving two young Jehovah's Witnesses who'd knocked on her door; so unremittingly did I press the Bible's absurdities on them that at last they fled downstairs as if pursued by the Devil! Slowly in place of my faith came a kind of sentimental pity for people, especially poor people, whose credulity left them victims to religious predators.

Bringing together many corrosive impulses from my humanities studies was a single book, *Candide*, by an author who had a tremendous impact on me, the philosophic joker Voltaire. That book is hilarious. Everything about it appealed to me. Wasn't I already a sort of humorist, and hadn't I attempted to write humorously? Here was a model of witty writing that has convulsed readers ever since its publication in 1759. Hadn't I, in my philosophy classes, wrestled for hours, for days, with the philosophical problem of Determinism? Here was a laugh-out-loud treatment of that subject, roaming through causality, necessity, and free will, all in parody of Leibniz's "Best of all Possible Worlds." Hadn't I cast off convention-al Christianity and become indignant about religious humbug? *Candide* is an all-out attack on religious mumbo-jumbo and the venality of priest-hoods. War?—was it not, like religion, just another cruelty practiced by the powerful for their own gain? On all these subjects, *Candide* won me over through its outrageous comedy and helped transform my belief-system, laying down a path that ran far into my future.

~

Yes, my worldview was being transformed. As a result of what I was learning and thinking about, a destruction and piecemeal rebuilding of my entire belief-system was taking place. What was going on was—isn't it obvious?—*liberal education!* That's just the sort of thing, a destruction and rebuilding of ideas, that happens to millions of college undergrads. But I didn't understand it at the time—and, for that matter, I think undergrads rarely do. But in my case, because of my insecure personality and because this slow intellectual revolution was going to transform my career aspira-tions in a major way, turning me from the law to the lectern, I experienced unusual turbulence during the transition. In fact I underwent a sort of identity crisis.

I can see its signs as early as the spring of my sophomore year, when I wrote in my diary, "I have entered a new era of self-assurance, my mind has quickened, become more analytical. I am assailed by the academic problems of existence, reality, Truth." Though bombastic, this signals that my belief-structure was starting to crumble. Confusion and depression fol-lowed: "8/18/58. Was depressed all day today, I can't understand myself at all, nor can I analyze the depression state's causes but I think it coupled with repercussions, disagreeable predictions of the future—in every aspect, romantic, occupational, monetary, etc."

Soon my mother was warning me about something new, my manic pursuit of a 4.0 GPA! "We were frankly upset," she wrote, "over your ex-cessive studying and are sure no 4-point is worth going without meals and sleep for. Don't be an extremist, honey. The happy, well-adjusted individual in this life is the one who avoids extremes—in food, drink, smoking, plea-sures—yes, even in studying." She continued: "Please listen to us. Don't skip meals or sleep. Your Dad says he isn't interested in your getting an A posthumously. He adds that he doesn't care about your grades—-just your education."

I'd begun slaving for a 4-point! Even into my diary I began talking like an academic blowhard: "It is difficult to see," I said (probably stroking my chin), "at the most sensuous level, any sort of pervading spirit which links all minds with all objects. The most that I can see now is an occasional analogy between the operations of natural things and forces, with mental, emotional phenomena." Blah, Blah. In my term papers also I was losing my light touch in favor of indigestible bookish formulations. Here's an embarrassing excerpt from a paper I wrote for Professor Eby of the English Department, an analysis of Emerson's essay, 'Napoleon, Man of the World.'

> Napoleon calls the spade; he invokes no supernatural intervention in life (if that is possible), but mobilizes his own enlightened capacities and concentrates them in full upon his material objectives: the enemy dissolves before the internal might of Napoleon. We are not yet sure what is this internal might, but does it not appear to be an extensive faith in one's own ability? Perhaps, then, it is self-reliance—that profound and extraordinary quality so seldom found among men. If so, we may be sure that when it is found, it is always the stamp of excellence—regardless of which field of human conflict it enters. Genghis Khan; Caesar; Churchill; Copernicus and Spinoza; Pelagius and Bruno; Savonarola and John Hus and Drake and Nelson and Darwin and John Brown—such men incarnate that brilliant inner power which manifests itself in great bold strokes, blazing on many planes, the single, only trail of history.

What a load of ponderous pseudo-academic BS! I was going off the rails! The same stuff was invading my correspondence and personal letters. I was just then breaking up with one of my nicest girlfriends, Sharon Lund, who'd been my steady date for many months; or rather, to tell the truth, she was breaking up with me. She was a very sweet girl, charming, not at all stupid. It's with mortification that I discover the same pomposity in a resentful letter I wrote her:

> Dear Sharon,
> I'd apologize for not having written sooner, but can't help but feel that it is more fortunate for both of us that I have delayed. I shall vary my predictably boring (as I am told) form of letter-writing style in this letter and the get the 'light' ¼ off first, because this

may entice you to read to the end of the letter—whereas otherwise the recondite (excuse me—'difficult to understand'—'complex'— for further explanation consult Webster's) style that I employ might have discouraged you from reading the entire thing. . . .

What a sneering, insecure, full-of-himself S.O.B.! These literary remains reveal the sweeping identity crisis I diagnosed above. They show me throwing off my character of *le bon bourgeois* and, though noticeably eaten by self-doubt, attempting to conform to what I apparently imagined to be the persona of the high-toned professor, throwing "perhapses" and "shalls" and "we may be sures" this way and that in stilted "observations." Ye gods, what an insufferable prig I was becoming!

Let's think about that. From today, at this distance, the whole evolution seems obvious. I'd arrived at the university as a fairly typical high school graduate, I'd come from a typical middle-class family living in a typical western town, I'd been raised with typical middle-class American values, which in the 1950s meant patriotism, materialism, religious piety, and personal ambition, all tending toward a future that would include such things as a successful career as a lawyer, a happy marriage with two or three children, civic activities probably as a young Republican member of some local Jaycees, social acceptance in a Rotary or Kiwanis club, and gradual promotion over time to become a judge or senior member of a law firm. At the end I'd settle into happy retirement as a valued member of an essentially white, materialistic,

With Sharon Lund

respectable, and bourgeois community. I'd become what my mother, in the letter quoted above, hoped for—"a happy, well-adjusted individual . . . who avoids extremes."

My years as a Deke reinforced all this, shaping my personality in that direction and equipping me with tools for realizing those goals. My fraternity taught me how to fit into an essentially conservative-minded group of upwardly mobile young men destined to operate and become successful in the American business culture. It taught me how to converse, dress, and think like them. It taught me how to become the rounded young Deke underclassman, earning a "gentleman's B" in class while keeping his eye on the really important things—pretty sorority girls, nice cars, and fraternal connections that would land me a nice job with a plush future.

But meanwhile, as I said, there was occurring, bit by bit, perhaps partly because of my distinctive "maverick" susceptibilities, but more largely as the simple result of *what my classes were making me learn and think about*, a revolution in my entire belief-system. It was a soft revolution, a time-lapse occurrence, something I wasn't very aware of even though it was going to affect my career aspirations and turn them almost upside-down. And hand in hand with all this, my role-modeling, the presentation of myself to my friends and to the world, was going to undergo very significant change also.

In sum, my worldview was changing from that of a conventional 1950s bourgeois young white American to that of a critical, skeptical, anti-bourgeois rationalist and social critic; my career aspirations were changing from the study of law as a respectable meal-ticket, to the scholarly investigation of philosophy, history, and literature *for their own sake*; and the patterns of social thinking and imitative behavior connected with these new patterns were shifting accordingly, so that every day I was less the gregarious "Slewob" of the Deke house, and more the grade-grubbing workaholic with pedantic affectations, altering his self-concept, figuratively sewing leather patches onto his elbows, throwing around big words and insulting his pretty coed girlfriends, and slowly withdrawing from the country-club-bound world of Fraternity Row. By the middle of my senior year I'd be rejecting nearly everything the Deke house stood for.

There's no telling how dreadful an academic stuffed-shirt I might have become were it not for Giovanni Costigan, who deflated my bombast and edged me toward the nest I'd been unwittingly preparing for myself almost since birth. Giovanni Costigan was one of the greatest teachers of all time. Of Irish parentage, educated at Oxford, acquiring his PhD at the University of Wisconsin in 1930, he taught English History at Washington for 41 years till mandatory retirement at age 70. Then, thanks to "the Costigan bill" specially passed by the state legislature, he continued to teach, lecture, and travel the world under the auspices of the UW Alumni Association until his death in 1990 at the age of 85.

When I first experienced this remarkable man he was 53 years old. Because his field was English History, I was obliged, as a pre-law major, to take his year-long course in English political and constitutional development. In consequence, for three academic quarters, from the fall of 1958 through the spring of 1959, I sat for five days a week observing him, taking copious notes on his lectures, scribbling down his eloquent remarks and *bons mots*. At the end of this very long experience I wrote, on the last page of my last term paper for him, "Thank you for giving me one of the richest, most pleasurable experiences of my whole life." For me, Costigan was a wonderful revelation. His year-long class was the last decisive step in the complete change of life and vocation that had already begun stirring within me.

Giovanni Costigan

He was a short, stocky man with curly snow-white hair, an English accent, and always a manner of politeness, interest, and sympathy. His voice was slightly raspy, and he could modulate it as well as any actor or poet. His lectures were spell-binding. He had an Irishman's instinct for words, and with conscious effect lowered or raised his voice in his accounts of kings, battles, preachers, wars. Though a man of letters, of grace and erudition and tremendous reading, a man by nature scholarly and gentle, he was also a passionate being who felt such indignation against injustice and the abuse of power that he infected us all with the same emotions. His silences, after describing some horrid historic massacre or abominably cruel event—his long silences, as he searched for words to describe something indescribably inhuman—those long silences, the room absolutely still as we took in his somehow beseeching expression conveying incomprehension at the enormity of human folly—such silences spoke more eloquently even than his words.

On the other hand, there'd be a twinkle in his eye when there was something to laugh at. I remember pulling a fast one on him. The class had learned from his lectures that he deplored the young Winston Churchill (before he became Prime Minister) because of his racism, imperialism, and bigotry against the downtrodden Irish. So some of us got a big poster showing Churchill's World War II face, glaring and looking angry and smoking a cigar. We taped this onto the rolled-up map of England that Costigan, after entering the classroom, would always pull down just before beginning a lecture. That day he pulled down the map to find the furious-looking Churchill glaring at him as if warning against further uncomplimentary remarks! It was a great joke, and he appreciated it.

Costigan taught his course in one of the largest lecture rooms in Smith Hall. All the seats, every year, were filled. He was famous not only on campus, not only even in the entire Pacific Northwest. Adlai Stevenson, the Democratic presidential candidate against Eisenhower in 1952 and 1956, justly called him "the most eloquent man in the western hemisphere." A decade later Costigan debated the American conservative idol William F. Buckley in Edmundson Pavilion before 10,000 people and absolutely demolished him.

I copied down verbatim some of the aphorisms he tossed off in lectures. They were often subversive; like Plato, he undermined the idols of the tribe: "Heresy is a sign of intellectual life." "It is foolish to say that humans have outgrown any stage of primitive habit, no matter how stupid." "Cruelty is a rule of nature." "No wonder man has projected pity into heaven, hoping to find it there." "The founders of the slave trade were only human beings . . . that is to say, ourselves." "The Puritans associated beauty with the devil. No wonder the devil is so attractive." "The Crusaders sanctified barbarism in the name of faith." "Out of good comes evil—and out of evil comes good unawares." "It is human nature to hate those whom we have injured."

Costigan required long term papers each quarter from each student—there were at least 70 students in his classroom—and he marked virtually every single mistake in mine, often *rewriting* every infelicitous phrase. And he was a brutal critic! Never had I received such devastating criticism. Over that entire year I wrote nearly 90 typewritten pages for him, and in his tiny spider-like handwriting he covered those pages with ego-shriveling comments ("cumbrous—rewrite"; "lurid"; "mixed metaphor"), often going on to scratch a thin line through my own prose to substitute his own, which *always* captured my thought more clearly and elegantly.

Although many of his comments dealt with my papers' historical content, what I want to emphasize here is his savage criticism of my writing style. Above, I wrote that I'd been veering toward some kind of pseudo-academic stuffed-shirt Germanic bombast. That was before I began taking his classes. But then like a knife to my gizzard this wonderful man ripped my writer's ego to shreds with comments like this: "You need to discipline your writing & control a too great luxuriousness of imagination as expressed in words. <u>Learn to write more simply</u>. It will increase the force of your writing. A stimulating and original paper . . ." He was still more brutally direct about my second term paper: "Your writing evidently gives you great difficulty—it tends to be exaggerated, over-emphatic, circumlocutious, altogether lacking in grace & ease, far too serious. Read such people as Llewelyn Powys or W. H. Hudson for a wonderful ease and mastery of style." His initial comment on my third term paper was: "This paper is of course not worth much—you did not intend that it should be. But I realize that your work is of 'A' calibre." And then after extremely lengthy comments he concluded: "Please forget about this last paper anyway—it does not in the least affect my judgment of your abilities."

This was the man who, later, told my mother I was "the best student he'd ever had over more than two decades of teaching." For all I know, he said the same thing to every parent he met. But is it any wonder that my "identity crisis" was now rapidly resolving itself? I'd come not only to idolize Costigan and take his every criticism to heart, reworking my writing and thinking, but also I'd begun attaching myself to him as my role model, adopting perspectives from him and beginning to shape my future toward becoming, like him, a professor of English history, an academic professional with a special bent toward lecturing and teaching; and perhaps, if I had it in me, with the capacity to write something important about England.

Just one more thing before leaving this account of my studies: It's my amusement that the paper I described as terrible, that turgid discussion of Ralph Waldo Emerson's essay on Napoleon—an egregious piece of pseudo-academic BS, I called it—greatly impressed the professor for whom I'd written it! Professor Eby actually *liked* that ridiculous and ponderous bullshit! His verdict, scrawled on my first page, was "A. Good, possibly profound. Beware of too much technical jargon. See the current usage in

Education and Sociology." *Possibly profound!* I guess I fooled him! Either that, or he didn't read my slop carefully—which, having joined the academic club myself, I think entirely possible.

On the other hand, maybe his mind had turned to cheese. During the preceding decade, poor Eby had been hounded by the House Un-American Activities Committee, whose members had accused him of communist sympathies. The Canwell Committee, run by a dreadful Spokane Republican demagogue, in 1948 had acted on an accusation that the UW faculty contained at least 100 Communists. Eby had been dragged before that committee and made to admit his membership in the Party. The online account reads: "Prof. Harold Eby admits to being former member of Party but refuses to name others." They'd caught him but hadn't broken the poor man. Revisiting all this makes me remember how, when Eby lectured, his eyes would shift around strangely like pinballs bouncing off rubber bumpers. After the Canwell hearings he remained a man under stress. But he hadn't lost *all* his marbles, as was indicated by his perceptive warning to me, to "beware of too much technical terminology"!

I'd entered college with a fuzzy career idea, the notion that I'd become a lawyer, and replaced it with a much clearer one: I wanted to become a professor of history. That meant I'd have to get much smarter than I was, and soon. Furiously I tried to read all the books I'd ignored or passed over earlier. And at the same time, while trying to fill in what I considered enormous gaps in my knowledge, my attitudes about life and politics continued to evolve. I began to shun and privately disparage fraternity life as "superficial," and to spend such spare time as I had with two new friends a little older than I, a married couple, Dave and Lizzy Davis.

Dave and Lizzy were highly educated and well-traveled English majors who'd met each other while knocking around Europe. Dave was from Seattle, the son of a school principal, from a family distinguished for learning. He himself was a wonderful writer, a poet, a humorist. Lizzy was from Largs, a small town in Scotland; she was pretty, sensitive, a fine writer— she's now one of Britain's best children's-story writers. I'd met this couple in English classes, and, enjoying their company in their little cabin down the hill behind the Deke house, greatly enlarged my understanding of how well-educated young people live—how they talk, what they read, the sort of stuff they cook, their pastimes, what things they appreciate. Their friendship was my introduction to the life of books and literate conversation.

The effect of all these changes was that by the spring of 1960 when I graduated with a B.A., my career compass was firmly set. I'd just turned 21. Looking back from that 21st birthday, supposedly the most important in life because it marks the end of childhood, I can say that from my parents I'd learned how to work, behave myself, and appreciate family life; from my childhood friends I'd learned sportsmanship, companionship, courage, competitive rivalry, and how to have fun; from my teachers I'd learned how to think, admire intellect, write better, and strive for excellence; from my frat brothers I'd learned about how to succeed in the adult world, to cooperate, to lead, and to make a better impression on the fairer sex; and from people like Dave and Lizzy Davis, and Dr. Costigan and his wife Amne, I learned something about the lives and tastes of people whose houses were crammed with books. In 1960 I was at last officially an adult, and in November of that year was about to cast my first vote in a presidential election. With Kennedy against Nixon it'd be a no-brainer.

∼

Over in Ellensburg, my mom, dad, and sister were also changing. My parents were then in their forties, in good health, and extremely active. I've discussed how hard they customarily worked, but they'd begun to relax a little. They partied, played cards in a bridge club, went to regular dances in a dance club called Rigadoon, frequented the Elks Lodge for fancy dinners, and occasionally played golf. My mother was also involved in a few civic clubs and other activities connected with the improvement of Ellensburg, and my dad was, for a while, a member of the Ellensburg Rodeo board. He also was invited onto the State Board of Veterinary Medicine, an honorary distinction. They were good citizens of the town, contributing to its high quality as a place in which to live.

They were also still raising Lynn, who was only 11 when I went off to college. She too was very busy most of the time. She studied hard and was good at her schoolwork, but was also busy with her horsemanship and spent many hours a week at piano practice—following the tradition laid down by her mother and grandmother, she'd been taking piano lessons since she was about five. I remember coming back to Ellensburg from the U just to witness her first piano recital on the big stage on the CWU campus. It was, I think, a Chopin scherzo. I always loved to listen to my dear lady relatives at the keyboard—Gramlin, Mom, Lynn, and now my granddaughter, Kate. For me the music is always better when they make it.

In June 1957 I landed a summer job helping to build the new Interstate highway (I-90) over Snoqualmie Pass, widening the existing two-lane mountain road. Daily I drove in my blue Deathmobile to the high area of Lake Keechelus, a distance of about 40 miles, and worked as a laborer in two basic jobs: pouring concrete, and "sloping"–that is, hanging from cliffs by a rope, to clear rocks and rubble from the steep mountain hillsides overlooking the new road. Getting that job made me a union man—I had to join the International Union of Hod Carriers—but once I'd done that, I began to make the colossal sum of $4.50 an hour ($30 a day), and the work would last every summer through my college years. That was *sweet*!

And as a bonus, that job added another layer to my general experience of the world. Every day for two summers I carried my lunch bucket up to Snoqualmie Pass and worked alongside common laborers, many of whom had never graduated from high school. They were men with rough lives and rocky marriages and narrow escapes from the law; they worked to make a living with their hands, with shovels and hammers, ropes and rakes. They were the sort whose lives are the tragic-funny stuff of country music, and I filled my diaries with descriptions of them. Being around them, hearing their stories and seeing their perspectives, deepened my knowledge of hardships borne by folks much less lucky than I. Already I'd been pushed in the same direction by the pity I felt for poor rubes taken in by itinerant preachers. And so, given also the softening effects of all the literature and history and philosophy I was studying, I see that my sympathies, like my ideas, were being greatly expanded during those college years.

~

And then there was that wonderful summer when I worked *only with my pen!* That was the summer of my trip to Europe, which made such a profound impression on me. I was 20. My companion was Mike Evans. He was a year older than I, a senior. He was thin, taller than average, unathletic; he wore his sandy hair in a crew-cut and had passable looks. He was very smart, very scholarly, a history major, and much more sophisticated than I—often he'd pass an afternoon arguing whether Mozart was a greater composer than Beethoven, or Titian a better painter than Tintoretto. I felt flattered when he asked me to join him on his trip to Europe.

That was some journey! It lasted nearly three months and carried us through 7,000 miles of driving in the new Simca that Mike's parents had bought for him and left stored in Paris. When we reached Paris he told me that I wasn't to drive it, that he would do all the driving; this was something his parents had insisted on, it had to do with insurance. Happily, that freed me to look closely at everything we passed. And certainly I was very lucky to be traveling with him. He elevated my tastes and we enjoyed each other's company. To travel with a trusted friend, comparing observations about the sights and sharing the pleasures, working together to solve the problems and plan the days, is such a great enhancement of one of life's best experiences. To travel to unknown parts is to know you're *alive,* and to do so with a talkative and observant friend is very heaven.

That trip was the most wonderful learning experience of my life. It took more than two and a half months. We left Seattle on June 15, 1959, bound for Paris, and returned on September 5. Our plane was propeller-driven, so we kept stopping to gas up! The outbound flight stopped first in North Dakota, then Delaware, then Greenland, then Shannon, Ireland. By that time Mike and I were so fed up that we bailed out and began touring the Emerald Isle. Of course I whipped out my pen, first thing. I was going to record everything I saw. Shannon airport is near Limerick, and we caught a cab into the city, driven by a garrulous old Mick who gave us in 20 minutes a complete account of Cromwell's outrages in Ireland. Then we reached the city:

> In Limerick we walked up to St. Mary's Church, watched a group of ragged, dirty children playing soccer in the street, listened to them plead for chewing gum & then squabble like starving animals for what little we had, saw 14-15-yr. old girls dressed in the most fashionable clothes with high heels and earrings, walking through narrow streets flecked with horse dung and covered with weaving motorcars, cyclists, draft horses with heavy wagons, and teeming pedestrians, all walking or standing, the light finally fading at 10 pm but still the endless body of pedestrians and cyclists, red-cheeked, cheery, loud, very many smoking cigarettes. . . . Priests, nuns, the Irish cross, were as plentiful as the Guinness stout signs.

We reached Paris a week later, and that's where I had my first date with a European. While Mike stayed in the hotel to wash his socks, I sallied out that evening to gawk at the Arc de Triomphe, only a few blocks away.

Standing in the crowd of tourists, I was joined by a very nice man, Pierre Bonjare, who proposed walking me over to the nearby Bois de Boulougne. I was too pleased by his offer and too star-struck by the gigantic illuminated Arch to be suspicious, but it should have been a tip-off when we passed one of the pissoirs, outdoor men's urinals, which looked, he said coyly, "très romantique!" I was still trying to figure that out when, a moment later, he offered to light my cigarette. As he did so, he groped me with his other hand. I jumped a foot. "Non, non," I cried, "J'aime LES FILLES!" He was crestfallen but walked me back to my hotel because by then I was thoroughly lost. He was, as I said, a nice man. He was also the first homosexual I ever met. Nowadays we'd call him gay, but I'd never heard of "gayness" till much later when I learned you could die from it.

We picked up the Simca and then toured the Continent in that little white car. We traveled 7,000 miles, visiting 13 countries, including tiny ones like Lichtenstein, San Marino, and Monaco. It's hard to believe we covered that much ground, but we did. I headed into it with the princely sum of $600 in American Express Traveler's Checks. It astonishes me now to be reminded of how cheap things were in the 1950s. Still, I complained about my travel expenditures: "I have never been so thrifty in my life! Admission to churches, art galleries, castles, public buildings, always run 25 cents. By the time I've spent $1.50 a day on these, plus $1.50 for a hotel room about every 5 days, to clean up & wash clothes, penny-counting is a necessity."

Egad, a dollar-fifty for a hotel room! Soon we began sleeping in the car. The Simca had seats that folded all the way back, so sometimes we slept side-by-side in it like a pair of mummies. Being young, it didn't bother us much. About every fifth night we'd find a room where we'd wash our clothes and fumigate ourselves. Conditions in such ratty places weren't ideal: "We checked into a cheap hotel in Luxembourg, showered finally after pounding on the locked bathroom door for 15 minutes . . . of course, baths cost extra."

We ate cheaply too. Sometimes we dined in inexpensive cafes and roadhouses, but often we prepared our own meals with a small burner. We weren't particular about food, this was no gastronomic tour. Unlike rich tourists, we didn't care what we ate: we preferred to spend money on admissions, film for our cameras, and slides to take home. "Dinners so far,"

I wrote, "have consisted of French bread, cheese, concentrated soup flakes boiled in water, and Nescafé coffee." A letter from Rotterdam captures our general routine in the bigger cities:

> We ate very cheaply in a snack bar at a department store, went to a cheap boarding house, unpacked, took sponge-baths (there is no bath), went back to town and had tiny pancakes in a fascinating little place, walked, & returned here, wrote till 3 a.m, got up at 10:00, wrote till now (12:40), will pack & take tour of city at 1:00—must rush, will head for the Hague tonite. Tomorrow in Amsterdam. Love you all, Jerry

That day, as you see, I spent about six hours writing a letter home; I usually spent only two or three. International phone calls were impossibly costly, so letters were our sole contact with our families. American Express offices all across Europe were not just our banks where we cashed Traveler's Checks, but our mailboxes too. I wrote at least 16 extremely long letters to my family; I retain 14 but know that at least two are lost, one from Salzburg describing that charming Austrian town and a Mozart symphony, the other from London detailing my impressions of Westminster Abbey and of a debate I attended in the House of Commons.

Fortunately my mother *typed out all my letters as she received them,* so I still have them in perfectly legible form. The pile is huge. The average length of one typewritten letter is seven pages; each page averages 700 words, so that's nearly 5,000 words per letter. Altogether, on that trip I wrote more than 80,000 words. That's nearly twice as long as *The Great Gatsby.* I was *a writing machine!* Here's something I posted from Austria: "Sorry I can't mail more often, but writing takes an enormous amount of time. A good job would take much more than the 2 or 2 ½ hours a day I can afford. Really, I can't even afford this. Things get so bad that I almost avoid experiences in order to avoid retelling them!"

Often I wrote these letters while sitting in cafes or rented rooms, but sometimes I wrote them at night in the car. This is from a letter written one July night in Switzerland:

> Right now I'm sitting in the stretched-out seat of the car, holding my pen-light between my teeth so that I can see this paper. It's about 1:30 a.m., and we're parked on the northern bank of Lac Le-

man. I can see lights across the water. The moon is low and it casts a shimmering yellow funnel toward us. We're parked in a grove of trees, the wind rustling their leaves, making the sound of distant waterfalls. Otherwise it's very quiet—now an airplane drones overhead—I'm quite isolated. Mike is stretched out alongside me, his feet jammed under the steering wheel. He's asleep. This is really a beautiful spot, and I don't mind staying up at all—except for my jawbone, which is losing sensitivity.

Why did I do all that writing? Well, as every diarist knows, to write something is to record something, hence to analyze and remember it. I was forcing myself to observe every detail, advancing my own education. I was also validating everything I'd read about Europe, that enchanted world where nearly all my admired writers and painters and musicians had lived their lives, and where nearly all the history I knew anything about had taken place. To observe and record everything was to fulfill a duty to myself.

But also I was trying to take my family to Europe too. *They* hadn't been there—remember that in those days before jet planes and the internet, Europe seemed impossibly far from the Pacific Northwest—and there was no assurance that they ever *would* go there. I wanted them to see what I saw, hear what I heard, learn what I was learning. There were no videographers in that era but I was straining to be one.

Here's a typical letter, posted on July 7, 1959. I began with my impressions of Holland in general, then of the Haag, the beach at Scheveningen, and Amsterdam. I pictured the countryside, a few cities, the beaches facing the Atlantic, our lodgings, several guided tours, art museums; I conveyed my growing love of Rubens and my sense that I was learning a lot about Flemish painting; I described innumerable ghastly instruments of pain in a medieval torture museum, I portrayed the Zeedike, the red-light district of Amsterdam. I also relayed my experiences in those places—my very unfavorable impressions of older American tourists, my amusing tête-à-tête with a young Dutch prostitute, a costly $3.00 visit to the Boer Restaurant in Amsterdam where I consumed an authentic Rijstaffel, a two-day binge with some charming American college girls which included a 4 a.m. drive to a beach, a cold-water swim, and a three-hour sunburned sleep on the beach afterwards. I signed the letter, "I love you, Cook," and added a P.S., "Write Heidelberg."

Here verbatim is a paragraph to give that letter's flavor. I've provided no sexy bits lately, so I'll choose my tête-à-tête with the young and beauti-ful Dutch girl I ran into in a bar:

> The girl was, as I had suspected, a high-class harlot. I asked her,
> for clarity, what she did. 'What you see,' she answered, glancing
> at herself. I asked her how she liked her job (fine), how long she'd
> been at it (4 years), whether or not she had student rates (no),
> whether she'd get married later (no), whether I was being rude
> (no), her price (75 guilden—about $20), and which way was the
> restroom. This afforded escape, and I made my way out to the
> beach, told all this to Mike, went to bed.

I tried to capture unfamiliar European customs. Here's a funny one that I called "The Dance of the Kissing Skippers." Mike and I were in the great cathedral town of Chartres just south of Paris. After marveling at the cathedral's amazing stained glass we stopped to watch merry-makers crowding a sidewalk café:

> Many looked as though they'd had a few wines too many, but
> all were singing & laughing. Before long, the whole group came
> bursting out, grabbed hands, and began skipping around in a large
> circle. As well as children and middle-aged people, there were 60
> and 70 year olds, I swear it, all skipping in a circle, singing some
> folksong. Then two men & two women broke out of the circle &
> into the center, forming their own skipping circle. Before long they
> each skipped to the outer circle, kissed a person on the left cheek,
> then on the right, and then the kissee took the other's place in the
> skipping circle till it was kissing time again. Occasionally a segment
> would break away and capture the hands of some bystander & pull
> him into the ever-growing outer circle.
>
> That made things even more amusing when we were dragged
> in! Although almost fainting from the body odor of the girl who
> held my hand, I laughed myself sick watching Mike skip around
> in the circle. The singing stopped & a horribly ugly girl kissed him
> on the cheeks. He went to the center ring and skipped there—hi-larious, since he is pigeon-toed. We dropped out in time to escape
> the melée into which the game had transformed, for every time the
> singing stopped, a colossal exchange of kisses took place!

I fell in love with many European cities. They were so old, so beautiful, so richly decorated, so full of history—I'd never seen cities so charming. Copenhagen, for example, enchanted me. Here's my first impression. I described the central square near the great town hall as if making a video, trying to capture the motion as evening faded into night:

> Tourists cluster around the iron statue-fountain, while across the street masses of pedestrians move both directions on the sidewalk. During rush hours, hundreds of bicycles zoom past, with charming young ladies competing ably in the midst of it, holding down their flowered dresses with one hand. Sunset casts a soft pinkish glow across this great area, and the bright blue awnings of age-blackened hotels and business establishments lighten in the dusk. From these buildings and the town hall, pale green spires stretch up and pierce the sky, seeming to hold it blue long after sundown. Yellow trolleys & busses load and unload, ceaselessly changing the faces of the crowd.

I was amazed at Tivoli Gardens and wrote a long, colorful description of that entertainment wonderland. I was only a 20-year-old hayseed from a cow town, and had never seen anything like it. And as to that particular description, I suspect that some of its gushiness flowed from what had happened the night before with a beautiful young woman I met there. All we had was an evening's innocent flirtation, but rereading the letter brought it all back.

She was 27, I wrote, but looked younger. Although married with two children, she offered to spend time with me before trotting home to her hubby and babies. She worked in the souvenir shop and invited me to return there at midnight closing time. I did; we carried her shop's money bag to the Tivoli office nearby, then set off on a moonlit stroll around the city. We stopped at a bar for a drink, and then, with her telling me about everything we saw, we visited monuments and landmarks till at last we arrived at the "Little Mermaid," the polished iron statue, resting on a rock beside the harbor, that honors Hans Christian Anderson's little story.

> After sitting a while we walked slowly towards her home, I still carrying her package of glassware under my arm. It was slowly becoming light, and while we lingered I felt that early-morning tingle

of cold air and isolation, of the loud bird-cries and early morning wakefulness, flooding me at that perfect hour. Under the street lights, with the wakening sky heralding the day ahead, she showed me the bus stop, I wrote her name in the frosty droplets on a car roof, Jonina Christenson. We shook hands, she drew close for an instant, brushed my mouth with hers, and then was gone.

Could I ever forget that moment? And marking her name in the morning dew? And that stolen kiss? Never. Ah, memory, where vanished things reappear, and dried flowers swell again with life.

Next, Germany. We wandered down the majestic valley of the Rhine and arrived in Cologne on a Sunday, just in time for Mass at the biggest of all European medieval cathedrals, the Kölner Dom:

> We watched richly costumed players run through their routines at the altar, sweating from the candles close by, shaking puffs of musky incense out of silver chain-swung braziers, ringing bells and otherwise giving God a first-class magic show. There was a choir seated high in a transept, and their voices rang throughout the great stone structure, miraculously blending with their own echoed tones. It's not difficult to appreciate the vast power enjoyed by medieval ecclesiastics, when they were the masters of these great beautiful fortresses dominating the countryside. One wonders how secularism ever triumphed.

Touring Germany meant evaluating Germans. Never forgetting the war that had ended only 14 years earlier, I sent home observations about the rubble I saw, the Germans' impressive rebuilding efforts, the Autobahns. One day I had an interesting conversation with a waiter who'd fought in Italy under Rommel, captured three Americans and sat all night with them in a foxhole near the front lines, then himself been captured. At war's end he came to Frankfurt "with nothing but my shoes, and it was all for nothing."

I sketched many quaint German towns and especially praised Heidelberg as my favorite place in Germany. I took a swim in the Neckar River, wandered through Heidelberg University, the castle, and an old student hangout called "The Cave." Enthusiastically I disclosed my new hobby of collecting cardboard beer coasters from every pub; I'd even learned the trick of flipping and quickly catching, with the same hand, whole stacks of those coasters. I can still do that today with as many as six at a time!

Reaching Switzerland, I was struck by the beauty of Berne with its traditional clock tower and bear pits, and told the story of how the town got its name. I pictured the Cathedral of St. Vincent and praised its music, which, like the Mass in Cologne, I luckily showed up just in time to experience. Then driving into high mountains, I tried to convey the immensity and majesty of the Alps. I explained how, as we drove, we found ourselves ascending a climbing, precipitous road full of switchbacks until at last we found ourselves, on a Sunday, in the small village of Les Haudères, where we watched soccer players battling at the foot of an enormous granite mountain. "Grassy knolls can be seen over the cliffs far above, and green expanses stretch even higher, like green-lapped giants; and above this rough setting, in the distance, a snow-crowned tooth with wind sweeping light clouds around its desolate peak—The Matterhorn."

After skiing on the Jungfrau we entered Austria and drove to Vienna, where I soon began encountering delegates to the Vienna Youth Festival. That was a week-long jamboree of sport, music, and propaganda sponsored by the Kremlin and aimed at influencing the world's young people—there were thousands in attendance from every continent. The event was, of course, heavily criticized in the U.S. My letter home, reporting on what I saw, prompted my mother to take it to the Ellensburg newspaper, which published it as a 19-paragraph eyewitness story under the headline, "Communist Youth Festival Briefed in Letter Here." I suppose it made my folks proud to have it known that their kid was half a world away, battling communists, waving the flag, trumpeting the American way of life.

But that's not what I was doing. I did send back criticisms of the festival's bungling organizers, but really I approached the event with a pretty open mind and a desire to learn about it. I even managed to get into the Festival grounds. "Entrance," I wrote, "is taboo for non-delegates, as you might suppose; but we managed to infiltrate a large group of Turkish students singing and marching thru the guarded gates. I made Turkish sounds as I passed the guard, and he smiled warmly." Soon I was in a great hall, with hundreds of lights and thousands of people. I met delegates from many countries and enjoyed talking with a Swedish delegate, then a young Iraqi socialist. We amiably debated a number of contemporary topics—the

Suez crisis, America's purchase of oil rights in Venezuela, Britain's domination of Iraq. I was learning, at first hand, about international politics from foreign students my age—something I'd rarely done at the U.

Then came "SUNNY ITALY!" I loved it. In Venice I went into epistolary overdrive, pouring out many pages, and then wrote many more about Ravenna, Rimini, Florence and Rome. (Good God, what a passel of work I would have saved if I'd had a digital camera and the internet!) Arriving in Rome, I wandered star-struck through all the ancient sights there, but what totally blew me away was three nights of Italian opera on the immense stage built over the ancient ruin of Caracalla's Baths! That stage, illuminated by spotlights, was half the size of a soccer field, and bounded on both wings by limestone columns 40 feet high. It was big enough for dozens of animals and hundreds of singers to move around on. "This was really an unforgettable spectacle: each day I looked forward with anticipation to the evening. I saw 3 operas, Carmen, Aida, and Rigoletto." I described "the 100-piece orchestra, melting and blending its own enchantment with that of the whole, with the rich and clear voices of leading singers, with the toreador of Carmen, with Aida, with the crippled Rigoletto in lament over the murder of his beloved daughter—it was an unmatched masterpiece of sound and color witnessed by 55,000 people in the starlit evening."

Aida's famous Triumphal March mesmerized me. Spotlighted trumpeters with long ceremonial trumpets "stood on ledges halfway up those 40-foot columns and sharply blew into the night air that signature theme: Da DAHH da da da DAHH DAHH DAHH, / Da Da Da DAHH Da Da!" And as they did so, there marched onstage, rank after rank, seemingly endless columns of participants—"200 people in colorful array, singing in choruses, dazzlingly clad rows of dancing girls & men, soldiers with gold and silver-encrusted armor, swords, buckles, plumes, all crowding the gigantic stage, marching in ranks, flourishing spears and tramping, singing in throaty unison while eight thundering horses pulling brilliant chariots rushed from the deep back-stage to its very front apron, then reared with hooves in the air. The applause was deafening!"

That, by Golly, was something! That was absolutely something to remember. I'd never experienced a single opera before, and now I was attending a brilliantly illuminated night-time operatic extravaganza, a Verdi Opera, at Caracalla's Baths in Rome! Three operas, in fact! Three from the top of the entire repertory! I was so lucky, so blessed to have been given that trip, so thankful to my parents for enabling it!

Like many Americans I found that I adored Italy and what I imagined to be the Italian national character. I described my feeling about Italians:

It's like the ribald, laughing, cussing, winking, griping type of association that might exist between two happy-go-lucky pick-pockets. Get the idea? It's my impression that for the Italian's birthday you don't give him candy and flowers, unless the candy is peppered and there's a squirt-bulb attached to the flower. What the Italians need: mass driving lessons, tourist trade in Southern Italy, Protestantism. What they don't need: lessons in salesmanship; gold, silver, or silk goods; thinner skins on their funny bones. I think Italians are the funniest group in the living business—it's all situation comedy, and facial expression, vocal tone, animation of hands—they strike me deep in the jocular jugular. What they don't have: gold earrings and red bandannas, fruit carts, every word ending in '...ah,' as in 'Youua wantah fruitah?' because some words end in 'o'—e.g., 'Pietro, youwa wanto fruitah?'"

Amusement led me to concoct a crazy video of Italian drivers. I recall that Mussolini, infuriated by his countrymen's faint-hearted military exploits, called Italy "a nation of waiters." Maybe so, but I never saw an Italian motorist wait for anything! So I asked my family back home to picture us driving our Simca up the Italian coastline, and characterized a two-lane road with a stone wall on one side and a steep cliff on the other, dropping down to the sea:

Now to introduce the human element—the vitality, the passion, the shrewdness and pride of the Italian native. Imagine first that this road has been converted by some gesticulating maniac into a precarious race-course. Realize that there are far too many entries for the slightest degree of safety, but realize further that safety is not in anyone's mind. 'The more the merrier' is the creed.

Now these cars are racing, bobbing, weaving along our sunny highway and we must add sound effects. The roar of the breakers below? Not a chance. Just horns. High horns, low horns, solo and duet horns, beeping sharply, lingering, squeaking (bicycles), or croaking like frogs (motor scooters). They love horns. Simply love 'em. Is any animosity aroused when one driver blares by another in passing? Not a bit. The second just honks back and prepares to re-pass the first. The game's rules are simple: Pass on all curves. Always have one hand on horn, blowing it violently for a minimum of 30 minutes each hour. If the driver ahead passes, pass him back at the crucial moment, creating that three-abreast effect while oncoming cars sound horns wildly, slamming on brakes. Sounds of scraping fenders to be disregarded. Only full-scale wrecks are eventful enough to stop for—and there is an abundance of these, as we often saw pile-ups of three and four cars, with motorcycles buried in their fenders.

Between wrecks there are crews of shirtless laborers excavating the road. They don't make repairs, they just dig up the roads. And they don't dig very often, preferring to spend most of their time staring at the cars streaking by, or urinating on their work.

So what sort of a picture now? High narrow road, cars & motorcycles racing, horns blaring, laborers digging, staring, urinating, wrecks occurring. Thru a small town now, same scene only with swarms of people standing, walking, talking, carrying loaves of bread or sacks of vegetables by hand or on bicycles, sailors whistling at pretty girls, white-clothed policemen peering at the sailors, other policemen in the center of the road, swinging arms in unintelligible signals, countless numbers of men in filthy undershirts, service station attendants wearing blue and yellow jumpers, and then there are those in the clerical profession, nuns and Benedictine monks, riding bicycles and motor scooters just as recklessly as anyone else.

Now add teams of street-cleaners, brandishing brooms or fire-hoses to purge the roadway, nimbly dodging out of each other's sprays, then add the sign-posters, who use paste and brush to cover every building with wine, cigarette, lottery, gasoline advertisements. Don't forget the watermelon sellers, the area around their stands heaped with the accumulated debris of a thousand seed-spitters. Then there are the tourist-catchers, who peer, black-eyed, like disgruntled skunks from their dens of waving silk scarves, jangling necklaces, beads, trinkets, postcards, slides, soup, nuts.

Throw all this together, add such dashes of roadway flavor as trucks backing down mile-long inclines, compelling all the lined-up cars behind them to do likewise; Renault Dauphines dropping like flies on the shoulders of the road, unable to climb further and unable to cross the road to coast down for another try—add these to cycling nuns, waving policemen, jumpered pumpers, insane drivers and tourist catchers, street cleaners, sign posters, melon sellers and seed-spitters, cycling monks and disgruntled skunks, walkers and talkers, peerers and leerers, whistlers and pisslers . . . and what do you have? A Big, Long, Laugh. At least I did.

Still laughing, we returned to magical Paris, where I gawked at the Tuileries, the Sorbonne, the Eiffel Tower. I marveled at the Louvre—I made two four-hour visits, there was so much to see—I navigated the Metro, I pitied war veterans washing themselves in the Seine, I described the Rue Pigalle, the haunt of Toulouse Lautrec whom I'd come to love. Then I revealed that near the Folies Bergère I'd met an American girl, a pretty college student, her name was Clare Something. Mike teamed up with her friend, so all four of us went wandering together, walking along the Seine, then up the Champs Élysées. We were four lucky American college kids at the end of a wonderful summer. Before we knew it, it became very late:

It was 4:00 a.m. when we sat down near the Egyptian obelisk at the Place de la Concorde, and from there we could see the dark figures of the Arch of Triumph and the Eiffel Tower against the blue light of morning. There was that autumn chill, that invigorating air, that pinkness at the horizon, the tiredness after a night pleasurably spent. I felt our isolation in that great roundabout with tree-lined streets leading off in every direction. The black iron street lamps slowly dimmed with the approach of dawn; at 5:30 they turned off, and lone cars began barreling around the great round intersection. Street-cleaning rigs rotated around the obelisk and its round platform, spraying away the previous day's debris.

Another day would begin, another day would end. I sense the philosophy, the acceptance, in that tableau. I knew as I penned those lines that although I was going away from Paris, all that I saw would continue and continue and continue. I know it continues now, 60 years later. The cars and drivers and street-cleaning rigs will change, but the scene itself is timeless. So long as that obelisk stands there, so long as night falls and morning creeps up over the Place de la Concorde, a little part of me will be there too, just a little whisper, just a tiny particle of that timeless mystic stuff that permeates all historic places and imparts a sense of invisible witnesses lingering there.

7

Master of Arts

SEATTLE AND BELLINGHAM, 1960-1966

I was 21 in 1960 when I graduated from the University of Washington. For America the decade ahead would be one of release from the conformity of the 50s, of protest against racism and overseas adventurism, and of new adventures in drugs, music and sex. The main drivers of all this were people my age, in their 20s, full of energy, lust for life, and zeal for general improvement. As for me personally, in one way or another my youth had equipped me with a certain self-confidence, a strong work ethic, a great fear of failure, a few skills in communication, tremendous admiration of effective teaching, and such a deep fascination with historical civilization that I wanted to make a profession out of studying it. I was ready to take the first steps toward building my career.

But not quite yet. At first, a fear of failure governed me. I began the 1960s nagged by self-doubt, thanks to my identity crisis and my late decision to make my career in Academe. I felt unprepared to enter grad school, and so decided to take a "break year" before entering the History Department's M.A. program. I found a lonely houseboat on Lake Union and there made my new home. It was small, still, dank, and mysterious; the waters of the lake lapped its foundations. Ducks went by in little flotillas, seagulls passed overhead, big boats and barges and tugs lumbered by toward the Ballard locks, often setting my little house in motion. Every night, my reading light burned late. To rest my eyes I'd get up and stare at my walls, on which I'd taped *bons mots* from the great French essayists Montaigne, La Rouchefoucald, La Bruyère. I'd memorize them, they'd help me hide my ignorance.

And so I read and read. History, sociology, literature, philosophy, book after book after book. I could have posted a "Man at Work" sign outside. Fascinated, I lived in a world of concepts. I had a *New Yorker* cartoon that amusingly captured that idea: it pictured a bald guy sitting in an arm-chair, gazing without focus at a blank wall, with, overhead, an enormous thought-bubble filled with something like interlinked gears and doodads and asterisks, stars, diagrams, and rings, all intermeshed and rotating in some giant design that only he could see. I framed that cartoon and for the next 15 years took it with me everywhere, chuckling as I stuck it up onto new walls.

I worked on myself as though I were a pig needing fattening. But I had to make a living, so I found a job working at a big discount store on East-lake Avenue. Jafco was named after its owner, Sid Jaffee. The company sold electronics and cameras, luggage, clothing, housewares, and cheap Asian imports. Dave Jaffee was my immediate boss. He was a small fellow, a few years older than I, brimming with good humor. He was the first Jewish guy I ever knew well and he became my friend. We were always joking, and like many Jews he had lots of Jewish jokes. I laughed till my sides ached at his story about how all Asia and half of Europe had been conquered by "Gh-engis Cohen." We invented silly names for each other in a crazy made-up Slavic language, "Prascȩnti Belàk," of which he, "Davyo Joppa," became the poet laureate.

I remember the cheap Asian gadgets in the Jafco catalog. There were "Elvis" pillows, "Minnie Mouse" shower slippers, and an unforgettable Ko-rean-made "Mood Meter," a clock dial with a spinning pointer attached, that couples were supposed to use when bashfully wanting to indicate whether they wanted to engage in love-making. "Headache," "Period," and "Bad Day" were at the bottom of the dial, "Strip Now," "Bang On" and "Quickie?" were at the top. That stuff sold surprisingly well. I was good at my job, and the boss gave me a handsome check as a holiday bonus. I think Jafco wanted to adopt me, and I was pleased to be greeted with "Happy Yom, Jerry!" at Yom Kippur even though they knew I wasn't Jewish. Prob-ably it's because I was so proud of my circumcision.

1960 also saw my first public political pronouncement. My opinions about everything political were evolving at warp speed, and as the decade passed, with civil rights issues and the Vietnam War intensifying, I moved farther Left, becoming particularly exasperated at the stupidity of people who charged idealistic activists with being "pro-communist." In February 1960 a series of student "sit-ins," non-violent protests against racial seg-regation, began in Kansas and North Carolina, and increasingly engaged the attention of young people like myself. The upholders of segregation, adopting the best weapon at hand, sought to smear students as communist dupes.

That sparked my first public attempt to "fix stupid." To counter that smear I sought in my *Post Intelligencer* letter, "A Student Speaks" (July 10, 1960), to respond to an ignorant writer's charge that college students were being brainwashed. Adopting a teacherly tone, I defended free inquiry and organized protests, and insisted that college education, far from being a form of brainwashing, was a vaccination against it.

As I wrote that piece, the 1960 presidential campaign was already underway. The contenders were the Republican Vice President, Richard Nixon, and the Massachusetts Democrat and playboy Senator, John F. Kennedy. The former, a Red-baiting Cold War warrior, stood for Anti-communism, Free Enterprise, and American military might. The latter, though his platform was similar, had a more compelling style and seemed more attractive on the stump, inspiring more and perspiring less before the national TV audience that witnessed their debates.

Two Cold War issues emerged. The first was a manufactured U.S. frenzy over Quemoy and Matsu, two tiny islands off the coast of Communist China that were claimed by China but also by Taiwan, America's client. Nixon, full of bravado, declared that if China invaded them, the U.S. should respond with nuclear weapons; Kennedy temporized. The other issue was "the missile gap," in which Kennedy pretended that the Republican Administration had weakened the U.S. by manufacturing fewer weapons than the Soviets. The charge was absurd but effective, like so many cooked up in the intellectual blur of the Cold War, and Kennedy won narrowly.

I, very much the young idealist, rejoiced, but my ecstasy was short-lived. Kennedy soon launched his ill-advised invasion of Cuba. He went on to establish the Peace Corps, chip away at his "New Frontier" agenda, and start a race to the moon, but after the Cuban fiasco and the worse one just beginning in Vietnam, where he was creating "Strategic Hamlets," my disenchantment increased.

In fact I was becoming angrier every day. I was maddened by the Cold War, the Arms Race, and the tendency of both Superpowers not only to build out their military alliances but to drag into them the small nations of the Third World. The two Superpowers were dividing Earth into two camps. They rushed to build radioactive weapons to destroy each other, and underground bomb shelters to save themselves. The more I saw, the more I felt another need to "fix stupid." And so, taking another public stab at it, I set about writing "A Martian's Guide to Earth," a bitter mock-history of the end of life on our planet. I was surprised when the *University of Washington Daily* printed it all without changing a word. It consumed an entire page of newsprint.

I presented it drily, as a guide written by Martian archaeologists for space tourists. "Travelers," I began, "wishing to beat the heat this summer might contemplate a trip to Earth, where the climate is mild and the radioactivity suitable for any Martian." There, from the "rubble of bygone civilizations," the visitor could see how humanity had ended. A gradual sundering of the Earth's population into two Camps had occurred, the two blocs engaging in "a Battle-For-Men's-Minds, then a Hunt-For-Armed-Friends." Crucial to their dividing-up of the world was the spread of bipolar thinking, promoted by ideologues and irresponsible newspapers. Incessantly propagandized, ordinary folks increasingly came to disbelieve Facts and credit Labels. Before long, in the two "Weapocentric" Camps, people took to "wearing helmets with radios in them, tuned to give momentary news of evacuation procedures; contactors began building whole cities underground; sensible people began wearing lead suits." Armageddon came by a fluke when one Head of State, dishing out routine threats against his counterpart, mistakenly took as actual truth one of the many outrageous lies churned out daily by the newspapers. This caused him to stroll out and buy one of the popular newspapers, hereditarily owned and published by a semi-literate—I had William Randolph Hearst, the owner of the *Post Intelligencer*, in mind. "Drawing his conclusions from the headlines, the Head of State went back to his office and pushed all the buttons."

~

That was a polemical satire, Voltairean in mockery, but its doomsday scenario captured the madness of the early 1960s. Educated people *did* feel like inmates in a madhouse. In fact, only a few months later, I found myself walking around the University District for a week with a transistor radio pressed to my ear, awaiting word of Doomsday! That was during the Cuban Missile Crisis, when Kennedy and Khrushchev faced off, threatening nuclear exchange. That showdown in August 1962 marked the supreme height of the Cold War.

It was also the high noon of hysterical American propaganda. After the postwar Soviet development of atomic weapons and China's fall to Communism in 1949, average Americans were horrified by the creeping

"Red Menace" and became weak as babies against mind-bludgeoning by demagogues like Senator Joseph McCarthy, who stopped at nothing in his anti-communist fulminations. At last, in 1955, McCarthy, a drunk, faded from view, but he left a poisonous legacy. Organizations like the John Birch Society spread charges that many of America's greatest leaders and *even President Eisenhower* were communists or communist dupes.

High schools began adopting anti-communist social studies curriculums. In the early 60s more than a dozen States enacted programs that mandated 30 school hours to study "Americanism vs. Communism." And while racists dressed their anti-civil rights attacks in anti-communist tropes, military kooks salted new "Troop Information Programs" for ordinary recruits with right-wing extremism. Extremism, though, was A-OK when practiced by Republican flag-wavers: "Extremism in defense of liberty is no vice," shouted their new presidential candidate, Barry Goldwater, at the Republican national convention of 1964.

The main target of all this anti-communist propaganda was domestic, not foreign: its unannounced purpose, its use by Republican politicians, was to smear civil rights agitators, trades union leaders, Democratic politicians in general, and anybody else who questioned the idea of our God-fearing white nation determining other countries' policies.

All this anti-communist madness landed like a bomb on Washington State, on *Seattle*, when Captain K.J. Sanger, commander of the naval air station at Sand Point, decided to launch a "Moral Leadership" program to indoctrinate not only all military personnel on his base but hundreds of students throughout high schools and colleges in the Northwest. The program featured the showing of an egregious movie, a powerful propaganda tool, called "Communism on the Map."

That movie was a terrifying but utterly misleading 75-minute portrayal of Communism's takeover of the entire world, step by step, in a plot supposedly nearing completion. Cunningly tricked out with altered quotations, true-sounding accounts of events, and impressive-looking footnotes from untrustworthy sources, that film was a masterpiece of misinformation and propaganda. Exposed to it, few ordinary Americans, historically ignorant and mentally defenseless, could withstand its impact. It ended with an ominous voice-over declaring that the United States "could fall at any time on the signal from Moscow." That was the sort of garbage that inspired the Columbia University historian Richard Hofstadter to publish *The Paranoid Style in American Politics* just two years later (1964).

The Pacific Northwest was much more conservative in the 1960s than now. The "pro-America" influence of the Boeing Aircraft Company (a giant defense contractor) was dominant, and influential also was the right-wing effect of huge military and naval installations all around Puget Sound. To expose and defeat the insidious efforts of Captain Sanger would require an intellectual warrior armed with an encyclopedic knowledge of recent world history, great personal courage, and a silver tongue.

Enter Giovanni Costigan. Enter the small, white-haired, Oxford-Debating-Society-trained University of Washington professor, filled with indignation at the suddenly spreading intellectual pollution of *his Northwest!* Already in just a few weeks, daily showings of "Communism on the Map" were being held everywhere, thanks to Boeing, Puget Sound Power and Light, a suspicious "Group of People Inc.," and various churches and affiliated groups like the Knights of Columbus. Costigan took up the gauntlet and led the attack. As a wide-ranging intellectual who knew the recent history of the world as few others did, he was perfectly situated to document and expose every single lie in that film (which had been made, by the way, at a Bible college in Arkansas). He lectured on its evils not only on the UW campus but in every town nearby. Thousands of people watched him rip it apart.

But it was now being shown *almost everywhere,* and soon there was a reaction by Republicans who accused *him* of being a communist! The controversy became violent after 92 other professors at the U and nine Seattle pastors also condemned the film. Right-wing death threats were leveled at professors, church pews were slashed, angry street demonstrations began.

If you look closely at political propaganda, you'll see that its power and persuasiveness often originate, as that film's did, in falsified history, or, more simply, historical lies. The most dangerous political propaganda springs from really big historical lies—myths, like Hitler's claim that Germany lost World War I because of domestic traitors, and Senator Joseph McCarthy's claim that China went Communist because of American traitors, and Donald Trump's similar claim that the presidential election of 2020 was stolen by traitors. In 1961 I was just beginning to understand this dangerous mechanism, and so, with my eyes newly opened at the dreadful power of uneducated people being stirred up by falsified history, my lifetime study of propaganda was just beginning.

I asked Costigan how I could help, and he gave me and four other grad students the job of writing and distributing a pamphlet documenting the teeming lies of "Communism on the Map." Here was a truly Herculean assignment to "fix stupid." I still have a copy of the pamphlet, "University of Washington Students PROTEST *Communism on the Map*," with my name heading the list of student authors. I remember driving to many places around Seattle to distribute it. That was dangerous, because while Costigan was admired by educated people, there were thousands who believed the slanders suddenly heaped upon him. As his helper, I also found myself reviled and physically threatened as a "comsymp," a communist sympathizer, and that was perilous when intruding, as I deliberately did, into right-wing street demonstrations.

I remember a Yugoslav immigrant, Josef Mlot-Mroz, who was a fixture at all those right-wing street gatherings. A very short, stubby, and always angry man with a Hitler mustache, he would stand with both his small feet widely and defiantly planted on a Soviet flag which he'd brought with him, and swear violently and loudly in fractured English against the evils of Communism, adducing horrors from his own life in Tito's Yugoslavia. I tried to hand him a copy of our pamphlet but he slapped it away and vociferously pledged his allegiance to "Communism on the Map." I wasn't going to push it. Those boots, though ridiculously small, seemed lethal, and even his Gilbert-and-Sullivan mustache looked dangerous.

～

I formally entered grad school in the Fall of 1961 and then sailed through my courses, never looking back at my houseboat fears. The UW History Department was then one of the best in the country. Stull Holt was nationally known as President of the American Historical Association. Max Savelle, a silver-haired gent with a speckled bow-tie, author of *Seeds of Liberty* and *A History of Colonial America,* was another luminary. Of course there was Costigan teaching English history, and we also had Donald Treadgold, author of *Twentieth Century Russia*—I wrote an "A+" paper for him on the Hungarian Revolution of 1956.

I eagerly took Scott Lytle's seminar on the French Revolution. Lytle was a New Yorker with a doctorate from Princeton who arrived at the U in 1949. His subject, the French Revolution, is one of the most fascinating events in all human history, brimming with heroes and villains, hopes and despairs, massacres, wars, the guillotine. I've always loved reading about it.

But the most memorable thing about Lytle's course was his lecturing style. He did it without notes, lost in thought, speaking slowly and carefully, and, much of the time, with his *eyes tightly close*d! And even that wasn't the totally oddest thing, for he did all this while *pacing side to side across the classroom*, abruptly spinning before he hit his head on one wall, and then, his eyes still closed, heading in the same manner toward the other!

To picture this, imagine a man walking railroad tracks while heading into a blizzard, his body bent forward into the wind, his face pointing down at the tracks, and then observe his walking gait as he takes very large but very slow meditative strides, planting one foot and then the other on every third tie of the track; and then, just before he bangs against an obstruction, picture him swinging around 180 degrees, still with his eyes closed, still talking, then treading in the opposite direction till at some point he reaches THE TWO GREAT AND GOLDEN WORDS, which, stopping to bob his head still farther down like a heron nabbing a fish and simultaneously rocking up his other leg behind him as a balance, he'd utter with great drama and a loud exhalation, "FURRENCHHH RREVOLUTIONNN." Undergrads took his lectures simply because they'd heard how hlarious this was.

Far more important to my development was another prof who arrived in 1949, Thomas J. Pressly. He and Costigan, though very different personalities, later became my twin role-models. He was a trim, handsome man in his forties. With his buttoned jacket and slim neck-tie he looked like a well-turned-out businessman, but he had a gravity about him. A southerner, he was courtly, dignified, serious, but hospitable and friendly. He'd grown up in Tennessee, gone to Harvard for his B.A. and M.A., and, after World War II, finished at Princeton and arrived at the U in 1949. He was the resident expert on the American Civil War, and in 1954 published a very important book, *Americans Interpret Their Civil War*, a history not of the war itself but of historians' writings about it. It was, in other words, a book of historiography, a study of the whole body of writing *about* the Civil War.

Now, in all American history-writing there's no subject more controversial than that, which helps explain why Pressly was so highly sensitive to *bias* in historical writing. In his book, clarifying what different writers down through the ages had thought about the Civil War, he showed great respect for their divergent views, even trying to reconcile them with each other in a search for agreed truths. Exactly the same qualities pervaded his classroom, where he unfailingly addressed with respect every question, however idiotic, by underclassmen. He thought history should be written and taught with a deep and humbling knowledge of the intrinsic *temporality of all understanding,* a consciousness that we can never fully enter the world-views of the past or live in the moral universes that past humans inhabited. History was to be respected for its own sake, rather than used as a weapon in political and ideological combat.

I worked hard in Dr. Pressly's advanced course, reading more than 1400 pages a week and writing many papers for him. I also profited immensely from his teachings, and later, as a professor, tried to emulate his objectivity. History, as Voltaire remarked, is a pack of tricks that we play upon the dead; but some players, from love of truth, play their cards face-up, as Pressly did. Unfortunately he didn't make Full Professor till 1960, 11 years after arriving at the U. Apart from his one great book, he published relatively little. Like Costigan, he was one of those professors for whom publishing was never the top priority; instead he devoted himself to teaching. In the later 1960s he became involved in NDEA summer institutes for high school history teachers, and later authored AHA booklets and sat on advisory boards promoting the teaching of history in the schools.

～

Dr. Pressly wanted me to become his Teaching Assistant ("T.A."), which meant that for the first time in my life I began evaluating tests, not just taking them. His other T.A. was Rick Painter, a New Yorker who had come all the way to Washington to study New York politics and write a master's thesis on Tammany Hall. I liked him a lot, and we soon became very good friends. He was a big guy, very slow and deliberate, with a deep, soft voice and a reassuring air; there was something senior, paternal, about him.

A third friend was Ralph Cheadle, a wayward Deke like myself, a guy who'd caught the spirit of the times, bought a harmonica and a guitar, and begun channeling Bob Dylan. I can still see his pleasant, open, boyish face, amber hair and blue eyes as he sings, mumbling, "Freight Train, Freight Train, goin' so fast," while strumming his guitar, then pausing to blow the melody on that mouth organ he'd ludicrously positioned with two bent coat hangers before his face.

Most of my new friends were eggheads or eccentrics. Robin was an exception. Ralph, from Spokane, knew a beautiful red-head from the same place, Robin Hardy, and she too became one of my pals—in fact I dated her and for a while we spent many days and nights together; she was my first long-term partner in that way. She was very sweet as well as very beautiful, and moreover, she was, or would become, very rich, as her father was, I think, the owner of a silver mining company in Idaho. But, thanks to my lucky upbringing, I've never been one to arrange plans around the getting of money; we lost interest and moved on.

We remained good friends, though, and that's how I met Ruth Genung, Robin's funny sidekick. The two had traveled around Europe together one summer, and were now living together in a small house in the U District. Another girl I knew was Margot Sullivan, the daughter of a prominent philosophy professor. Like her father she was unstable, and at one point accused me falsely of making her pregnant—I'd never even touched her! She was into Zen, pot, "natural" healing arts, and astrology like other wacky characters in the U District. I had no use for any of those and never even smoked a joint.

Wait! Except for once, when it drove me almost crazy! I pause to summon up that occasion. I smoked a joint in the company of Roger Jackson of Badger Pocket (like me he'd come to Seattle from the Kittitas Valley), an entirely crazy guy with prominent teeth and a daffy smile—he was also a fantastic impromptu piano player, he could play any Scott Joplin rag while bashing the keys and bouncing up and down on the piano bench—and Susie Johnson, another Ellensburg native; she'd been a prim high school cheerleader and was now in her hippie stage, loose as a boot-camp whore although Roger soon married her anyway.

We shared Roger's high-powered grass, then made our way out for "munchies" at the Bartell Drugstore on the corner of 45th and University Way. (It's still there.) The drug hitting me hard, I sat there in the company of these odd friends, furiously scarfing cookies while whipping out my trusty pen to write down page after page of brilliant insights! My mind was a crackling bonfire of ideas nobody had ever thought of before! But when I woke up next morning to look at what I'd written, I saw that it was garbage. After that one experience I stayed away from pot. Of course I continued getting drunk whenever I wished. Drink is the curse of the working class, and I was a worker.

I only knew Roger for a year or two. He was a druggie, very affable, a sunny hedonist. At some point he trailed down to Mexico in search of peyote. But I do have a funny story about him. Like other heavy pot users he was very loose in all his attitudes, and as regards politics he was an out-and-out anarchist. That's why I thought it hilarious when he told me, after we hadn't seen each other for several months, that in order to keep body and soul together he'd taken a job with the Seattle pet licensing bureau! His assignment was to put on a badge identifying himself, then roam Seattle's neighborhoods with a clipboard, a money sack, and a bag full of pet licenses, tracking down pet owners who'd not properly licensed their animals. This anarchist's job was to enforce petty laws against small-time violators! So out he'd go, selling licenses or issuing summonses when he uncovered criminal pet owners.

He told me his routine. He'd go up to a door and knock. The door would open. Then, imitating the dumpy, mean housewife who lurked within, her hair in rollers, he'd snarl, "Whaddya want?" He flashes his badge and inquires, in his own voice: "You got 'ny dogs or cats?" "No!" she shouts, trying to slam the door, but in her back room there's a yapping, then a smallish mongrel becomes visible. "Oho, so, what's *this*?" "Uh, it's a friend's dog, we're keepin' it for him." "Well, you gonna have to get it licensed!" and Roger scribbles a notice, rips it out of his book, hands it to the woman.

Clockwise from far left: Ralph Cheadle, Bill Daly, Me, Gordon Nickell (behind his girlfriend), Sandy and Dave Jaffee, Ruth on Rick's lap, Dave and Lizzy Davis

"But," I interrupted, "What if the owner's away, or at work?" "Sometimes," says Roger, there'd be no response when he'd knock at a door. Maybe the dog owner was hiding inside? He'd take out his pencil and enter coded notes in his record book for a follow-up trip later. The notes, he said, registered his suspicions. I was actually looking at a page in his record book at that very moment.

"What's this, 'S.O.D.,' after this address?"
"Scratches On Door," he replied.
"And this, what's this '4.N.S.D.'?"
"4 Neighbors Say Dog," he replied.
"And 'D.S.I.Y.?'"
"Dog Shit in Yard."

And that's how Roger supported himself, his anarchist girlfriend, and his own unlicensed cat.

Another new friend, very eggheady, was Gordon Nickell, a philosophy student. He was from Grandview, a small town south of Yakima. He was short, small, with a round head, short curly dishwater blond hair, and a wall eye—his left eyeball, disoriented since birth, looked up and off to one side, showing an abnormal amount of white, while, alarmingly, his blue right one looked right at me. He'd been raised in a lunatic evangelical church and was now, at the university, very much with the help of his philosophy studies, ditching everything about it. He was a year or two younger than I and firmly attached himself to me, seeking me out, asking far-out metaphysical questions and listening to my answers with attention and often enjoyment. He, or at least his right eye, was my first disciple, and that was okay with me because he stimulated and brought out my show-off tendencies. Gordon also, rather surprisingly given the extreme religious sobriety of his upbringing, played the ukulele, and, as I was just then beginning to fool around with a guitar, we murdered folk songs together.

Gordon had a girlfriend named Sandy, a pretty girl he'd known since his Grandview school days, so she too entered my widening circle of post-graduate friends. They actually got married a year or two later and lived happily for a while, but Gordon, a man of increasingly unorthodox views, was on that long and often reckless trajectory from evangelical youth to totally hell-raising adulthood, and these were, after all, the 1960s. He fell in love with a gorgeous and glossy long-haired brunette, a singer-guitarist with black leather boots and a body to kill for—she resembled the dazzling folk singer Joan Baez. Apparently she loved him back as they both departed into the drug trade, leaving poor Sandy behind.

I had another close friend from California, a smart guy named Bill Daly. There was a gentleness in his manner, though there was nothing gentle about his absolutely biting wit. Like most of us, he was looking around, trying to find himself. So, anyway, I had a lot of new buddies now, an entire ring of egghead pals with only the equally liberated Ralph Cheadle as a connection to my old home and social harbor, the Deke house. Of course I'd also carried over from undergraduate days my valuable friendship with that literary couple, Dave and Lizzy Davis, but all the rest were new friends, all benefiting and influencing me in one way or another.

It should be no surprise that Rick, Ralph, Bill, Gordon and I decided to move in together, rent an entire house on the main drag at 3924 University Way, divide up its bedrooms, and share each other's companionship and cooking while pushing on with our schooling. Two vivid recollections about living there are of Bill Daly in that kitchen, cooking that wonderful Spanish Rice he made, and, a very different memory, my utter shock that November 1963 morning when Bill came bursting into my bedroom to wake me with news that President Kennedy had been shot dead in Dallas.

My Teaching Assistantship gave me just enough income to get by on, so there was no need to find a summer job in 1962. My parents saw this as the perfect excuse to push Lynn and me out of the house for a lengthy period, so offered to support us in an auto tour of the U.S.A. We jumped at the chance. I was 23, Lynn 15. This was a great occasion to have quality time together and also, for Lynn, a golden opportunity to appreciate me more. Also she could hone her listening skills. She'd be trapped for six weeks in my tiny Morris Minor with the chance to enjoy, as few others have done freely, the volume of wit and wisdom that rolled out of me. This was to become the highlight of her entire life.

Our plan was quite simple. You could call it a box tour. Our plan was to drive east from Ellensburg to Boston, turn right and drive south to Georgia, turn right and drive west to Los Angeles, turn right and drive north to Ellensburg. That's a box, and that's pretty much what we did.

But in the box were events. The first was in the Midwest. I was the driver, Lynn the navigator, and we'd planned to stop for a night at the farmhouse of Harry and Ruth Lehrman, in Indiana. Harry was one of our dad's oldest friends. He was a character, a practical joker and a self-consciously shit-kicking rube. He wore bib overalls, his ears sprouted hair the way his fields sprouted corn. The Lehrmans lived three time-zones away from my folks, so Harry, the practical joker, enjoyed calling my father every

July 24th at the crack of dawn to wish him Happy Birthday. Of course the joke was that when it was sunup at six a.m. in Indiana it was three a.m. in Ellensburg, with the moon still overhead and coyotes howling on Thorp Prairie. Harry's chaffing would start as soon as my dad picked up the phone: "Len, you sound real groggy! You all right? Too much to drink?"

He was a character. But the "event" I spoke of was that Lynn navigated us to Decatur, Illinois, rather than Decatur, Indiana, which, we found when we reached the first destination, was 282 miles and five hours away from the second! That was annoying, and I believe the innocent party, the driver, made hurtful remarks to the navigator. To be required to drive five more hours on top of a long day of concentrating one's stare on the road was criminal. I remember that afterwards I bought Lynn, at the first opportunity, in order to register the magnitude of her mistake and impress upon her the importance of accurate navigation, an Army Surplus leather bombardier helmet with woolly ear flaps to fasten at the chin, the better to maintain concentration on her road map. With gratitude she wore that helmet every day for the rest of the trip.

Because it was nearly daybreak when we reached the Lehrmans', we stayed an extra day to stoke up on sleep and food. I remember the scene when Harry and I, the next morning, went out to his barn and found a stiffened cat's carcass on the hay-strewn floor. With his tractor he'd in-

advertently run over the poor thing 24 hours earlier. He reached down, took it by the tail, and whirled it spinning like a boomerang out the door of the barn into the barnyard, calling it "you pot-licker!" When we left he gave me, as a going-away present, a pair of small ceramic smiling green frogs, one with big girly eyelashes and the other with a smug look on its face. How nice, I said, but, I thought, how ugly. And then when I turned the frogs over I found them prominently equipped with hu-

man genitals, gaudily painted, the one sporting a large penis with testicles, the other a large, hairy vagina. I kept them ever afterwards and laughed every time I looked at them.

Harry's gone now, gone to meet his maker; but you never know, do you? Sometimes we receive a thing like that pair of ceramic green frogs, an insignificant thing. We invest it with memories till we die, at which point the remembering dies and the thing itself becomes just a thing again. It starts as a thing, becomes a souvenir (literally, a 'thing kept for remembering'), then it's just a thing again. Strange. Then suppose it winds up in an antique shop. You see where this line of thought leads, don't you? The antique shop is a morgue, a graveyard, of souvenirs. But a recycling center also, no? Perhaps a Dr. Frankenstein factory, then, for generating fresh souvenirs from dead ones? Hmmm. How many precious memories dwell in that millefiori paperweight you picked up at the flea market? . . . . But enough. Now, to put a stop to all this metaphysical rumination, let me state clearly that those ceramic frogs won't go to an antique shop when I die because I gave them to my young grandson to improve his uh, self-awareness.

From Indiana we drove to Boston, gawked at the Freedom Trail, the Old North Church and the grave of Paul Revere, we went to Lexington and Concord, gawked at the Minuteman statue, found Walden Pond, then made our way to the home of a family friend, the Rev. Miller Lovett.

Soon we headed to New York. In the big city we gawked at Fifth Avenue, the skyscrapers, Central Park, and went to Coney Island where we gawked some more, rode the roller coaster, and I won a pink plaster dog with rhinestone eyes and a chipped ear. (WHERE IS IT NOW??? MISSING ME IN SOME ANTIQUE SHOP? I WANT MY PLASTER DOG BACK!) From there we drove south through Richmond, Raleigh, and Charleston into Georgia, where our car broke down in a little burg named Claxton. We had to wait four days for repairs. This gave us the opportunity to learn that Claxton was world-famous for its fruitcakes. And now, dear reader, you've learned that too. I hide a surprise for you on every page.

The good Claxton people were leery because we were young white northerners. We didn't come in a bus, though, so maybe we didn't mean any harm? This was the era when mixed groups of black and white young people, mostly college students, were invading the South in Greyhound and Trailways buses, trying to break the calcified segregation of bus stations, waiting rooms, and affiliated eating facilities. They were called "Freedom Riders" because riding interstate bus lines governed by federal, not local, law, protected them in their attempts to disrupt and correct the local non-enforcement of Supreme Court rulings prohibiting segregation in interstate commerce. Those brave students were taking their lives in their hands because they faced angry mob violence often led by Ku Klux Klan members and even police authorities like Bull Connor, who beat them with chains and baseball bats, and tried to burn them alive in their buses.

With such things going on we missed the charm of Claxton and were anxious to hit the road again. Southern accents amused us, but bat-wielding southern hospitality didn't. Also, we were becoming fatigued; one can only take so much sameness on an American vacation, and that was before the chain-storing of the nation. So, moving on, we grabbed a quick look at New Orleans, regretted not having a quicker look at endless Texas, and at last arrived in Las Vegas flat broke. Devil-may-care, we plowed our last quarter into a slot machine, crossed the desert, and limped into L.A. where our great-aunt Ella McAfee fed us and pumped up our money supply. A last we returned to Ellensburg safe and sound, with lots of memories and, really, a much-deepened knowledge of our country.

The best part, though, was the togetherness, the sights, anxieties, frustrations, fears, and laughs we shared. Oh, and the watermelons. We consumed one nearly every day. I ate the red part but shared the seeds with Lynn. We ate so many that we called them "Its," as in "let's get an It and find a park for the butchering." We used to be quite silly before one of us lapsed into drink and typing.

～

Back at the U in the second year of my Teaching Assistantship, I was given a discussion section to lead. This was my first formal teaching gig. I was then also in what might be called my aesthetic phase, writing poetry and ostentatiously discovering beauty in small things—which may explain why, going onto campus, I always picked a glossy green laurel leaf for the lapel of that ghastly brown tweed jacket I wore. It was a stupid affectation. I think I resembled the ridiculous Bunthorne in Gilbert and Sullivan's *Patience:* "Though the Philistines may jostle, you will rank as an apostle in the high aesthetic band, If you walk down Piccadilly with a poppy or a lily in your me-de-evil hand . . . "

My discussion section met twice a week. I had a class of about 25 students. One of them was Ruth Genung. She, like her friend Robin, was already in my circle of friends. She had fine light brown hair, a pleasing face and devilish smile, a fine young figure, memorable legs, and a brain that cracked off witticisms the way a hot kettle pops corn. I think she had a little crush on Rick, who was older, fatherly, reassuring, and gently humorous. She certainly was very good company, and everybody felt happy and easy around her. She was somewhat in revolt against her parents, who were stereotypically conservative Republicans living in wealthy Broadmoor, a gated community of mansions between Madison St. and Lake Washington. She and I, outside my class, had a kind of joking, friendly relationship, but we weren't good pals. I was a few years older than she, and slightly resented her frequently cutting my class—it was, after all, a *discussion* class. Maybe she did it to annoy me. Anyway, she worked hard enough to earn a passing grade. At some point I set her up with my friend from Ellensburg, Jim Gosney, the amusing tennis-playing Bogart-imitating guy who'd been my campaign chairman in high school. They were both relaxed and amusing, played good tennis, and were a good fit.

I was also beginning to do research on my Master's Thesis. The history department set a very high standard for its M.A. degree and, as I discovered later, required considerably more work than similar programs elsewhere. It was assumed that a proper thesis should be at least 100 pages long, heavily footnoted, and defensible afterwards by its author facing a battery of professors. What was ultimately to become my 215-page Master's Thesis, *THE GROUP MIND: A CONCEPT IN MODERN INTELLECTUAL HISTORY*, began as a seminar paper in Costigan's advanced course on the Philosophy of History.

Earlier I mentioned that my engagement with "Communism on the Map" initiated my lifelong interest in the relationships between historical myths and political propaganda. My thesis was the first formal step down that road. I took as my subject a German thinker, Johann Gottfried Herder, born in 1744. Herder was a religious man with an unshakable conviction in the existence of "souls." As a young scholar he sat down to speculate about the tremendous importance to a group of its cultural heritage—its distinctive language, folk tales, mythology, and so on. And he was onto something. An ideal or spiritual inheritance does indeed inhabit and shape a people in some way. We loosely call it the "spirit" of a people, the "soul" of a people, and that's precisely what Herder did, it was a *Volksgeist*, a people's-spirit. There was a German soul just as there were others, and these were silent trainers of personal character, they helped to shape each

German or French or English child simply by virtue of birth and encultur-
ation. In fact, didn't they somehow *determine* the individual's personality
and action as a member of the national group?

In my gigantic thesis I tracked that idea through a myriad of thinkers
including Kant, Hegel, Bosanquet, Le Bon, Tonniës, Wundt, Tarde, All-
port, Freud, Durkheim, Lévy-Bruhl, Lazarus, and Steinthal. At last I came
to, and ended with, the Scottish social psychologist William McDougall,
whose *The Group Mind* (1920) provided the title of my book and captured
in a phrase the long historic evolution I'd unearthed and brought to light.
What McDougall and his imitators taught was that the group was, and
ought to be, almost totally in charge of the individual. They'd taken Herder's idea and turned it on its head, so that, in their teachings, the "national spirit" was treated as *inescapably dominating* each national citizen. This
was to be the root idea of Nazism. Poor Herder's ideas were bastardized,
and before long mixed with the "Superman" idea of Friedrich Nietzsche to
form the racist ideology of Adolf Hitler.

It took me nearly two years to work all that out. My finished thesis
was, as I mentioned, 215 pages long and based on extremely arduous reading from the 100-plus sources listed in my six-page bibliography. It was
quite as scholarly and ambitious as many doctoral dissertations I've seen.

But that obsessive work was taking me off the rails. My head in a fog,
I resembled the egghead in the cartoon on my wall, I exhibited all the un-
sociable mannerisms of the stereotypically absent-minded professor. Rick
Painter's girlfriend said to me, in a matter-of-fact way, "You'd rather read
a book than see a friend," and Ralph Cheadle, in a letter, sternly warned,
"Don't kill yourself under the Group Mind." It's as though they were trying to warn a neurotic against jumping off a cliff. I was indeed in peril. I
was losing perspective, sociability, elasticity, the ability to slow down and
stop. And if someone were to stand between me and finishing that thesis,
wouldn't I lose patience with them? Soon there'd come a test.

～

At Central in Ellensburg my mother was finding time to take some
interesting English classes. Now in her mid-40s, she was resuming pursuit
of a bachelor's degree, something she'd missed at Pullman by virtue of her
departure for the Orient in 1938. She didn't need a college degree, she was
already educated, but she wanted one anyway, and had sufficient leisure to
take courses till she'd filled the requirements. Besides which, she enjoyed

learning and was an inveterate reader, so why not read for Dr. Vifian's English course?

In class she met a young woman named Lila Nelson, very pretty and very smart. Her family lived in Seattle; she was an only child. Lila had come to study at Central and did very well, but she was unhappily married. My mother liked her, admired her intelligence and perception, and sympathized with her as, step by step, she got herself a divorce. Lila decided to return to Seattle and finish her studies there; my mother invited me to welcome her to the U, and recommended her as possibly an interesting date.

It was late 1963. I was living on University Way with my buddies, still teaching my discussion section, still wrestling with my thesis. Lila and I hit it off immediately. In a letter I described her as "a very interesting, very refined, very sensitive, complex being, poetic, with an entirely quiet, cheerful, passive temperament"—although, I noted, "spoiled as a child and sometimes astonishingly willful." She took a solo apartment only a few blocks from me and before long I was living there half the time.

Her parents knew she was seeing someone but had no idea she was resuming the conjugal life she'd just left, and she didn't want to tell them. I think they worried about her doing something nutty on the rebound from her first marriage. Keeping our arrangement quiet was okay with me, but the situation led to awkward moments when they dropped by to find me reading a book with my shoes off, or, worse, finding my shoes near the door with me under the bed.

Lila didn't like Cigarettes

The winter passed into the spring of 1964. We hadn't known each other long, but feelings were developing. The unvarnished truth, even though it's unbecoming for me to say so, is that Lila loved me and wanted to get married again. I'm not sure I loved her, but I was as fond of her as I'd ever been of anybody, and wasn't that love? Anyway, at 25 I figured it was about time, and so, with me not thinking clearly about anything but German historical propaganda, we wandered into marriage on July 20, 1964. We moved to larger quarters at 4101 Roosevelt Way, a three-storied ancient brown wooden house just next to Vic's G&R Grocery—Vic Rossi was a short, rotund, jolly Italian who fed cops in the back room. Soon the summer ended and Fall Quarter began, so with marriage and nest-making finished, I got back in earnest to my thesis; and that's when, and why, the trouble began.

As Lila saw it, I began neglecting her needs, failing to provide the love and attention she required, impatiently pushing her away. As I saw it, she began placing intolerable demands on me and getting uncontrollably emotional when I failed to go for a beer with her, or to bed at the same time— she was, as I put it a few months later in my diary, "forever tugging my sleeve, wanting to drag me out on a trip that I would rather skip, getting drunk and hysterical and wild and sick." This all led to worsening relations, emotional fireworks on her side, withdrawal and coldness on mine. If for me this had begun as a marriage of convenience, it was so no longer. My diary entry continued: "I could as well have lectured a fencepost as prohibit her going over to the tavern, bringing back beer, and then proceeding to wail and harass me all night. She told me she boozed because she feared to lose me. If true, it's tragic, because I loved her before she took to drink."

After many bouts of sobering her up and holding her and staring into the cosmos, gradually my distress and sympathy turned to revulsion and contempt. There was nothing left, nothing but the possibility that by separation she might gain strength and pride. One night I simply picked up my books and moved out to a motel three miles away. I took up residence there, buried myself in my thesis, and coldly ignored her. I felt I'd made a terrible mistake, I wanted out of the marriage, and told her so.

On December 10, 1964, she wrote me a letter pleading for another chance: "If we could live together again for one month without me making demands, or clinging, I believe it would provide some hope for the future. We did enter into this marriage with our eyes wide open. And it is primarily because I feel that I haven't done justice to it that I'm asking for more time with you. Actually, I'm not asking, I'm imploring; our marriage has some fine potential, and it seems to me that it deserves to have as much effort devoted to making it work as to finding adequate reasons for a separation."

It makes me ashamed to read her letter again, because there's so much goodness and deep feeling and contrition and love in it. It makes me ashamed because it didn't move me to accept her offer. I reacted to it hard-heartedly, and I'm touched with regret because possibly she was right, possibly with mutual adjustments we might have made a very happy life together. She was, after all, a gem. But I mistrusted her and feared that if the trial month proved unsatisfactory, I'd find it that much more difficult to rid myself of her.

Lila went off to New York to become a copyeditor for Macmillan, and, after a bloodless divorce, that was that. In my diary I see that I held out a vague promise of reconciliation later, but after a few months of postcard exchanges I never heard from her again.

That damned *GROUP MIND!* That damned thesis was a major cause of the failure of my marriage. Would Lila have gone off the rails if it hadn't been eating me alive? Wouldn't I have been more patient and loving, less hard-hearted and unforgiving, if I hadn't been caught like an animal in its coils?

But wait. Stop and think a little longer. Wasn't that thesis just one link in a much longer chain? Wouldn't my doctoral dissertation, later, and my scholarly journal articles, and my book, and that massive 800-page encyclopedia—wouldn't those efforts be just as absorbing? As I think back, reviewing my writing obsession, I wonder whether the end of our marriage wasn't a blessing for Lila. That *New Yorker* cartoon, with the bald guy sitting abstracted in his armchair, captures my sickness perfectly. Ever since that hot summer of 1950 when I learned from my dad how to work without stopping, I've lived with this sick thing that Lila would have had to live with. No woman would ever have been ready to accept me in the long term if she hadn't been ready to dwell in her own sphere while I was up to my eyeballs in mine. What I needed was an indefatigable writer like me.

I remember the spring of 1965 as unusually sunny and bright. I was ready to catch up with the world that'd been passing me by while I slaved on my thesis. I went to a Seattle Rainiers baseball game, took a ferry ride, went out to Golden Gate Park in Ballard and drank beer with my buddies, wrote more poetry, returned to the pleasure of reading novels, and resumed writing heavily in my diary. There I find snatches from *Steppenwolf* and Pope's *Essay on Criticism*, observations about Polly Garter in Dylan Thomas's *Under Milkwood*, thoughts on P. B. Shelley, *Harper's Magazine*, Emily Dickinson, *Barchester Towers*, Saul Bellow; long and short poems of my own creation; idle bits of doggerel. I even spent enjoyable hours just sitting around and *remembering things* ("Last night I spent more than six hours in Memoryville, more than I have at any time, perhaps, in my life").

But also, in spite of my general euphoria, I occasionally fell into very dark moods; I felt turbulence, lingering fears, bitter self-accusations, continuing feelings of inadequacy and inferiority. All young writers, I suppose, are eaten by such feelings, but in these private pages I see the desperation of an ambitious young man who knows too well his own inadequacy and intellectual inferiority. Outwardly, however, and in my lighter moods, which were much more common, I was insouciant and self-confident, and it was in that spirit that I made my diary a play-pen. I produced aphorisms, sketched University District eccentrics, jotted down reflections on how I'd teach history: "When I do begin to teach, I'll use literature a lot, with not only the biographical flavoring & memorabilia, but also the great works: 'All right, chickadees, let's see *your* history of England. You're going to *imagine* it and use your poetic faculties. Prizes for the best re-creation of an historical mood, in short pieces of prose or poetry.'"

And then came my big break. That spring a teaching vacancy appeared at Western Washington State University in Bellingham. Although I was now just a Master of Arts in History, Dr. Costigan wrote a letter recommending me. I was interviewed, accepted the offer, and happily looked forward to my first teaching job. My title would be "Instructor of History," my pay would be $6,600, I'd be bound to work from September 1965 to June 1966.

I drove to Bellingham in late summer. It's a pretty seaport in the state's northwestern corner, about 90 miles from Seattle and the same from the Canadian border. The city faces Bellingham Bay, Puget Sound, and the San Juan Islands; behind it to the east lie the Cascade mountains. Bellingham is much larger now than in 1965. At that time its industries included fishing, canning, mining, paper-making, and of course, at the university, sheep-processing, by which I mean beating critical thinking into the heads of high-school graduates.

I rented a bungalow near the university and furnished it cheaply, knowing I'd spend most of my time on campus anyway. The campus is green and pretty, and sits atop one of the larger hills, with a grand view of the Bay. When I arrived, the History Department, with about a dozen tenured faculty, offered classes in the usual academic areas, but also partnered with the English Department in running a very good year-long Humanities course that assigned literary and philosophical classics from early history to recent times. My job was to teach sections in that course.

There were 1700 students, mostly freshmen, enrolled in it. To take it was to earn, each quarter, seven credits. That's *a lot of credits*, indicating what great emphasis the school put on the course. Its main lectures were delivered by the best professors on campus, grandees of the lecture hall, in a giant auditorium that seated 850 students (the lecture would be given twice the same day), after which "section leaders" like me would fill in with supplementary material, conduct discussions by prodding students to talk about what they were learning, assign writing projects, and give exams. Each quarter I taught three sections, each with 30 students, for nine hours a week; my classes met on Mondays, Wednesdays, and Fridays, at eleven, one, and three.

I liked teaching a lot, and discovered I was pretty good at it. In a letter to friends after the first midterm exam, I wrote: "You might be proud of me when I mention that although the size of my entire group (89 students out of 1700) equals only 5% of the total, they took 17% of the highest marks on the midterm." Impishly I sent assurances that I was breaking up inherited prejudices: "You might be amused if you could station yourselves down the hall from my classroom, from which vantage point you could note, amid clouds of dung and agonized bellows, the stampeding exoduses of sacred cows." Reviewing this in old age, and from the platform provided by this book, I'd say it looks as though I'd begun fixing stupid, and enjoying every minute of it.

Friends become more valuable when you live alone and far from them. I kept mine close by rigging up a network of letter-writing. In that bygone era we had no wireless phones, long-distance calling was expensive, and texting, which has killed genuine long-distance contact for millions born too late to know their loss, would have been thought rude and inelegant. So we wrote each other long letters and relished receiving long replies. (Yes, replies: we actually acknowledged receiving communications—another fossil in the 'Dead Politeness' gallery of the Forgotten Manners Museum.)

Such correspondence was pursued routinely by everyone as a necessity, but among the literati it was, in addition, a living art, a venerable art form that stretched back to ancient times, encouraging educated people to put out their best in order not just to convey news but to impress and entertain their friends, and even make them sorry they didn't live closer!

I sit here sorting through a nice collection of letters from that year. My mother, of course, kept up the stream of information from Ellensburg, Gramlin sent instructions on how to prepare her amazing fried chicken, Bill Daly sent Seattle theatre news along with his prized Spanish Rice recipe for my "bachelorhood," Dave Jaffee laughingly told me about his promotion to become Jafco's chief driller of bowling balls (yes, really, since each hand is different), Purnell, from Los Angeles, revealed that he too had just bought a motorcycle and "loved riding in the warm sunshine up the seashore and into the mountains," and Ralph Cheadle reviewed a new biography of Dylan Thomas—apparently at age 19 the Welsh poet had knelt on the cobbles of Swansea and probed some of his own hocked-up phlegm, "hoping to discover specks of blood which would prove him the proud possessor of the poet's affliction, consumption."

Most prolific were my literary pals Dave and Lizzy Davis. His letters were short, often lampooning the idiocy of students and the pretentiousness of academics, but the best letters of all were from Lizzy, who, sometimes vacationing in Scotland, wrote long and beautiful reflections about her Scottish family, sheep-shearing, her father and brothers and seven-year-old sister, Rose, and of course always about authors—Yeats, Melville, Aeschylus, Dos Passos—and about friendship, and love, and how romantic love can be dulled by time and then reignited after an absence.

All these letters by all those old friends—friends now lost, or dead, or unreachable—these letters bring back that era with more force than memory alone could ever do. Fortunately I kept copies of some of my own, for I wrote letters, too, lots of them. One of Lizzy's begins, "Dear Jerry—Your last hundred letters have been delightful—and I won't even attempt to match them." At no other time in my life did I maintain such a huge correspondence as that one which I carried on from my office in the History Department. Rather than go home after work I often stayed there because it was a fine place in which to prepare the next day's lessons and compose those letters to friends. I was reading, every week, as the central part of my work, long passages of the world's classic literature, so although not much was going on in my everyday life, I had, as raw material for my letters, not only observations about students and faculty but commentaries on what I was experiencing intellectually. Despite occasional loneliness, that year in Bellingham, holding my Master's degree, was an extremely happy one. I was free from all former burdens as a student, and immensely enjoyed my high-quality reading and the new fun and authority of teaching.

Here's one of my first Bellingham letters, written on university letterhead and dated September 26, 1965. In it I give my first giddy impressions of college teaching, explain what it was like to have my own classes, and convey my happiness at joining other young academics, learning their lingo, and experiencing their banter, humor, and craziness. I see now that this letter could almost be read as a come-on to join a most exciting and delightful profession:

Dear Friends,

It's a different world here. Smaller. Richer. Prouder. Quicker. Deeper. Fuller. More people have room in their lives for other people. There's a kind of connectedness that I didn't know, and a kind of opportunity. Being Faculty is a credential, a letter of recommendation, a badge of merit, a breast-pocket catechism, a season ticket and a key to all kinds of unexpected and exciting inner sanctums.

But instead of generalizing, let me just sketch the last couple of days. I could start with the classroom. There, I'm just plain Bwanah. A wave of my hand, they all bend their heads and commence writing furiously. A word, and they come bearing typewritten gifts. (My first assignment, "Relate the Hulla Hoop to the Concept of the Dignity of Man," has netted my weekend reading more than a few chuckles.) With my little finger I could break the Christian faith of almost any one of them. Which could lead directly, if I wished it, to other conquests less cerebral. But besides encouraging megalomania, the classroom is a challenge to engage, inspire, entertain, deepen these guests at my table.

Faculty status can be rewarding in other ways. Take the fact that Mrs. Johnson, who works in the library here, has offered to give me an informal course in Using the Library, however detailed and extensive I want it. Believe me, that's valuable, because what she doesn't know about libraries ain't worth knowing. Or again, I've been invited to lecture seminars of graduates in social theory, or, if I don't care to lecture, to just come and discuss late 19th century social thought with them. Me—a "specialist." Wow.

And of course things like this work in reverse: I want to know something about Roman verse forms? Walk upstairs a flight and invite one hell of a smart muthah, R. D. Brown, head of the English Dept., for a stroll. Wanna know about cave painting? Ask the man next door, he'll hand you a cave-full of illustrated disquisitions on the subject. Economic history of the U.S.? Yesterday I helped the local expert haul away the trash in his yard. We began beer-drinking with the first load, about 10:00 a.m., and were snockered by five. Then we dropped in on Bob Michener, painter and teacher in the art dept., in his downtown studio. Smock, paints, canvases, brushes, and much gab, not all of it weighty, about art. After dinner, a run over to Bob Huff's pad. The poet. His house littered with objets d'art—gifts of friends or creations by his interesting wife. No reproductions, except a Breughel in the bathroom and a couple of ankle-biters watching TV.

Everything's an occasion for words—though sometimes one comes up with the wrong ones. For example, Al Roe, this historian, has a painting over his fireplace, it's a prone nude with enormous casabas, a red bandanna thing on her hair, a bluish coloration along her face. In the background there's something like what you see on a pack of Camels—pyramids, palms, sand piles. So there I was at Michener's painting studio, drinking a beer, exchanging gab. Besides Michener and Roe, there's another guy whose name I didn't remember because he didn't look like much, but who'd been introduced to me as a Prof. in the art dept., a sculptor.

Now, I knew Michener hadn't painted the nude, so I says to him, Hey, who's this cat who painted Roe's mantelpiece, you know, the neo-pop art Sphinx that looks like the Phantom on the make? Good gravy. The third guy—I should mention that artists can become terribly keen on their own work—turned purple. His face swelled. He looked like a gila monster pickled while digesting a hornet. Michener gave me an enchanted smile—how he relished this—and silently, with a broad introductory wave of the hand, indicated said gila monster. Somovagum. Even though I know I'll be crazy appreciative about his sculpture, should I ever accidentally see it, nothing could unsay this remark. And though Michener later confided that it *is* an abominable painting, very well described, I was hardly consoled.

Prof. Schlesnik, in the Physics Dept., last Friday was lecturing on Seismography. A student told me about it. Seems that Schlesnik, an animated speaker, loves demonstrations. If he keeps them up after this, he must. He was demonstrating how seismographs are anchored to bedrock by concrete, so they won't shake so much during earthquakes. Dense material, says he, resists motion and vibration. To prove which he jerks a piece of paper out from under a bunch of upright blocks of wood. The blocks fall to his feet. Class snickers. Undaunted, Schlesnik goes on to prove how this principle holds for even denser materials. He lays a wood shingle on his head, and on top of this, a plate of two-inch concrete. With a hammer he smashes the concrete—which disintegrates in dust and little fragments falling all over him. Class in uproar. Schlesnik, picking up his glasses, brushing concrete particles from his ears, smiles apologetically. Experiment will be performed with new plate Monday. I can't wait.

The faculty here really surprises me. A few duds; but mainly they're very much in touch, very sophisticated, lots of class. It's a little disheartening to see how caring for ivy, yards, the rain gutters, and especially children, stops their pores. By 35, most of them have ceased to be historians and writers, though perhaps the artists are less vulnerable to the trap; anyway, they become teachers of history, of English, and so forth. Of this, Costigan made a virtue. Others, though, are not so wonderfully equipped as he, and the success of their homes becomes the downfall of their hopes for a career. The lesson for me in this is becoming increasingly clear: get out of Bellingham next year, no matter how much I like it here. Keep moving. Get the doctorate.

~

Every History Department, like every zoo, contains a collection of individuals ranging from odd to colorful to outrageous. At Western my most conventional colleague was Al Rowe, who lived just a block away from me. He was in his thirties, easy-going. He and his wife often invited me for dinner on Friday nights. Invariably we'd have steak—T-bones, round steak, rib eye, sirloin. Al was a big steak-eater. However, the first time I went for one of these dinners I saw the Rowes' three boys eating peanut butter sandwiches at the foot of the table. I was about to compliment the chef on the steaks when he hushed me up and whispered that they were raising the kids to be vegetarians. This was my first clue that teaching wasn't going to make me rich.

A favorite colleague was Elliot Benowitz, the Russia historian. He was small and weasel-faced, with a vinegary sense of humor. His rank was the same as my own; he was an Instructor because, though he'd been at Western for years, he hadn't finished his dissertation. He'd begun it a decade earlier at Wisconsin. He joked that "his daughter was born the year he began his dissertation, and now she's old enough to read it!" His ironic sense of humor made its way into his test questions too. In his world survey course he posed the most memorable exam question I've ever seen: "Name Japan's war aims before World War II and explain how they were realized by 1950."

No Department would be complete without the curmudgeon who makes it his business to take down new arrivals. Quirt Slapperman undertook this duty at Western. He was about forty, stocky, round-faced, arrogant, and sour. In my diary I described him: "Fastidious. Dresses with great care. Clothes always well-tailored and pressed. Dapper black hat. Coat always buttoned. Military order of his office. Compulsive habits of straightening and tidying." I tried to avoid him but his office was close to mine and just up a narrow hallway, so I frequently had to pass it. "My impression," I told my diary, "is that he has sought to draw me into some kind of trap." He'd lounge by the door of his own office, engage me in conversation as I was proceeding up the hall, then gradually retreat into his own office, fussing with papers and arranging things until, in order to hear him and not wishing to be impolite, I'd have to enter, after which he'd start posing irritating questions about my life or my teaching. I recall that when I first arrived in the department he brought up my M.A. thesis, which he'd perused before my arrival. He offered this weighty criticism: "You are always using the subjective 'I'." To which I replied that, because it was a history of ideas, it contained more speculative argument than the standard narrative prose of most historical works. His own dissertation, never published, was, I sniffed in my diary, "on airplane styles, WW II, no doubt useful in the extreme."

The colleague I got to know best was Jim McAree. A Scotsman born in Canada, he'd received his PhD at Minnesota and then wandered around before landing in Bellingham. He'd gotten the "Outstanding Teacher Award" in 1964, the year before I arrived. He was some 17 years older than I, but we got along swimmingly and he unofficially mentored me. He was one of the most colorful personalities I've ever met—a showman, an outstanding raconteur, an individual who could hold the undivided attention of dozens with his funny stories.

His genius was that he stole them. The secret of his stories was that he appropriated the best, retouched and shamelessly recycled them. I remember telling him, shortly after I arrived, about a frog hunt I'd gone on with Gordon Nickell. I told him how, one night, we'd driven to a weedy pond near Bothell, heard a chorus of croaking bullfrogs, removed the battery from Gordon's car and mounted it in a small rowboat, attached it to a powerful searchlight, then rowed around the pond for hours, shining the light into the shallow places near the bank where we'd catch sight of a bullfrog, its eyes big and glowing like yellow headlamps as it floated there mesmerized by the searchlight; how I'd slowly row backwards toward it until Gordon, in the prow of the boat, thrusting with a twelve-foot spear, would try to skewer it; and how I, getting tired of doing the rowing, got Gordon to switch places with me, but when it came time to make my spear-thrust, I'd overbalanced, fallen over into the pond up to my left armpit, and wound up with no frog but only a water-ruined Bulova wristwatch.

Darned if I didn't overhear McAree tell the same story two weeks later! He was sitting around the corner in the Viking Union, having lunch with his back to me. To a group of English professors he told that story *as if it had happened to him*. They roared with laughter as he lunged with imaginary spear in his left hand, his right accidentally plunging into the pond. The only difference between my story and his was the hand holding the spear: he was a southpaw.

But you can't help loving a guy like that. He'd had dramatic training and directed local theatrical productions, so he knew how to juice up his stories with mimicry. Also he could take on almost any accent—his French was hilarious. I remember his story about a Frenchman charged in a paternity suit. The suit was supposedly brought by the mother of an innocent young woman whom the Frenchman had been kissing in the park; from this encounter she'd brought forth a baby. The joke is set in the courtroom where the paternity case is to be judged by a listening jury. McAree, impersonating the Frenchman's defense attorney, admits the kissing in the bushes but stoutly denies his client's responsibility for the impregnation, laying the blame elsewhere: "Oui oui, mon cliont (client) and zee young ladie **did** go into zee *booshes*, and zay **were** gissing; but ze **Muzzer** [the young woman's mother], who vass **following** ze young ladie, SNUCK UP BEHIND

MON CLIONT and **keeked** him *from behind* just at *ze CRITICAL MOMENT OF ZE GISSING*, **pooshing him forward**! And so, ladies and chentlemen of ze jury, it is ze contention of ze Defense, ... zat . . . ***ZE MUZZER IS ZE FOZZER OF ZE CHILD!"***

As you might imagine, McAree had lots of pals, and one week a friend from London flew in to visit him. The friend, a very timid and withdrawn academic, had never eaten Chinese food, so McAree, very much a man of the world, invited us both to accompany him to Vancouver B.C. for dinner at a Chinese restaurant. When we reached the restaurant, McAree took over the ordering. He requested several dishes. One was a steamed rock cod, which, it turned out, would be presented whole, with the head still on. I was too wet-behind-the-ears to anticipate this, and the visitor was, too.

We sat at the table, pleasantly chatting and waiting for the food to arrive. A waiter brought the large and ugly codfish on a platter, setting it down directly in front of the timid academic visitor. The cod was positioned in such a way that its large eyes seemed to stare up accusingly at him. There was a silence. "Er, . . . Good Evening," he slowly ventured, staring back at it apologetically. I nearly fell off my chair laughing. It's too bad McAree can't be here to recycle that story for me, because, enriched with his mugging, you'd appreciate how hilarious that comment was, that shy welcome to the bug-eyed and very unamused codfish.

⁓

Fall Quarter ended in December. My students had read large extracts from the Bible, Homer, Sophocles, Aristotle, St. Augustine, Chaucer, and others. I decided to prepare them a Christmas present, a seven-page essay that I entitled TRUTHS OF THE ANCIENTS. With warm holiday wishes I handed out a copy to each student after the final exam. It contained a few paragraphs about each reading we'd studied. I tried to draw a single memorable point from each, to help them remember what they'd studied. Here was my comment on Chaucer:

Central to the genius of **CHAUCER**, that merry beachcomber, is the knack of reading character by spotting the *significant detail*. This means that in eight words, in the observation that the red-faced and snowy-bearded Franklin 'loved a sop of cake in wine,' Chaucer implies more about the man than most of us could say in a hundred. The same is true of the Wife of Bath, who 'had a flowing mantle that concealed large hips, her heels spurred sharply under that.' Chaucer, in a twinkling, individualizes and yet, by invoking a familiar type, universalizes his characters. And aren't we all, after a fashion, similar hunters of signs and symbols? The diamond cutter, the wine taster, the art collector, all traffic in nuances; the employer will deduce shoddy workmanship from a scuff on a shoe-top; women know wealth from other women's coats; men choose liquor, tennis rackets and even girlfriends by hints of sound, taste, sight, scent, touch.

Such stuff was fun to write, and in January, after the break, half a dozen students wandered by to say they'd enjoyed their Christmas present. I really had great fun teaching that Humanities course. I loved reading and talking about the world's classics, but what I enjoyed most was the discussions I ran, in which I tried to make students dig deep into themselves to answer tough questions on the materials. I spent a lot of time thinking up good questions.

For example, with the *Book of Job* behind us, we read *Oedipus Rex*. I then asked students to compare Job's misery with that of Oedipus, hoping they'd see that in the former case it's the impersonal universe that brings the hero down, in the latter it's the actor himself, his perseverance in a chosen ideal. To lecture students is easy. It's a lot harder to get them to *arrive by*

themselves at intelligent insights. Arduous personal brain-work like that will stick with them longer and make their learning more fun. I take no credit for inventing that technique; it's called the Socratic method.

Because I liked teaching so much, I'm puzzled about my concluding thoughts in that long letter I quoted above, the one describing my first impressions of teaching and faculty life. Obviously I enjoyed my gig in Bellingham and the life I found there, and I was at a crossroads. Why did I decide to abandon teaching Humanities in that pretty Washington port? Why did I say I wanted to "get out of Bellingham next year, keep moving, get the doctorate?"

I don't know. And it's frustrating not to understand or perhaps even really *like* one's own earlier decisions! But without even thinking about it I applied for admission to two universities' doctoral programs. I'd decided that I wanted to pursue a doctorate in Victorian Studies—that is, to specialize in nineteenth-century English history and civilization. The most important places for doing that were at Indiana University, which had a big library of Victorian materials and was home to the main journal in the field, *Victorian Studies*; and Harvard University in Cambridge, Mass., whose libraries contained the largest body of Victorian research material anywhere in the U.S.

To follow up my applications I took a train to San Francisco in December to attend the American Historical Association's annual meeting and talk to a few profs from both universities. Apart from meeting the famous Harvard historians Crane Brinton and H. Stuart Hughes, the thing I remember most vividly was the conversation I had on that train with another traveler, an older historian from Oregon, who was heading to the same meeting. We sat chatting as the landscape rolled by. I asked him what he thought of the two universities, and which I should choose if accepted by both. He didn't think long. "Well," he drawled, "Harvard is Harvard."

The other major development was that I'd been falling in love. Ruth Genung and I had come to know each other much better in late 1965. As I mentioned earlier, I first met her in 1962 when I was dating her friend and roommate, Robin Hardy. Ruth was quick and funny. She had, like Emilie Duwe, a gift for fashioning spur-of-the-moment jokes, cracking quips like lightning from stuff always right there at the top of her consciousness; and, also like Emilie, she was often the butt of her own humor.

But there was much more to her. She was proud and could be a resourceful fighter, just like her pugnacious dad, a long-distance Olympic runner. Like him also, she hated losing. I remember how, some weeks after I first met her, we ran into each other again at some boozy party and jousted over French pronunciation—neither of us gave an inch, my reason being that I was right, hers being that she was stubborn as a mule. However, that was just one incident, and although there was often a little friction between us, it was part of a bantering relationship beneath which there was growing affection.

Ruth was a little younger than I, and occasionally consulted me about things. I remember, back in those Seattle days, advising her like a Dutch Uncle over how to handle Milt Rowe when she was dating him. After Ralph and Rick and Bill and Gordon and I moved into the University Way group house, she become not just one of our regular visitors but a favorite because of her likeability, humor and easy charm. She often came around in the afternoon after classes, and had a much closer relationship with Rick and Bill than with me—they were more relaxed than I, and had more time to sit around and gab. Later she signed up for my Discussion Section (which she frequently cut, which led to more banter), after which at some point I set her up with Jim Gosney, and the two of them attended my wedding.

Ruth liked Lou Ella, but took my side when that marriage broke up. There were various odd meetings, sometimes by chance—I remember moaning into a cup of coffee with her after taking my Graduate Record Exams, thinking, in my doomsday mode, that I'd flunked; we drank beer a couple times at the Blue Moon; we had a good time laughing together at Rick's wedding reception. When, in the spring of 1965, her boyfriend Jim Gosney departed, leaving her unhappy and desperate, I gave crucial help for which she was very grateful. I was then alone too, and that misfortune of hers, so traumatic, brought us much closer together. All in all, over the course of three years we'd become very fond of each other as reliable and amusing old friends. There was no big spark, and I think we had no clue that we'd get married later. We'd both been disappointed in love, we were gun-shy, we were both heading off, in the summer of 1965, to new pastures far away.

For, while I was driving to Bellingham to teach, she was departing to San Francisco State to pursue a Master's in English. I was 26, she 23. As I left for Bellingham she handed me an amusing letter that reveals much about how she saw herself. "How very much I'll miss you," she wrote. "I feel as though something meaningful is ending for me. There are lots of Ruths around, they can be amusing pets, they're clean, gregarious, and bright enough to be taught tricks to entertain your guests, but trim their claws often: they are especially good with children, and hardly ever bite." She concluded fondly: "There will only be one Jerry in my life. I'm so much the richer because of you. With love, Ruth."

And so began a weekly, sometimes a daily correspondence. In the exchange of letters and phone calls we were falling in love. I planned for her to come visit me at Christmas: "Nobody in Bellingham can hold a candle

to you. You'll be an absolute sensation, and already I'm afraid for Jim McAree when he meets you, you're just the kind of chick he missed out on. Hit the books, kiddo, because with all my heavy reading I'll be so smart you won't understand a word I say unless you do. Ciao, Columbine, your Harlequin."

We saw each other at Christmas, again in March 1966 when I flew to San Francisco and we marched in anti-war parades together, and then again two months later very unexpectedly in May when, after I'd sent her one of my rare but depressed and soul-searching letters, she impulsively flew to Seattle, took a bus to Bellingham, and showed up totally out of the blue late one night. "Last night I was wakened from deep slumber at 3:30 in the morning by a pounding on the door. I staggered into a pair of pants, groped to the door, and lo! Ruth! The dear impulsive creature had telephoned me earlier in the evening, and as I didn't answer, she decided to hop a plane up here to see what was wrong."

She stayed a few days and attended one of my classes. "We were gay and happy, last night we sat down here in my living room and played a silly game, the name of which would be 'What if money was really Peanut Butter?'—we played this till we were sick from laughter and absurdity; and then Ruth washed the dishes and I brought in my guitar and we sang some songs as she finished."

Meanwhile, on that other front, I'd received word from both Indiana and Harvard. Indiana offered not only admission but a big scholarship and the assistant editorship of *Victorian Studies*—a wonderful opportunity. Harvard offered admission and a $3,000 Harvard Fellowship. I debated a while, but Harvard, as the man said, was Harvard. I wrote Costigan to thank him for his letter of recommendation, and followed up with Pressly, who also had done so.

So now everything was coming together at the same time. We decided to get hitched on Saturday, June 19, at the University Unitarian Church in Seattle, with our friends and families in attendance. We'd honeymoon with all our friends, camping and fishing on the Snoqualmie River; Ruth and I would drive to San Francisco for me to take a crash course in German to fulfill Harvard's two foreign language requirements; and Ruth would try to persuade her profs to let her fudge her M.A. requirements so as to permit her to go east with me in early September. And that, all that, is just what did happen.

8

Doctor of Philosophy

CAMBRIDGE, MASS., AND HARVARD UNIVERSITY,

1966-1970

We set off for Massachusetts on Labor Day weekend in my aged blue Morris Minor, and for six days camped till we reached Boston. The closer we got, the more anxious I became. I thought of all the famous people Harvard had recently produced—Kennedy, Bundy, McNamara, Galbraith, Schlesinger, Langer, Reischauer, Erikson, Moynihan—the list was intimidating.

Widener Library

It was a warm September evening when we entered Boston and started driving up Massachusetts Ave. It was my first time on that long, wandering street. We drove slowly, and wondered whether M.I.T. was Harvard as we passed it. I envied all the beautiful people strolling the dusky streets, I observed all the signs—Harvard Delicatessen, Harvard Trust, Harvard Cleaners, Harvard Flag and Awning, even buses with "Harvard" in the little window up front. Then there at last it was, shadowy and dark with enchanting little lights here and there among the trees, and in a belfry, and along darkened walks between those ancient buildings. We stopped to sit on the steps of Widener Library, feeling awe in the warm historic silence. Harvard Yard.

Next day, we found Harvard Square. It was thronged with infinitely wonderful people. Every one of them was beautiful. The air shimmered with brain waves. In one acre there was more wit than in all of Texas. Every middle-aged man carrying a briefcase was a Nobel Prize winner. Every gray-haired oldster could have been Nathan Pusey himself, the President of Harvard University. Every bearded mouth belonged to an oracle, every newsboy was a Socrates. What did I know, what could I say, what was my business here? Where was Seattle, what was the name of that school out there? I was from the antipodes, born in a sty, learned only in crawdads and the making of whistles.

It was the same feeling of unworthiness I'd had before, when entering the M.A. program at the U, and when beginning to teach at Western. But now I knew I'd succeed anyway. I didn't know how, but I would. Also, I had a great teammate. Punning on the 23rd Psalm, I told my diary: "I do have my staff to comfort me. A staff of one, but how I love her, how she brightens my life and makes it worth living, Harvard or no."

We found an apartment about ten minutes by bus from Harvard Square, in a nice little neighborhood full of big elms, crooked brick sidewalks, and tiny green "yards" fronting houses built big because of Catholicism. Our neighbor was Tom Flynn, an old man with a long, vivid memory of growing up in Boston, living through the Depression, and loving Red Sox baseball. He was a sweet man, and his stories about his youth were compelling. He'd never taken a drink, was a hidebound Democrat, loved the Kennedy name, had seen Babe Ruth pitch for the Red Sox, could tell you what the 1929 stock plunge had meant to him as a Boston office boy, and also how, when the circus came to town, you could buy, for only one quarter, three throws with a baseball at the dodging head, poked through a canvas target, of an African-American man. Boston before the Civil Rights movement.

Three days after arriving we met a nice young couple on a nearby tennis court, Dick and Lucy Bulliet. It so happened that Dick was also a Harvard grad student. He'd just returned from Iran, where he'd spent the summer making aerial photographs of the dust, rubble, and barely visible remains of the vanished medieval city of Nishapur. He told me he was going to use them to help him finish his *social history* of that historic city. "How on earth would aerial photos help you write a *social* history?" I asked. "Good question," he said. "They help me figure out the terrain, and where people lived, and the pathways of the water and sewer systems. Rich people always live on hilltops, you know, and their garbage and sewage always flow down to the lower classes." Dick went on to become a star of the Columbia University history department, where he wrote a great synthetic history book, *The Camel and the Wheel* (1990).

Shoveling Snow with Ruth, Mr. Flynn and his Grandson

Before the semester started we went out to take a gander at greater Boston and found ourselves charmed by the ponds and leafy beauty of Boston Common, the mixture of brick and brownstone buildings at the city's heart, the tony grandeur of Back Bay, the diversity of workaday Dorchester and the honky-tonk flavor of Revere Beach. The local people, so far as we could tell, were, first, primarily of Irish extraction, then of Italian. We found the ethnic mix strange, and the Boston accent funny. It was odd the way the locals dropped their "r's" in one place while adding them in another, as if to compensate for the first error by making a second. The word "year" was 'yeah' with the 'r' barely audible, but a "hernia" was a 'hernier.' The locals were also rude in an easy, habitual way; impudence almost passed for an agreed social relationship. Once I was getting a haircut and some geezer wandered in and greeted the barbers. They said "Hullo, where ya bin keepin' yourself?" and the geezer asked "Where's Joe, anyway?" and the barber by the window replied without batting an eyelid, "Ya think I folla him around all day?" Just like that, mouthy.

On the Boston wharves we found a lobster warehouse and wandered in. It was near closing time. There was a guy behind a window, counting money. Lobsters were in long watery tanks, climbing all over each other, and there were wooden pins and rubber bands attached to their claws. So I moseyed over to the guy and asked him what the pins and rubber bands were for? Were they to identify each lobster in some way, or to keep them from hurting each other, or maybe to keep them from pinching guys who had to handle them? Slowly putting down his pencil and his fist-full of money, he threw up his hands, rolled his eyes, looked skyward as if praying for patience, then erupted: "What am I, some kind of lobstah psychiatrist??!!!"

After a while he warmed up to us. In fact he became almost as cordial as he had been rude. He wound up explaining everything we might like to know about cooking a lobster, throwing in a lot of "Sees?" as if we might not be familiar with boiling water, or beer, which he recommended as a side dish. When we left, he said apologetically that it had been a long day, and then asked, as we stood sympathizing, why we thought he and his partner worked late like this, after the warehouse closed? "It's our *wives*," he chortled, with an appreciative leer at mine. "How would you like to go home to a fifty-year-old wife?"

One day a gang of sewer workmen dug a huge hole in the street outside our house, big enough for six men to stand in, and worked to repair a major breach in the ancient sewer line. They were jabbering and gesturing a lot, the way Italians do. I walked up and stood there watching. Beside me was the foreman, also a Boston-Italian guy, giving orders. In the hole, five guys in yellow hard hats were just standing there leaning on their shovels. The sixth, looking down, reached into the muck, idly picked up several prophylactic rubbers, and silently flung them over the top of the pit onto the dirt pile. I asked the foreman, "Are those *rubbers*?" "Yeah," says he. So, says I, "How come that guy's throwing them out of the pit?" Thinking, he turns to me and says, with a smirk, pressing down with both hands as if testing the springs of a mattress, "They make-a the road-a too *SPONGY*."

The lobster and sewer people weren't the only exotics in the area. One day the Bulliets asked whether we'd like to attend a party. We said "sure," so next evening we accompanied them to this soirée. I described it in a letter to Dave Jaffee:

We went to a party the other night, invited by a couple we met on a nearby tennis court. The host looked very cordially at someone else as he shook hands with me. The talk swirled from computers to psychoanalytic transference to private school teaching to oral examinations to sound equipment to the relative merits of this or that biological microscope, to the American Revolution, woodcuts, encaustic, and, most of all, Harvard. There were three psychiatrists there, all interns, and a computer analyst for New York Life, and a managing consultant, and two graduate students in history. The wives had almost all of them gone to Radcliffe, as their husbands had been undergrads at Harvard College; only one of them, I think, was without a Master's degree, and two were working toward the doctorate.

The computer analyst told me lengthily about his work, and I nodded and chewed and puffed furiously on my pipe, understanding not a word of it. In the next room, a large Arab with a spot on his tie explained how the Arabic word "ashem" came to be "hippos" in Greek—the "a" became the glottal stop "h," the "s" was dropped for some other reason, and the palate flimflam remorbs to a glotular pos, the final "t" sunken underground as it were. Ruth said she thought it had been misspelled in the first place, which made some laugh and some stare.

For some pressing reason I referred to the Aeneid and a smallish girl with big spectacles and a double-edged smile stepped in to correct my pronunciation—it wasn't "i-nead," it was "ah-nead." I said, defensively, that where I learned Latin, "ae" was pronounced "eye." She grumbled and went off to ask her husband; who, it seems, exonerated me, but salved her wounded vanity by saying that "in the English," it's "ah-nead." She told me that people noticed such mistakes at Harvard, and I replied that thank God I had been shaped in such a way that it could never bother me, that I would lose no sleep over such peccadilloes so long as I was happy, and that required only my wife and my cultural and sporting interests. She declared she found this very refreshing.

While she thus conversationally patted my head, I noted that one of the psychiatrists was conversationally patting Ruth's breasts; but before I could think about that, someone walked up to the Gauguin reproduction hanging beside me and remarked that the painter "must have been very poor at the time he painted it," since the colors were not of the best quality. Now *there* is discrimination: to dredge biography from a three-dollar pressboard reproduction. I left thinking it was a wonderful group of people and wishing I could blow the whole place up.

What's it's like to pursue a doctoral degree in the Harvard History Department? I can't say what it's like now, but in my time it was like living in a system of terror. That was made plain at the first meeting of the Henry Adams History Club. There, at the beginning of the semester, all the incoming history grad students were officially greeted by Professor Donald Fleming, Chair of the Department. He was short, with bandy legs, a larger trunk, and still thicker neck and head—something like a standing-up tadpole.

He began on an ominous note: "I welcome you to Harvard and to the History Club. Your years here will be exciting—those of you who remain— and rewarding—even if you might not have leisure to notice it at the time." Momentarily he praised us as holders of prestigious scholarships and said we'd been "intensively screened and selected from a total of more than 450 serious applications—when I say serious, I mean all that were more than indulgences in, ah, fantasy (nervous laughter)." Some of us, he allowed, "will be leading historians of the coming generation," but we were now put on notice that "many of you will not be with us this time next year. In June you will be sent a closed letter indicating our will as to the continuance of your education here." Some "will be barred from further study—last year, out of a group of 40, ten were barred, and we have decided that our regulations need drastic tightening this year."

The current standards, he said, were pitifully lax: "I for one am utterly dissatisfied with the quality of certain candidates who have been allowed to scrape through their generals successfully, and there will be no more of that." The faculty's "evaluations, which take each of you up in turn, and at length, are thorough and rigorous," but he offered no apology for their lateness in the academic year: "You may complain that June is late to be making plans for finishing your education elsewhere than at Harvard, but we can't evaluate your work until it is finished, can we?" And if that was unsatisfactory? "You should begin early to think about some other career for which you might be better suited. And now, having welcomed you to Harvard University, I turn you over to the president of the History Club." (Silence) "That's all, I'm finished now." (Silence; a tentative rustle; a clap; then one of the most extorted "hands" in recent history.)

"I'm still scared," a fellow student told me two hours later, after three double-bourbons. Fleming, it seemed, was the leader of the Pharisees, with enough Mosaic authority to cast out Hellenistic little old me! And what, you ask, was the purpose of this terrifying regime he'd announced? That's elementary, my dear Watson. It was to save faculty the trouble of teaching! To escape getting kicked out, the terrified student *taught himself*. "A professor's fame is no guarantee of his usefulness to the student," I declared after two years' experience in Cambridge.

The terror system permitted faculty to do absolutely nothing teaching-wise but lecture once or twice a week—to walk in, take out a 15-page script, read it aloud, walk out. The Harvard faculty I was acquainted with knew almost nothing about teaching history. I don't think they'd even read a one-page handout about *how* to teach it. They were employed to do research and write books, to polish their own names and that of the university. "Publish or perish" was the watchword in that era, and for younger Harvard faculty and grad students that was like living on death row. To maximize research time, most faculty only "taught" one semester out of every two, and the terror system let them escape serious teaching *even during that one semester when they were paid to do it*. I will freely admit that many, including Fleming whose lectures I later attended, were exceptionally good, even brilliant, at the lectern. But a good lecture is something you may write once and then simply repeat for decades. As for kicking people out, I never saw Harvard do that, either. Being kicked out was a threat used to intimidate and isolate us, and make us ready to cut each other's throats in our seminars.

I'm not saying that to divert suspicion that I performed badly. As a matter of fact, I performed very well—I totally bluffed my way through. After that first semester I reported to Dr. Pressly that my colloquium professor, Patrice Higonnet, "told me that I had been the best discussant in the group last semester." My diary a month later: "Colloquium and me as usual a big hit. Professor Landes only tells an anecdote now and then, almost leaving the discussion-leading to me." But I saw how the terror system worked. Worst was the Kafka-like *uncertainty* packed into it, which sharpened the student's worries. "The students' papers," I wrote, "never get turned back, and the profs never assign you a grade as you go along, which allows a lot of subjectivity in the final grading. Much of the terror of the system," I wrote, "would be relieved if students knew how they're doing. But then, that might require more effort on the part of the teachers, and everyone knows how totally devoted they are to conducting their own research."

There was one shining exception. In another letter I revealed how much I liked one of my profs, David Owen, who taught a seminar on Victorian London in which he actually led me and three other grad students into Widener's stacks to show us how to get at *Hansard*, the record of British Parliamentary Debates, and other primary sources. "He's extremely popular with graduate students, for he's very willing to open his door and talk with them, and is very sympathetic toward their many grievances." Professor Owen, I continued, "has an almost religious attraction for students, given their usual isolation and their berserk worry about grades. A friend of mine, a fellow from Lebanon, very bright, named Basin Musallem, says that without Prof. Owen, who has helped and encouraged him through a jungle of red tape and administrative indifference, his life would be very black indeed. Musallem told me this *when I visited him in the infirmary*—the doctor put him there for three days, since Musallem, sitting in a chair and not moving for two weeks (so he says), had reached a sort of pathological state, not to mention exhaustion. Owen is an older man, quite secure in his reputation, and more interested in his students than in writing more books."

Right after Fleming's hair-raising welcome, the history department hosted a cocktail party to introduce the faculty. My diary: "They're a pack of icy bastards, so far as I can tell, and, worse than that, I met my adviser, John Clive. He's nervous, excitable, eccentric, an overgrown 35-year-old bachelor with thick lips, bug eyes, and the sweet disposition of maybe King George III, with all the easy sociability of a suspicious bear. It's too bad he's not older; he's been here only a short time and still has that hunted look of the untenured and unestablished." Two years later I walked into his office to discuss the dissertation I planned to write. I asked him, "Approximately how long a work should it be, how many pages, more or less?" He carelessly gestured toward somebody else's dissertation on his desk. It was very big and fat. With both hands I hefted it, putting my legs into the job; I looked to see how many pages it ran. Six hundred and three. Mine, which he very readily approved more than two years later, was only five hundred and ninety-eight. I've always believed in brevity. They say it's the soul of wit.

For me the best things about Harvard were its massive research libraries and the excellence of my peer group. As I wrote to Jim McAree, "My greatest pleasure here has been meeting and talking with the other students. On the whole, they're a very good lot. No geniuses so far, but a generally high caliber of thought and understanding. There's a closeness among first-year grad students too, owing to the common feeling of sympathy that the system engenders."

Clockwise from left: Sarah Luft, Sharon Grant, Ruth, John and Eleanor Toews, Steve Grant, Dave Luft (kneeling)

The most important course I took that first year was the "Colloquium on the Interpretation of Modern European History since 1714." It stretched through both semesters and brought together all students who aimed to specialize in modern European historical studies. It was run by Prof. David Landes, who specialized in economic history, and Prof. Patrice Higonnet, who specialized in French history. There were nine students; many became my good friends. Among them were Stanley Palmer (the son of the great European historian R.R. Palmer, incidentally), who, like me, specialized in British history—he was my best friend that first year, and arranged a surprise birthday party for me; Steve Grant, a Californian specializing in Russian history; Dave Luft, keen on Austrian intellectual history; and, finally, John Toews, a Canadian who, like me, was drawn to European Intellectual History. There's a photo of us, with our spouses, on the beach at Gloucester.

The colloquium met once a week in what I called "The Barracuda Tank." There, after we'd privately digested some book and written a paper about it, we'd quarrel over what we'd written, being prodded to tear each other apart by Landes—the Barracuda Tank was his special creation. But aggressive criticism was a virtue throughout the department: "Harvard," I noted, "is where brutal criticism is a good, and passive amiability one of the cardinal sins." Landes, however, took this to extremes, and was disliked even by some professors. Part of his attitude was a deliberate pose, but I do judge him the most pugnaciously warlike tyrant I ever met on a college campus. I called him "Mephistopheles" because he was "all warty, black, malevolent, pugnacious and smiling." Frustratingly, he refused to say how we were doing—"You will be notified," he'd growl. My distaste grew when I found that his historical interpretations always seemed to favor rich institutions over poor people, and in the spirit of his own Barracuda Tank I once told him so. His reply: "You seem hostile, Mr. Newman."

I did acquire his respect, though, and later learned that when other students went to see him to complain about grades, he told them they "should speak up more and take the lead, like Mr. Newman." A year later I was regularly meeting him to play squash.

The first time I became openly aggressive with a professor was when I attacked Henry Kissinger. Before explaining that, let me review some of my earlier anti-war activities. In Bellingham I'd begun condemning the Vietnam War even before March 1965 when our first combat troops and bombers began operations there. In August 1965 I declared that "the stupidity and pointlessness of this war should be recognized, we've done our worst and that didn't work, now we should stop the murdering and lying and get out." In November I indignantly rebuked the Bellingham *Herald* for smearing anti-war protesters as "communist sympathizers." In February 1966 the campus newspaper printed my full-page satire, 'Vietnam, the Threat to Humbug." In April I helped organize 250 students and faculty in an anti-war march through Bellingham's streets, and wrote the pamphlets we distributed. My diary conveys what educated grad students were thinking: "The Vietnamese only want peace, want us to stop raining as many as 23,000 plane-loads of bombs on their heads in a single week. People crisped in napalm, driven like cattle to refugee pens on the coast, more than a million of them—that is, the rural peasants, who are the Viet Cong. How fruitless our so-called peace feelers are bound to be, so long as we refuse to recognize the authenticity of the home-bred rebel movement as *primarily a nationalist rather than a Communist movement.*" And yet, I wrote contemptuously, the war continued with support from "the American mob, with their shibboleths and intellectual baggage, appallingly unreachable through logical discourse."

Kissinger, when he walked into our colloquium that day, wasn't yet the evil genius behind American war policy. He was a respected history professor, and our topic was his book, *A World Restored* (1954). Like everybody else in the room I'd read that book, but I didn't like it. Its subject was the setting-up in 1815 of a repressive ultra-conservative organization, 'the Concert of Europe,' to stamp out what remained of the revolutionary enthusiasm that had rocked Europe for 25 years. The Concert's purpose was, in the name of "stability," to crush all popular nationalist movements, using spies, troops, and bullets to do so. Kissinger's attitude toward this was clear from his book's title; he saw the Concert's work as the *restoration* of something worth preserving, namely the undemocratic and anti-nationalist European order of pre-1789.

Our colloquium's task was to discuss that book, but the Vietnam War was always on everybody's mind, and there was an obvious parallel between post-1815 Europe, where rebels had been crushed by the Concert, and the situation in Vietnam, where rebels were now being crushed by our own government and the South Vietnamese dictatorship. Feeling like jousting, I asked Kissinger whether he hadn't, when writing his book, "leaned rather too much toward praising and endorsing the bloody work of the Concert and its leaders, while minimizing the passion and later victory of the European nationalist movements." After all, I added, "those movements, you know, in 1848 exploded in a pan-European revolution that threw out the kings and chancellors who'd run the Concert of Europe, even forcing Metternich, its creator, to escape from Vienna in disguise!"

Pensively he stared at me, batting his eyes and looking froggy through his horn-rimmed glasses. He understood my disapproval of his interpretation but decided to handle me gently. Finding the right words, he slowly stated that he didn't *morally* overrate organizations like the Concert; what he wanted to stress was "their importance to the *maintenance of peace and stability*." I regarded that as an evasion but didn't say so. In fact his book *does* laud anti-nationalist repression, exhibiting moral approval for it.

It's only fair to acknowledge, though, that with his background as a fugitive from Nazi Germany, every sort of nationalism was anathema to Kissinger: he shared a blindness, or what I've called a group-blindness stupidity bubble, that was then common among many Americans. This might be the place to mention that I was just then starting to become an expert on the thing that he habitually ignored, nationalism. And, further, let me point out that the parallel I suggested that day, that Vietnamese rebels would throw out the Americans just as European rebels had thrown out Kissinger's admired "Concert," proved itself true nine years later.

The continuing tragedy of Richard Nixon's foreign policy requires me to state that Kissinger, after becoming National Security Advisory (1969) and then Secretary of State (1973), continued to favor balance-of-power "stability" over popular democratic-nationalist movements. Although he continued the disastrous Vietnam War even to its humiliating end, he received the Nobel Peace Prize—received it in such bitter controversy that some in the Nobel committee resigned in protest. Kissinger had a blind spot, a stupid spot, and although in 1966 I saw it and pointed it out to him, there was nothing more to do afterwards but watch the disaster unfold. Sometimes you just can't fix stupid.

Looking back, I see that I was, in general, becoming more intolerant toward defenders of what I regarded as pernicious ideas and practices. I was becoming annoying. But those years were so full of war, official lies, and the abuse of public trust! Besides Kissinger, I skewered the eminent professor Bernard Bailyn (and made other grad students laugh out loud) when I attacked his slipshod presentation of an idiotic lecture. I clashed with a third professor, the illustrious Tudor-Stuart expert, W. K. Jordan, when taking my general exams in 1968. That confrontation lasted an hour or so. I wasn't openly impolite, but afterwards in a letter I excoriated him as one who "bombastically celebrates the greatness of the Tudor sovereigns without ever acknowledging that their success was rooted in the hard work of the lower classes, to which he gives almost no attention." During the exam, Jordan, responding to my criticism, had excused his indifference with what he regarded as a good reason for it: "Our knowledge of these people," he said, "is almost nil. What they did, what they thought, these things are virtually unknown to the historian. We can only guess. Fortunately, Mr. Newman, this makes little ultimate difference to our picture of Tudor history, because they contributed almost nothing to the country."

Yes, *he actually said that!* Jordan, inhabiting his fond academic bubble, was still mired in the "trumpets and drums" perspective that had dominated historical studies since the Bronze Age, according to which history was, pure and simple, the study of political power. Poor Jordan was incapable of imagining how social historians would revolutionize the understanding of English history just a few decades hence. To him, history was all kings and queens, or what I dismissed as "whores and wars."

And so he was, of course, a huge fan of Henry VIII, whom he idolized and incessantly praised. He leaned forward in his chair and invitingly asked me, "Was Henry VIII a great king, would you describe him as a great man, Mr. Newman?" I was ready for that. "Those, of course, are two separate questions, Professor Jordan. As a man, Henry VIII was detestable. Power corrupted him, as it has corrupted many similar personalities. His lust, his egotism, his personal brutality, his cynicism, knew no bounds." I gave numerous examples of what I meant. Jordan interrupted: "But Erasmus, Mr. Newman, praised him highly." To which I replied: "Erasmus was a notorious flatterer, wasn't he."

I rattled on, parading my knowledge (it was, after all, an important examination), displaying my knowledge of Henry's VIII's dealings with Wolsey, Cromwell, the Scots, France, Sir Thomas More, and much else; and I concluded thus: "In any event, Henry VIII turned out to be a bad man and a very lucky king, successful almost despite his lack of good judgment." To which, Jordan: "Harrummmpphhh. Well. That is one view that might be taken of the matter. Tell me, Mr. Newman, would Henry VIII have been a great king in your mind if he had died in 1529 instead of 1547?" Newman: "Then," I said, relishing this, "He would have been a *total* flop." To which, Jordan: "Harrumph. But wouldn't you agree on his fine intuition into the characters of men, his great judgment, his instinctive recognition of personality and worth?" Newman: "Well, he struck down his two greatest ministers, beheading one of them, so I wonder. But it's strange, isn't it, that with such great insight into the characters of men, he was such a hapless bungler when it came to the characters of women?"

～

Writing my doctoral dissertation was like writing my M.A. thesis, an endless mental grind. Again I resembled the egghead in the New Yorker cartoon, a thought-bubble full of rotating doodads occupying my every waking thought. In the autumn, slogging away in my carrel in Widener Library, a pile of books beside me, I'd sometimes stagger out to the front steps and sit there watching but barely seeing the leaves fall. In the winter, slogging away in my carrel, I'd wander out to watch but not see the snow falling on barren branches. In the spring, slogging away in my carrel, I'd wander out to witness the barren branches starting to bud, then stagger back to record the three sentences I'd found budding between them.

But one evening in early April 1969 was very different. It was nearly dark when I exited Widener, lugging my briefcase of books. Outside the quiet library I first heard loud yelling, and then, farther through the south gate, I saw a maelstrom of students pushing their way west on Mass. Ave. It was a stampede, and, unable to cross it, I was swept along with it. "The pigs! The pigs are coming!" was the cry, and I saw, marching grimly toward us, squads of uniformed policemen wearing helmets and face masks, the light reflecting off their billy clubs.

I'd been so sunk in work that I wasn't even aware of the fact that student protesters, determined to force the university to abandon its ROTC program, had taken over University Hall. They'd ejected its administrators and begun what they intended to be a long occupation till their demands were satisfied. But President Pusey, a hard-liner, called in the state police to remove them. What I'd walked into was the aftermath of their forcible removal—a continuing confrontation between angry protesters and the forces sent out to disband them.

With the police marching fast up Mass. Ave., the crowds broke south down the narrow side streets and then slowed their pace, lingering to see which ones the police would enter. Those streets housed shops of all kinds, and I, with my heavy briefcase, happened to be standing near a men's clothing shop when I saw two individuals suddenly break its window and begin helping themselves to its contents—new shoes, leather belts, a raincoat. With my judgment dislocated by the descending police force, I confess I didn't have the presence of mind that one young undergrad student did. He loudly attacked the looters, crying, "Hey, cut that out! That has nothing to do with us! What the hell you doing!?! Get outta here!" They stopped, dropped the loot, and melted away into the crowd.

There's a history lesson there. That event stuck in my mind as an example of how a single individual can turn a crowd, take control of its thinking, and lead it to do the right thing. Without that young man taking charge, others might have joined the looting and so brought public disapproval down on students instead of the policemen bent on clubbing them. At times, the decisiveness of a single individual becomes crucial.

I got home late that evening and found Ruth worrying about me. While she warmed up my dinner, I told her about my experience. On our little black-and-white TV we watched the so-called "riot" in Harvard Square, shaking our heads at its misrepresentation. Of course we little dreamed that 13 months later, on the same TV, we'd be watching with utter dismay a similar "riot" on the campus of Kent State University in Ohio.

~

When we first arrived in Cambridge, Ruth found a secretarial job in the university, but she kept looking for a teaching gig. She'd gotten a Master's Degree from San Francisco State after writing a thesis on Hamlet's father's ghost: Had Shakespeare intended the ghost to be understood as an hallucination? Probably not, because the ghost, in Act I, scene v, reveals something Hamlet didn't know, the nasty poisoned-eardrop method by which uncle Claudius had knocked off his dad. So was the ghost genuine?—a true paternal hell-hound? Maybe a mischievous angel instead? Was Shakespeare more religious than everybody has always thought? How much credence did ghosts enjoy in 1609? Is a ghost a wraith or a specter, a goblin or an imp? And so on. It was an English department, after all.

As I said, she kept looking for a teaching post. One day, with no teaching certificate but more clarity than the average goofball about 17th-century ghosts, she trotted into the Melrose High School hiring office and applied for that job teaching English. They were sorry, but did she know anything about field hockey? She lunged and signed on, though she didn't know a hockey stick from a crowbar. She soon learned, though. The first day she met her class, she interrogated them on every aspect of the game. "Now, class, this is a hockey stick. Which end do we hold, and how do we hold it? All right, very good, what's your name, Susan, yes, very good. Now, Susan—and everybody else is quite free to chime in if you wish— what is the best offensive strategy, how do we maneuver, what is the best passing plan, for getting the ball into the opponents' goal? Mary, what's the answer to that, and by the way, how many players on a team?"

After she plugged away for months at field hockey, actually enjoying it, a vacancy opened in the English Department. She hopped onto it and spent two years teaching English to eleventh-graders and subverting some of their more stupid beliefs. In June 1969 I informed Dr. and Mrs. Costigan that "the suspicion has arisen that Mrs. Newman has strayed from the explication of gerunds and the propounding of participles," and cheerfully concluded that "we look for the day when I may write you anecdotes of the doings of 'the controversial Mrs. Newman.'" That, I knew, would please them, because like all good educators they welcomed controversy as a sign of critical thinking.

Meanwhile, I too was working hard. With my course work finished I began writing my doctoral dissertation, *VOLTAIRE AND VICTORIAN IDEOLOGY: A STUDY OF ENGLISH INTELLECTUAL AND SOCIAL VALUES, 1760-1890.* That project engrossed me for three years. As I remarked earlier, the finished product was 598 pages long and represented, like *THE GROUP MIND*, another giant piece of historical investigation. True to my "maverick" roots, I developed an entire set of new theories about what I considered the hitherto misunderstood patterns of English literary and cultural life. In my next chapter I'll say a little about the published book that emerged from that work, *The Rise of English Nationalism.*

In early January 1970 I asked my diary, "Will life ever become more pleasant than it has been these past four years? Nothing but deadlines, anxiety, and restless dreams of the far frontier." I'd taken the hard path of many an American grad student. My constant diet of work wore me down and sometimes made me depressed, and Ruth also became depressed because of problems at work. And we had other things to worry about too. The winters were very hard and made getting-around difficult, we didn't have much money, our car was always in need of repairs, a doctor discovered that Ruth had a heart murmur (he hastened to caution us that it wasn't serious), and on top of that, she fought a continuing battle against psoriasis.

On the other hand, we had each other and were very much in love. I wrote my parents: "You might think that conditions are not ideal for perfect marriage with Ruth working, me working, the whole forced-labor psychology of it all. But really we have very few quarrels, we make up quickly and without bearing grudges, and we enjoy our real moments together during the day at dinner and thru the evening. We remain sold on each other, and I for one think I have never been so happy ever, on a day-to-day basis, as here now, despite the confounded slavery."

Our pleasures *were* limited. We played tennis occasionally, we drove once to Lexington, more commonly we'd simply go for a walk; we went on a few picnics, we traveled with our friends to the Gloucester shore where we goofed off on the beach, we held an amusing costume party (it was "Come As Your Repressed Desire" and I came as "Voltaire, Hammer of the Jesuits"), we often sang songs together in our little apartment as I scratched out a tune on my guitar, we had a few dinner parties with our friends. We became Celtics fans, Bruins fans, Red Sox fans; we attended the crucial seventh game of the 1967 World Series, and when poor Yaz blooped and Lonborg fizzled, we sat there in Fenway with everybody else, stunned and speechless.

~

What else was going on in the world, beyond our small part in it? Well, those were the late 1960s, years of continuing political turmoil and war. 1968 was the deadliest and most expensive year of the war, and saw the shameful My Lai massacre and the disastrous Tet Offensive. On the Home Front, racial protest and ever-larger anti-war demonstrations were eclipsed by the assassinations of Martin Luther King, Jr., and Robert Kennedy. There were bloody riots at the Democrats' convention in Chicago, and the startling withdrawal of Lyndon Johnson from the presidential race, and the zombie re-emergence of the ghastly Republican hero Richard Nixon. More totally disillusioned than ever, I wrote in 1969: "War and more war; racism, violence, separatism, poverty and hunger, the selfishness of the comfortable. Nixon, a horrid mock-sentimental incompetent with, I think, no sense of purpose beyond getting himself re-elected. And nothing seems to get any better."

But despite all that turbulence, life was going on for the people I cared about out West—except for one of them, my dear Grandma Nellie, with whom I'd spent so much time in childhood. I attended her funeral at the lonely Thorp cemetery and was overcome with feeling, not only for my loss but also, in that cemetery, for all my dead relatives laid to rest there, and for the Valley, my homeland, and even the cemetery itself where I too would, in time, be laid to rest. Washington State, the West, the Kittitas Valley, they were always at the back of our minds as we labored there in the East. But my mother and my old friends kept me posted during those years. They wrote of changes occurring in their own lives, and commented on my own news. My mother sent reports about my old Ellensburg buddies, her gardens and civic activities, my dad's pheasant and elk hunting expeditions, the purchase of a motorboat, Lynn's schooling.

Lynn, however, had important news of her own. Studying literature at the U, she'd met a fellow named Tom Benediktsson and they hit it off. He was beginning doctoral work in English. That summer, in July 1969, she wrote me about their relationship but was, as I complained in my return letter, vague and indecisive about Tom. She said he was smart, independent, even intimidating. "Exposure to Tom can be nothing but good for you," I wrote. My favorable opinion, always the most important thing in her life, cemented their relationship. Otherwise they might not have fallen in love or begun riding horses together or hunting shaggy manes in the Manastash Canyon or cruising the Columbia River with our parents in their new boat or looking for a Seattle apartment or planning their wedding for December 26.

Ruth and I flew west on Dec. 17. We'd asked our Seattle friends to hold a party where we could reunite with them. I asked Lynn and her fiancé to come also, so I met Tom for the first time there. Noting his sense of humor and thinking he'd let me get away with a rough joke, I pulled him into a corner, softened my voice, and, adopting a Mexican accent, whispered, "Señor, for one hundred pesos you can sleep with my seester." He laughed and we began a bond that has continued for half a century.

Walnut Farm was beautifully decorated for the wedding with wreaths and candles and red satin. The Benediktsson clan were there looking spruce and happy. My mother was proud but nervous because the somewhat daffy minister was late. Undaunted, my dad managed to look like the happiest man on earth as he proudly brought his daughter up the aisle, or rather down the stairs. Lynn, who'd cleaned up for the event, looked very beautiful, composed, and, as they say, "radiant" as

she descended into the crowd of close friends which by December had ballooned into three thousand. Tom played his part perfectly. "The wedding," I later wrote, "was a beautiful one, it was moving. The couple were full of joy and a prankish attitude that seemed to keep them in stitches during certain moments of the ceremony." Gramlin, I remembered, had been "very composed, only emitting a sob or two, and that strategically, during the music."

~

John Clive, though a cold fish, warmed up a lot as I turned in, one by one, the 17 chapters of my dissertation. He said it was "rather good, rather important, and rather engagingly written." My first taste of this nice treatment was on April 22, 1969, when he returned my first chapter with very few criticisms and "said he liked it well enough; he was affable, and called me 'Jerry' when I left his office." I was astonished. That "Jerry" was a landmark. I continued to slave away until, by December, the end of my dissertation was in sight. With my doctorate in the offing, the next step was to find a teaching job. I flew to the American Historical Association meeting at the Sheraton Hotel in Washington D.C. to interview for a job to begin in the Fall of 1970. Two hundred people, mostly young men, entered that "slave market," as we called it. I was soon invited to three campuses to interview for openings in British History.

My letters of reference were very strong. I know that because the whole bundle was shipped to me by mistake. "It would be very nice," I told my diary, "to believe all the nice words spoken about me by the six professors who wrote letters of recommendation for me—letters which, by an error of some secretary at Fairhaven school in Bellingham, were sent to me and which I've read. But I can't really believe all these kind words." Professor Henry Hanham had replaced the much-loved David Owen as Harvard's Modern Britain expert, and what I relished most was his statement that "Newman takes nothing for granted, he must prove to himself even conventional wisdom before adopting it." He liked the maverick in me. But I also recall that he once cautioned me, as we were walking across campus, against "dragging my coat," referring to an Irish pub custom of willingly provoking a brawl. Fight only when you have to.

There were three good job opportunities for a British historian: at Fordham University in New York City, the University of Saskatchewan in Saskatoon in central Canada, and Kent State University in northeastern

Ohio. I was invited to all three campuses, flew to them, was interviewed and offered a job at all three. Ruth and I decided to choose either Saskatchewan or Kent. The choice would be difficult because, on the one hand, the Canadian university stood on a beautiful campus, its library was full of fine research materials, its history faculty were very friendly, Canadian students were more serious, the teaching year would be a month shorter, and Saskatoon was considerably closer to Washington State. On the other hand, I was treated well by the Kent faculty, that department was much larger than the Canadian one, the Kent campus was attractive also, the pay would be better, professors at both UW and Harvard urged me toward Kent, Ohio's winters were infinitely nicer than those of frozen central Canada, Ruth and I both worried that the bitter cold and dryness of Saskatoon would make her psoriasis a nightmare for her, and, further, that she'd have much more trouble finding a job there than in the much more heavily populated Kent area.

Together, on the last day possible, Thursday January 29, we chose Kent State. We chose it even though, that same day, I told my diary that "Saskatchewan is definitely a better school than Kent—it's a university, but I'm afraid Kent is simply a factory." I worried myself crazy about that decision, and ever since that time I've thought about how it changed our lives. In fact, haunted by misgivings, I called the Canadian department chairman twelve days later and, as my diary records, "said I discovered I'd made a mistake, and did I still have a chance to accept? No. Offer is out to someone else." I beat myself up some more: "The only reason we are not going there is that we decline to brave the unknown—the cold, the standard of living, the shortage of 'culture.' I know Ruth would follow cheerfully to the North Pole and try to make the best of it there on blubber and seals' flippers but I couldn't ask her to do it—not because my happiness depends on hers, which it does, but because I too remain divided in my own mind as to what life would be like, perched up there on the edge of the great North American wilderness."

It was a failure of nerve and imagination. But with the decision made, I stopped thinking about it and returned to work on my dissertation. Dimly I began to see a release from that prisoner's life, a return to something I'd loved before, a career of teaching students. "Life in graduate school," I told myself, "has been a back-breaking experience. Will teaching regularly do something to restore me? How could it not?"

~

It was a memorable spring day when I received my doctorate, the last milestone in my student life. My mother flew in from Washington. The

commencement ceremony was in the Tercentenary Theatre, the big tree-canopied open space in front of Widener Library. It was a warm and comfortable day, the air seemed cheerful and expectant. First there came, winding into that open space, a long procession of Harvard grads, the oldest of them in front, hobbling their way to their seats of honor. Faculty members came next, wearing their academic robes, then graduate students, then undergrads. Everywhere there were crimson robes, decorated with black hash marks and small blue insignias indicating various faculties and subdivisions of the university. Music was played, songs were sung, speeches were delivered. The undergraduate part of the ceremony always includes one speech entirely in Latin, after which there will be important addresses by university dignitaries and internationally famous guests—Alan Paton, the South African novelist and author of *Cry, the Beloved Country*, was the featured speaker at my graduation.

Something quite special is reserved for graduating doctoral students. For me the crowning moment came when I stood in my crimson robe before my family and the entire seated congregation of students, faculty, alumni, and domestic and foreign dignitaries. Accompanying me in his own crimson robe (for he too had received his doctorate from Harvard) was my smiling advisor, John Clive. From his hand there hung a part of my doctoral costume, a long black hood. The moment of "hooding" is, for a doctoral

student, the symbolic equivalent of moving the tassel from right to left on a "mor-
tar board" cap for less exalted graduates;
it's a physical gesture to mark the candidate's achievements and new status.
Clive stood ready to "hood" me, to loop
the hood over my head and let it hang
down my back, whenever Franklin Ford,
Dean of the Faculty of Arts and Sciences,

gave the signal. Which, when all was ready, he did, saying to me and the
few others standing near me, with the entire congregation listening, these
remarkable words: "Welcome to the Ancient and Venerable Community of
Scholars!"

That was pretty unforgettable. Afterwards, families gathered around
the honored graduates, and photos were taken at "the Spreads," that is,
a delicious luncheon there under the trees, provided by the university for
all honored guests and graduating students. It was a proud and happy moment, and I was delighted that my mother had come to share it.

There's no use denying the fact that Harvard University is an object
of enduring American curiosity. And so before leaving this chapter I'll offer two concluding reflections about it. The first is that all the ordinary
people in the Boston area utterly reverenced it. Mr. Flynn, my barber, my
grocer, the lobster guy and the sewer workers—nobody, not even I, the grad
student in the barber chair, would be suffered to say a word against it. To
them, Harvard was so much more than a name, it was a presence, regnant,
majestic, mysterious behind its gates, enchanting behind those hallowed
traditions and high brick walls. "We sweaty and unworthy masses, we barbers, grocers, delivery men, tailors, we hide our faces and abase ourselves
under her honored gaze," I imagine them saying.

And it would be unfair not to recognize the near-universality of that
sentiment among Americans in general. The veneration felt even by well-educated America was captured in that remark made to me on that train as I
was heading to the history convention in San Francisco: "Well, Harvard is
Harvard." No one could disagree with that, but what's strange is that few
would disagree with what was *meant*. I went to school there for four long
years, I knew the campus like my own hand, and I know now—in fact I had

a pretty good idea *then*—that the professors there were no better than those at any other big American university, and that the teaching there was *much* inferior to that provided by many small liberal arts colleges. Yet no one, so far as I know, has ever written the exposé that Harvard deserves. Its vulnerability is one of the best-guarded secrets in America, and the reason is simple. Harvard's defects are only felt by those who pass through its gates, and for them, their reward for secrecy is borrowed reputation. Who would desecrate his own passport to the world's esteem?

The other reflection is both a proof of what I've said and, I guess, a confession. Toward the end of our years in Cambridge, Ruth and I, together with Steve and Sharon Grant, drove to New York and spent two perfectly wonderful days strolling around Manhattan, visiting the Guggenheim, walking around the Bronx Zoo, lounging in Battery Park. We found a little restaurant in Greenwich Village and sat there eating and drinking, staring happily at the passers-by and hoping for a glimpse of any of the resident geniuses—Norman Mailer, Nat Hentoff, Leroi Jones, Barbra Streisand, Robert Merrill, Julie Andrews, Truman Capote, Gore Vidal. What could be more wonderful than this crowd passing by on the sidewalk, these golden people with their talents, their enviable lives, these marvelous urban animals?

And it was only then, strange as this may seem, that I became aware of a subtle change in myself, something slowly born in me during my four years of struggle. Back there in Cambridge there'd been all that endless work, that terrible slogging through sleet and snow and slush those many months and years, lugging my battered valise full of books through those hallowed Harvard gates and halls, grinding out my endless hours and already failing eyesight in all those Harvard libraries that were *so admired by everybody who hadn't been to school there!*

Sitting there in wonderful Manhattan, in Greenwich Village, I blinked, looked around at the talent show strolling by, and felt 100% happy, with no sneaking sense whatsoever, none, of envy! Totally *happy!* Looking within, trying to understand this sensation of bliss, I saw that I had no envy of those shining people walking around Greenwich Village, they had no easy claim on my worship. I felt that in some way *I* had been to the mountain, I'd received my sign of election to grace. And so, in fine, at the end of it all, I saw, with some embarrassment, that I myself, despite knowing the trickery in it, had bought into the Harvard mystique. Harvard was, even for me, in that other sense, Harvard. Which is exactly where I'd begun four years earlier, sitting on Widener's steps that first warm and magical night in town.

PART THREE

Years in the Saddle

9

A Second-Rate Academic

KENT, OHIO, 1970s

At last, after all that preparation, I ended up, in the summer of 1970, in Kent, Ohio, to begin my career as a professor of history. Kent, in northeast Ohio, is a pretty little college town, hilly and green. It sits in the expansive green middle of an urban triangle formed by Cleveland to the north, Akron to the west, and Youngstown to the east. In 1970 the area's economy was prosperous because of steel, rubber, and auto manufacturing. Its people were open, friendly, and patriotic. In politics they leaned Republican.

The school that hired me, Kent State University (KSU), was one of several cornerstone institutions of the state-wide Ohio system of higher education. Founded in 1910 as a normal school, it grew to become a full-blown university, then expanded to become a large research institution with many degree programs and regional campuses. It had already begun this postwar growth spurt when I arrived.

Part of the Kent State University campus

Its growth was part of a much larger nationwide pattern. Before 1945 the typical state university enrollment was 3,000 to 6,000 students, but after the war, student populations burgeoned with the rising birthrate, extension of college admissions, lowering of entrance requirements, growth of financial aid, and intense Cold War emphasis on advanced research. By 1970 the student population of Ohio State University, the flagship institution in Columbus, was 50,000; Kent State's was 21,000 and growing.

The U.S. was in what's called the Golden Age of American Higher Education. Building-construction was a sign of it. About three-quarters of today's campus buildings were constructed between 1960 and 1985. Other signs were the crowded dormitory, the vast impersonal lecture hall, the manic faculty emphasis on research and publication, and the criminal inattention to undergraduate education.

I've got to admit that by that era's standards I was a pretty second-rate academic. When I retired, no endowments were started in my name, there was no new "Gerald Newman Chair of British Studies." I wasn't hot stuff, I wasn't hired away by top-notch university head-hunters, I was no superstar, I wasn't even a star. That didn't stop me, though, and, happily, I didn't know it yet. So, as a fully certified educator who took his job seriously, I set out for the first time in my life to "fix stupid" as a professional teacher and to do so in teacherly ways—as I said in my Preface, to dispense information and impose critical thinking, or, more simply, to fill blank minds and promote open ones. I didn't yet realize that there'd be some "group-blindness stupidity" to fix too, even in my own history department.

Most of the senior members of my department were baked into what I'd call a research-and-writing mindset while blind to its incongruity with other priorities more important. Many had, as grad students in big universities, laboriously researched and written their dissertations, and then after taking up state university jobs they naturally continued to operate as though original research, the one thing they were trained to do, was the proper be-all and end-all of university work. Supporting that belief and adding respectability to it were the empire-building ambitions of departmental chairmen, the research emphasis brought by the Cold War, the salaries and merit-reward systems of the academic departments, and the glacial effects of customary outlook and behavior.

The over-all result was very inferior undergraduate teaching but tons of published research, of which a fraction was more than trivial. Faculty blindness to that problem was understandable: it's hard to see the bubble you're a part of. But if, like me, you're a misfit to start with—and, remembering my past, something of a noisy newcomer to boot—you might feel its constraints more than other people and start annoying them about it. That may explain some of my doings in the Kent State University History Department. I tried to fix, in addition to the usual types, some "bubbled" stupidity.

~

But first, Ruth and I, as junior faculty people, had to get a house, a dog, and some babies. Arriving in August 1970 we found a small house in a quiet neighborhood and soon met the old lady who lived next door, Mrs. Zaniewski. Chatting in the driveway, she asked where I'd come from. I mentioned that although born in Singapore, I'd lived in the U.S. since I was three. She looked so puzzled that I had to ask what was the matter. Embarrassed, she looked aside as though averting her gaze from a deformity, and assured me that I "didn't look Asian." I laughed and told her I wasn't. She looked relieved: after all, I was going to be living *next door*. I'd known Kent wasn't Seattle or Boston, but now I realized I'd really moved into the hinterland. Then the old gent on the other side told me he'd never once been out of Ohio, and proud of it. Well, well. But, seeing no profit in fixing my neighbors, I resisted the impulse.

Next, a dog. I bought a beagle puppy and named him Bounder. He was hardly bigger than a teacup. What a wonderful playmate he was, bless his doggy little soul! When I came home from work, we'd play, or else I'd teach him tricks. I taught him to perform them in one continuous sequence, so that he'd sit up, shake hands, lie down, roll over, and then sit up again in a single dazzling show. He became the treasured third member of our household and a model for training our babies.

Peter Montgomery Newman was born on September 10, 1972. He was tiny and bald but promisingly fuzzy, and at first had a wizened, very old-man look about him that was hilarious. We doted on him and before long began making faces and funny noises at him, making him laugh. I feared it might affect his happiness to learn that in French, "péter" means "to fart," so I never told him. Cognitively he was above average: at age one he could utter a few words like "ma-ma," "da-da," and "sesquipedalian." I got a tremendous kick out of him. Before long, with Bounder role-modeling, I could get him to sit up, shake hands, lie down, roll over, and then sit up again in a single dazzling show. By age three he'd even developed one trick on his own. I reported it to my diary:

I'll be reading the paper when Peter will approach me, throw back his head, open his mouth so wide I can see his tonsils, and emit a screech that actually assaults my ears: "RAOOR!" In mock fright I clap my hands to my ears, shrink back with terror on my face, and yelp, in a high voice of my own, "Oh! So loud! Help me—! Oh!" He'll throw his head back even farther, open his mouth even wider, and emit an even more overpowering "RAAOOORR." To which I respond by begging him to roar softly, like the Lion-Bird-ie—and then illustrate as he looks on, his eyes flashing with amuse-ment at the absurdity (which he perfectly understands), pursing and rounding my lips, clasping my hands to my bosom like an enchanted lady bird-watcher discovering a new species on a limb high above her, and roaring a very tiny, sweet, and almost inau-dible little "roarr." He bursts out laughing, imitates this, bursts out laughing again, sobers up, then tilts back his head, opens his mouth big as a pie-plate, and emits another tremendous and ear-splitting "RRAAAOOOOORRR," at which I collapse in trauma and beg him not to terrify me any more. To which, as often as not, he'll answer with a screech as loud as the last. Somehow the game ends after variations with the Mouse-Birdie and Flea-Birdie.

For comic relief we got him a baby sister. We prepared him by pointing out how he'd be able to show her stuff. Avidly he began building his list—he'd show her his animals, his toys, the alphabet. His eyes lit up when I asked if he knew why I'd gotten the new chest of drawers: "It's for the baby," he said, smiling. We started thinking about names. When I mentioned the one suggested by Don Wade, our departmental specialist on Ancient Rome, we all liked it. Wade had suggested "Livia," the name of the spouse of the great Roman emperor Augustus, and I loved its rippling sound. Tacitus, the Roman historian, had accused Livia of poisoning her enemies, which added roguishness.

Livia Alice Newman was born on June 21, 1975. She was, of course, adorable. Pete was very protective. As she grew older he loved hauling her in his wagon, but also teasing her—picking her up from behind and carrying her around, her arms sticking up helplessly. She'd yell bloody murder but that didn't faze him, and soon they'd be happily playing again. Sometimes we bathed them together in the bathtub; there'd be lots of screeching at rubber duckies, then mock-hysterical terror at the rubber shark Pete had snuck into it. At some point Livia acquired a Barbie Doll named "Gertrude," which got beheaded, then painted various colors, then made the victim of sadistic tortures. They sharpened their wits by making up stories about the little brute's misfortunes. There was lots of laughter in our little house. Soon I started reading children's stories to them together, one on either side of me as we lay on a bed, with Peter always insisting, his face lighting up in anticipation, "Read it funny, Dad, Read it funny!"

I laugh when I thumb through pictures of Livia when she was a toddler. She was a comedian from the start. At her first birthday party she played the perfect hostess when other kids and their mothers came by. She sat quietly in her high chair, her eye glued to the double-decker chocolate cake with "Livia" on it—chocolate was her favorite taste, color, birthstone and state bird. After the cake was cut she began transferring it at high speed from plate to gullet, hands, face, and bib, all the while laughing through gobs in her mouth. It was grisly. Later she revolted against drinking milk unless flavored with chocolate, and there's a family story about how, when we were camping near the ocean and having a meal—Livia was about four at the time—I got philosophically expansive about how great the moment was, with the scenery and the ocean and the sea birds and us together enjoying each other, at which point Livia chimed in, with her face deep in a glass of her favorite beverage, to gurgle her hearty agreement: "VERY CHOCOLATY!" She never lost her focus.

Nearly everyone in America has heard of the Kent State Shooting of May 4th, 1970. That event and its aftermath affected my working life for decades, so I've got to talk about it here.

Its background was the Vietnam War, which ran from the early 1960s to 1975. People who didn't live in that era must understand that with ever-mounting casualties and no "light at the end of the tunnel," frustration had built up tremendously by 1970 in the hearts of war-protesters who indignantly regarded themselves as just as patriotic as anyone else, even more so, because they saw their country, which itself had begun in revolution, departing from its own values as it battled a revolutionary enemy it didn't understand. Against them, the anger of all those patriotic people who supported our country "right or wrong" grew, too, in opposition to "bums" and "hippies," people like me. They thirsted to crack our heads and make us good Americans.

The war needed to be stopped. Nixon was elected with "a plan" to do so, but soon was up to his neck in it. The central fact prolonging wars is that leaders, *once their own prestige becomes entangled with the promised goal of victory*, lose sight of all else and overrule compromise endings. And so Nixon, on Thursday, April 30, 1970, astonished America by announcing his new initiative: we'd win the war by carrying it into a new country, Cambodia! That was like throwing a match into gasoline. Students on 800 campuses from Maine to California erupted in protest. But the only place where they were *mown down* for reacting was at Kent State University, on Monday, May 4, when at 12:24 p.m. the Ohio National Guard fired 61 bullets, for 30 seconds, into an unarmed crowd of 1500 students.

I was still at Harvard then, but already under contract to go teach at Kent State. The train of events that led up to the May 4th Shooting has been described in many books and documentaries. The day after Nixon's announcement, KSU grad students buried a copy of the Constitution near the school's Victory Bell. Protests continued that evening when anti-war students set small street bonfires downtown and broke the windows of several businesses. The next day (Saturday, May 2), while some students cleaned up the glass, Kent's mayor called for National Guard troops to come protect the town, a decision that contributed to a still more fateful act that evening, the burning-down of a small campus ROTC building by persons unknown.

Next day, Sunday, May 3, the campus was fully taken over by the Guard, equipped with rifles, tanks, tear gas, bayonets, and circling helicopters. That converted the issue from "expansion of the war" to the more inflammatory "troops on campus," that is, to the use of soldiers to suppress political dissent *not downtown but on the campus where the students themselves lived*. James Rhodes, the ultra-rightwing Republican governor, then laid down an ambiguous directive saying that all outdoor events were prohibited, even while student activists were planning a Monday rally by the Victory Bell.

Confrontation became inevitable late Monday morning when Guardsmen were ordered to walk in a broad phalanx across the Commons and up Blanket Hill to "disperse the crowd." By that time of day the crowd consisted not only of demonstrators but of hundreds of other students simply moving from one class to another. The Guard fired tear gas canisters, protesters returned them with some rocks, the Guardsmen maneuvered and began firing bullets. After a colossal din, 13 students lay bleeding on the ground, some dying.

Photo courtesy of commons.wikimedia.org

Everywhere, massive sympathy actions followed. In Washington D.C., more than 100,000 people marched. The biggest student strike in U.S. history followed; at KSU and elsewhere the uproar was so great that classes were simply canceled until autumn. No one but crackpots defended the shooting—a presidential commission confirmed that the Guard's acts "certainly cannot be justified."

The historical importance of May 4th is that it dramatically changed U.S. consciousness of the war, making the whole nation, the thinking part of it anyway, realize that anti-war protesters weren't simply "bums" and "hippies" as Nixon and Kissinger maintained, but, rather, serious young Americans who demanded an end to the war and got killed for it. One of the murdered students had been an ROTC student himself, and most of the people shot were simply caught in the hail of bullets.

Throughout, the behavior of the University Administration was naïve and reprehensible. The President, Robert White, was "totally unqualified to handle a crisis," according to the foremost expert on the shooting—Jerry Lewis, a distinguished sociologist, my neighbor and one of my oldest friends in Kent. The top administrators were literally "out to lunch" during the event, eating together at the Brown Derby; according to Lewis, the highest university official on the scene was a fourth-level "Conduct Code" guy, Ralph Oates. It was a geology professor, Glenn Frank, who stepped between guardsmen and students, preventing more loss of life.

And, following suit, during the next decade the top brass did everything to make the public forget the event, to pretend it didn't happen: they were terrified of worsening the school's undeserved image as "a hotbed of student radicalism," and scared the conservative state legislature would cut off its public funding, at that time about 60% of its income.

After 1970 came two decades of protests, controversy and litigation. The legal aftermath was driven by outraged parents of the dead and wounded, who sued the university, the National Guard, and the state of Ohio; their lawsuits resulted in federal and civil trials in 1974 and 1975, and then, in 1979, a settlement including a half-hearted "apology" from the state with a measly $675,000 payment *in total* to the weary plaintiffs.

Meanwhile the familiar anti-war protests continued too because the war itself lasted *five more years* to 1975. I remember the student leader in 1972, Jerry Persky, who'd taken my Victorian England course and written a mediocre paper on Karl Marx. He had curly black locks that stuck out below his red do-rag. He was no orator but his outdoor harangues were, at least, LOUD. He was never without his bull-horn—he even brought it to class. A bull-horn was a license to interpret May 4th. Shouting through his, and interpreting May 4th as a mandate to shut down ROTC, Persky organized a sit-in on the steps of Rockwell Hall. I remember the police arrests because I was there as a volunteer Faculty Marshal. Persky had skipped out. Is he now selling plumbing supplies somewhere, with one eye on the stock market and the other on his receding hairline?—or maybe he hides it under a star-spangled do-rag.

One year the protests were dominated by Yippies, the anarchist sect devoted to street theater, pot, and free love. One of their leaders was Jane Brower, a red-haired History grad student. Carrying her bull-horn she led crowds in that sad self-contradictory chant, "The people, united, will never be defeated."

Every year brought an official commemoration of the shooting, but when the war ended in 1975, the administration said there'd be no more official remembering. That led to the forming of the May 4th Task Force, a student-faculty group devoted to continuing the tradition. Following a candle-light vigil on May 3, there'd be, next day on the Commons, a moment of silence for the dead and wounded, recognition of survivors like Dean Kahler (paralyzed for life by a bullet to the back), and speeches by invited guests. At such gatherings I met famous dignitaries like Senators Eugene McCarthy and George McGovern, and also witnessed the partici-

pation of national figures such
as Jane Fonda, William Kun-
stler, Abbie Hoffman, and Tom
Hayden.

Passionate protests had
died down by 1983 when I
myself was invited by the May
4th Task Force to deliver the
45-minute keynote speech on
the Commons. That was quite
an honor, and I worked hard to produce something worth listening to.
My speech, "Some Thoughts on Killings in World History," is, I believe,
maybe the best lecture I ever wrote. It addresses many questions arising
from large-scale massacres, and so, for anyone interested, I was recently
surprised to find that it can be googled at "Kent State Gerald Newman."

A new controversy, the Gym Dispute, arose in 1977 when the administration abruptly announced its decision to bulldoze one part of the shooting area, and build there a sparkling new gym annex and swimming pool.
The very earth where people had died became the scene of battle, with the
bigwigs, on one side, wanting to obliterate it, while students, locking arms
in protest, "sat in" and soon began pitching tents there. One of their leaders was Nancy Grim, one of the best students I ever had. She was deadly
serious about confronting injustice—she later studied law and began her
own law office in Kent, specializing in discrimination and whistle-blowers'
rights. Every day I'd walk over to Blanket Hill and talk with her and the
others holding out in "Tent City."

The administration decided to drive them out. Nancy's group had
warned students everywhere about this possibility, and so, an amazing
thing, supporters showed up in astonishingly great numbers, ready for battle. Fleets of buses came to Kent, hauling students from hundreds of miles
away. I'll never forget the vivid impression made one May 4th afternoon by
hundreds of visitors running downhill in a disciplined snake-dancing column, down steep Blanket Hill onto the Commons from above Taylor Hall,
pumping their fists in the air and shouting in unison, "Move the Gym,
Get off the Site, New York-New Jersey's here to fight!" They'd driven 500
miles, from Newark and the Bronx, to snake-dance down that hill, to join
the never-ending parade of protest at Kent State University. Naturally they
were tear-gassed and arrested.

Later, I often went swimming in the new pool. Over time, humans come to accept almost anything.

Then came the Monument Dispute. Many students and faculty felt that something imposing should be erected as a May 4th memorial, but the administration, always fretting about the university's image and enrollments, stubbornly resisted and even turned down a wonderfully evocative monument donated by the noted sculptor George Segal: it portrayed the Biblical patriarch Abraham, knife in hand, standing over his son, Isaac, in obedience to a divine command to slaughter him. As a comment on the Shooting, that sculpture would have inspired deep thoughts about authority, patriarchy, love, and duty—which is about all one could expect from any monument. But the bigwigs refused the gift, so now it stands in a sculpture garden at Princeton.

That was in 1979, but then in 1980 the new university president, Brage Golding, amazingly did a 180-degree-turn and decided to erect a large $30,000 commemorative arch, even vowing that he'd build, with his own hands, benches where people could sit and contemplate it. Immediately an outraged cry went up against it by leftist students and their supporters, backed by the student editors of the *Daily Kent Stater*, objecting because, they said, an arch meant "triumph," which they interpreted as "the State's triumph over the hapless individual." The arch would sanctify more "oppression."

That was a stereotypical case of what I've called bubbled stupidity—in this case, of lefty campus Group-Think. I tried to fix it. I wrote a long *Stater* blast arguing that "the proposed marker, by its largeness alone, should serve to focus thought on the tragedy and even the glory of May 4, 1970, and on those young people, dead now these ten years, whose lives ended there. It should also serve to prove beyond any lingering doubt that the university community as a whole takes those events most seriously. Now is our opportunity, and I think we ought to take it." That had zero effect against the imbecilic "oppression" argument, and four days later the *Stater's* headline read: "Negative opinions scuttle May 4 Arch."

Two years later, in 1982, the national Vietnam Veterans War memorial was unveiled in Washington D.C. Again I spoke out in the *Stater*, saying that if the nation was prepared at last to erect a Vietnam War memorial, then maybe one could hope that opponents of a Kent memorial would "think twice this time before running to their soap boxes" and support one.

I can't say I fixed anything, but I do believe the faculty's steadfast support helped to undergird the administration's decision in 1985 to launch a big national competition to build a permanent memorial. Hundreds of designs were submitted by gifted architects. But alas, another disastrously mishandled mess resulted. The winning architect was, it turned out, Canadian, which violated the rules, so the runner-up got the job, which resulted in a lawsuit by the first guy, more years of bellyaching, and, finally, the squeezing-out of a pitifully tiny and ugly monument that cost less than one-thirteenth of what had originally been authorized.

Go visit that thing and you'll see nothing to convey the importance of May 4th. Instead you'll see on the ground five black stone disks about the size of manhole covers, a low wall, a tile patio, four more stone blocks, and an irrelevant planting of 58,000 daffodils to represent American soldiers killed in Vietnam. The memorial, after so much sound and fury, is mute, reflecting the university's fear of political criticism, and even the inscription is an ambiguous head-scratcher: *"Inquire. Learn. Reflect."* Bah. Inquire about what? Learn about what? Reflect about what?

At least some hopes were later fulfilled. In 2010 the National Register of Historic Places finally added the Shooting site to its list. In 2014 a May 4th Visitors Center was opened in Taylor Hall, full of displays that also promote civil rights and democratic protest. A Center for Peaceful Change, established in 1971, expanded so much that today it's an entire "School of Peace and Conflict Studies," annually teaching a thousand students about conflict management and nonviolent change.

I've been asked what it was like to teach history at Kent State during that era. It was a wonderful bonus! Professors can't often teach world history on a world-historical spot. Historians teach about lots of things—discoveries, empires, treaties, personalities—but ever-prominent topics are wars, protests, violent events, political struggle, propaganda, politics, and the mentalities and tactics of every sort of group.

So? Picture me one fine spring afternoon in Bowman Hall, a piece of chalk in my hand, talking about such stuff, and being interrupted by a racket of speech-making with bull-horns, and yelling crowds of protesters, and radicals attacking conservatives and America-firsters, and police breaking up sit-ins, and even, during the first half of the 70s, national guardsmen with weapons pushing people against chain-link fences, and the smell of tear gas drifting through an open window. KSU was a living history lab, a perch overlooking the behaviors and processes of historical action, and there I was to point them out. That was the bonus.

~

Discussing May 4th has carried me well past my first arrival in Kent, so let's return to that. In early September 1970 I found my way to Bowman Hall and climbed three floors to the History Department. Its office space had been expanded to both ends of the building to accommodate my 32 colleagues, all men; and I was one of three Assistant Professors hired that year. That's a stunning reminder of how dramatically higher education had mushroomed during its "Golden Age."

Henry Whitney, the departmental Chairperson, was an interesting study. A trim, polite man with thinning hair and a pleasant Boston accent, he was a gentleman of the old school, interested in his colleagues' lives, children, and especially their publishing successes, those being the contemporary standard of departmental quality. His ambition was to lead the best department in the school of Arts and Sciences, and he didn't fall far short of it. His method was to cater to a few prima donnas, build up their salaries, give them extra secretarial help, and cut back their classroom hours to support their research, which would add luster to the department's standing.

That made it harder, though, for him to deal with others who resented the overlarge influence of the prima donnas. That's where his mastery became apparent. Whitney's wife called him "Biff" in reference to some amateur fighting he'd done; I think he'd worked to perfect what's called the "bob and weave," the dancing and feinting and air-punching that marks the boxer who rarely lands a blow but wins anyway by slipping every punch till his opponent keels over exhausted. That's how Henry dealt with those who'd buttonhole him in the hallway with questions about this or that, things as big as the future of the History of Civilization series (our bread-and-butter course), or as small as "who's going to get the fishes and loaves during the next salary discussions?"

That's when you'd see "Biff" at his best, spryly bobbing and weaving. His genius was to listen respectfully, all ears, emitting sympathetic noises, and then to begin a meandering monologue, discussing some transitional movement of departmental affairs, which he'd illustrate by drawing an imaginary diagram with his finger on a nearby wall, and then, running his hand through his thinning hair while delivering small and seemingly painful grunts as he forecast disappointing turns in the road and possibly disastrous outcomes ahead, he'd continue on until you started to get weak in the knees and felt ready for bed-rest or at least your own office chair. And so you'd drag yourself away, feeling perhaps slightly pleased and hopeful, but also confused and a little scared about horrible things you'd never known about before.

He led me down the hall to a large office with a big window and a wall of bookcases. Sitting there was my new roommate, Ken Calkins, our Germany expert. I found myself shaking hands with a pleasantly smiling young man with sleek dark hair and a boyish face. I took to him immediately, and also saw how lucky I was to share an office with that big window facing onto the Bowman parking lot. Later I'd look out and laugh at Philosophy professors searching for their cars.

I met other good people nearby, nearly all with doctorates from the country's most prestigious schools—Chicago, Northwestern, Wisconsin, Indiana, Illinois, the Ivies. The two oldest were Maury Baker, the Latin Americanist, and Sherman Barnes, who specialized in Early Modern Europe. Baker, a very sweet man, retired soon after I arrived, and I remember him saying wistfully that "it seemed as though he'd just arrived, and now it was time to retire—where did the years go?" Barnes was a merry old character whose most surprising asset was his eccentric wife; once I dropped in on them and found her emerging from their basement covered in shavings from some odd wood hobby, carving dildoes or chain-sawing grizzly bears.

Glee Wilson kidding around at my desk in Bowman 321

Across the hall I met Vic Papacosma, Glee Wilson, and John Hubbell, all about my age. Vic was likeable, polished, our Balkans specialist, one of the best-liked guys in the department. His office mate, Glee Wilson, the specialist in Ancient Greece, later became one of my best friends. A small, trim, bearded guy with a drily ironic sense of humor, a man with artistic tastes and a collector's instincts, he would have made an ideal liberal-arts-college prof if he hadn't despised students' laziness. John Hubbell, the Civil War man, had been a Marine and exhibited the slightly peremptory and combative attitude typical of the breed. Blunt but funny, he showed me around the campus, cracking me up with irreverent observations about administrators. Another joker was Bill Kenney, the Colonial America guy. I asked him what the local historians did for fun. "Well," he said, "our most exciting thing is lining up at the railroad depot to greet the evening shipment of Preparation H." Bill got into major trouble with the Black United Students group when he failed to endorse their exaggerated count of Africans carried in death ships to the New World. He was no slavery-denier, but BUS harassed him anyway for a month or two as a borderline racist.

Three other colleagues my age, people who became my good friends, were Henry Leonard, Jim Louis, and Barry Beer. Leonard was a cheerful, ruddy, humorous sort of guy, penguin-shaped, a New Englander, with a jaunty manner reminiscent of any fictional character in P.G. Wodehouse's "Drones Club." He was the type who might have greeted me with a "What Ho, Gerald!" Louis was a pipe-smoker, and the story was that one day before entering his classroom he'd knocked burning tobacco from his pipe, stuck the pipe into his jacket pocket, strolled in and begun lecturing, but soon found himself a raging inferno! Of course that led to waggish comments about firing up the students. He later moved into the central administration and became an Assistant Vice President (ASSVIPE).

Beer, a first-rate scholar, loved to pose provocative questions just to see how you'd answer them: "Do you REALLY BELIEVE you should PAY TAXES to BUILD ROADS IN UTAH?" I loved chatting with him because he knew the latest gossip and would convey it humorously. He and his wife Jill were more staid than other couples, and I chuckle when I remember that shortly after becoming acquainted we accompanied them to see Marlon Brando's X-rated "Last Tango in Paris." It included a rape scene and other sorts of depravity with, as I dimly recall, a stick of butter playing some role. As we emerged from the theatre, all four of us embarrassed at what we'd seen together, Jill loudly remarked, "Well!!! Nobody WE KNOW is like that!"

I feared they wouldn't invite us over afterwards.

My best story about any of my dear old KSU colleagues is the one about our Chinese History guy, Yeh-Chien Wang, who liked to be called "Gene" because his real name was hard for some people to pronounce. Actually his own pronunciation of English, especially of "r" words, was dodgy— "Rome" was "Wome." He was a very nice guy, a specialist on land taxes under the Qing Dynasty, but though he was an Einstein on that, he was totally

Bill Kenney and Ruth

clueless about even the simplest technology. That became apparent to me one evening when we were both preparing to teach night classes. He came running up to me, looking very agitated, and asked whether he could use my office key to open his office door. I explained that that was impossible, each office had a different lock. On another evening he came running up for help to unthread a ripped-up educational film from the department's 16mm projector—he'd pushed film into the wrong end, slivered it, and couldn't extricate what was left.

But the lollapalooza was when John Lanigan, the broadcaster at WMJI in Cleveland, reported one morning, on his program "Knuckleheads in the News," that "Gene Wang, a Kent State professor, yesterday ran his car through 20 yards of freshly poured concrete roadway, even though a road crew was shouting and gesturing that he should stop!" Oh, no, I thought! Poor Gene! I figured he was going to get hit with a huge fine. Next day I came up to him, expressed my sympathy, and then asked why he'd paid no attention to the road crew? "No woad cwew!" he said. "No crew?" I asked—"Then what made you stop?" His reply: "Woad *soft.*" Some wag said Gene had made a genius move: he'd get 100,000 miles out of those tires.

The resident curmudgeons were Harold Schwartz and Augie Meier. If Academe were a zoo, Schwartz would have starred in the Poisonous Reptile Exhibit; Meier, famous for chest-pounding and earth-shaking grunts, would have featured as Silverback Crested Gorilla.

Schwartz carried a personal grievance against me that dated back to before I ever laid eyes on him. Back in January of 1970, while I was still job-shopping, he'd been in Boston on some kind of trip. While there, he called me up to see whether I'd have lunch with him, his purpose undoubtedly being to look me over as a potential colleague. Swamped with work and uncertain about heading to Kent anyway, I politely declined, and he never, for the next 30 years, forgot this refusal, which he insisted on regarding as a terrible personal slight. It was nothing of the kind, but he gave me the cold shoulder when I arrived and never addressed a word to me for years afterwards. He was a petty man, his disposition notoriously sour; students disliked him, and he relished it as proof of his superiority. Four years after I arrived in Kent, I was astonished to find a note from him in my mailbox. This was the first communication from him, of any sort. I opened it to find the following two sentences: "A student told me you're a dedicated teacher. I presume he meant this as a compliment."

That was, at least, witty, though it acknowledged his disdain for teaching. Why, I asked myself, was he even there at KSU? Was it only because it gave him an income? After students, the second group on his "Most Disliked" list was faculty wives. Following a faculty meeting I noted that "Schwartz most unexpectedly, and in a spirit of nervous agitation, began to complain bitterly of the role faculty wives play in office politics and appointments." At which Bill Kenney came up with a clever put-down. He coolly eyed the printed agenda and then asked, "Are we down to 'Miscellaneous' already?"

And then there was Augie Meier, the chest-pounding crested gorilla. With his official title as "University Professor" he was the top prima donna of the department, the most celestial being to kowtow to as provider of departmental glory. To his credit, he was indeed an important pioneer of African-American studies, and his fruitful collaboration with his life partner, Elliot Rudwick, resulted in tons of informative printed paper, especially when you consider the productions of their often very good doctoral students.

But like other individuals who accomplish a lot—Edison, Ford, Howard Hughes, Jeffrey Dahmer—Augie was slightly off his rocker, and got worse as he aged. In my mind, his exaltation over everyone else typified the History Department's off-the-trolley value system, which laid such massive emphasis on publication and so little on undergraduate teaching. To the outer world he was a great man, to me he was unimaginably vain, wildly abrasive, insulting, sometimes hysterical. My office door was only 20 feet from his, and what I remember most vividly about this publishing colossus was his childish rage in 1983 when it was officially announced that Martin Luther King Jr. would have a federal holiday named after him. "He wasn't that important!" was what I heard Augie yell in his office, kicking his wastebasket across the room. What an appalling reaction. Kicking his wastebasket was a fairly common occurrence, but once I actually saw him do a twofer—*I saw* him *throwing his telephone while kicking his wastebasket!* Whatever fit he threw, you knew his ego was at its center.

Those were some of my colleagues and this was the history department I'd chosen to spend 30 years working in. This is what I got when I decided to spurn the University of Saskatchewan because of its remoteness and cold winters and Canadian "mmeh." This was the end of the line for the guy who, with his humble Master's degree, had had so much fun teaching Great Books of the Humanities at Western Washington State University. My new colleagues were generally good people, generous friends, decent scholars, but there were things that warned of something bad about the atmosphere. I'd just have to wait and see.

My official KSU job description comprised three supposedly equal categories—teaching, publishing, and service (which meant committee work and community outreach). But, in fact, publishing towered over the others. And that's what I'd feared even when I signed my contract. I'd worried that dedicated teaching, which I'd admired so much at UW, and enjoyed attempting at Western, and seen so little of at Harvard, would be relatively unimportant, that I'd signed myself into a "factory" where classes were larger and students less interested than at my other main choice, the University of Saskatchewan; and that my worth would be judged more by my publications than by my effectiveness at building the skills of young adults.

My worries were justified, and it's a matter of lasting regret. A year after arriving at KSU I wrote in my diary: "I was right about Kent, it *is* a factory, and I don't like the school and have an unoptimistic view of the students." I must say that afterwards, with higher entrance requirements, the situation significantly improved, but KSU in 1971, its eye on fat enrollments, sometimes admitted students who should never have been let into any university without further preparation; and the same motive led to classes, even specialized upper-division classes, being so huge that many students would have been better off if they'd simply read a few books.

In the early years I had a few appallingly unprepared students every semester. I remember one who, while I was lecturing about the Japanese attack on Pearl Harbor, looked so perplexed that I had to ask what was wrong. "Where's Pearl Harbor?" he asked. "Right here," I said, pointing for the second time at the large map right there beside me, a world map with the Pacific Ocean in the middle. I pointed directly at Oahu in the Hawaiian chain. He still looked alarmed and dumbfounded. *"Right here,"* I said, more loudly, stabbing my finger at Oahu. *"I've never been there!"* he squealed. That was his excuse for looking baffled—he'd never been there! Seeing his, um, innocence, I had him stop after class for a map tutorial. If I hadn't fixed him, that poor student might have grown up to become just like Mrs. Zaniewski, the neighbor I saved from living next to an Asian.

The problem wasn't just lack of intellectual preparation. There was a manners issue, too. Some students just didn't care about history at all, and didn't bother to conceal it. There's a saying for such students: "You can always tell a sophomore, but you can't tell him much!" In fact some students hadn't a clue even about how to *behave* at a university. The first time I taught my Victorian England course, a student in the front row finished his cigarette (yes, students were permitted to smoke!), then stubbed it out and *flipped it up against the blackboard wall not ten feet away from me as I stood at the lectern!* Astonished, I demanded he pick it up and remove himself from my presence; he looked offended.

Another incident four years later: "This morning I got so furious in my Victorian class that I almost choked this idiot student, name of Karp. He comes in and habitually sits directly in front of me, sprawled out, yawning and sleeping, his mouth a giant open cavern into which I more than once have nearly pitched a large stick of chalk. The more I looked at him, the louder my voice got, I got angrier and angrier, shouting louder and louder as he sat sprawling there in a near trance. I think I'll flunk the bastard."

And then there were the ones who sat for 50 minutes, bouncing their knees. Sometimes, what with bouncers, yawners, and people clueless about maps, I had to talk with my eyes closed like dear old Prof. Lytle lecturing on the "FURRENCHHH RREVOLUTIONNN." Well, yes, I'm exaggerating, but come on, it's hard to concentrate on your work when there are such distractions.

However, I must admit that I too went overboard occasionally. A ludicrous example comes to mind. As the years passed I discovered, every semester, an ever-larger number of male students sitting in the classroom, *wearing hats!* Now in my own student days, to wear a hat in a classroom would have been considered ill-bred and disrespectful. So one day, with several male students sitting with their hats on, I kind of blew up and yelled that they should for goodness sake *"remove their hats in class! Nobody wears hats in university classes!"* Chastened, they followed my orders and took their hats off.

But then, next week, several came up before class, all sporting ridiculous hats, and held up a picture of a medieval engraving of students, in the dead of winter, at the Sorbonne, every one of them wearing a massive headgear to keep warm! I laughed, and my students did too. They'd hoisted the stuffy prof by his own historical petard. I admired the research they'd done and was reminded of the time, back at the U, when we'd confronted poor Dr. Costigan with the angry face of Winston Churchill, smoking a stogy! After further exchanges I also learned why they so often came to class with their hats on. It meant they didn't have to comb their hair after crawling out of bed.

I knew I was working sometimes with rough material, but I never got cynical, as many another professor did. Maybe it's because I inwardly know what a dummy I am myself, or maybe it's because I devoutly believe that each mind ripens at its own pace and may suddenly become open today to things of no interest yesterday. Anyway, I knew that if I persisted, I could get through to many students; I could help them think more clearly about the world, and, what's equally important, help them enjoy it much more. Education is the ticket to a richer, fuller life, a ticket to the box seats.

I wanted to reach them, but sadly like all the other professors in the History Department, even in the entire university, I'd never had a single class in how to teach. We'd all gone to graduate schools, done a dissertation or something like it, received our diploma, and were then expected to know how to teach students. *But that's another science all by itself!*—I'd learned that from educators as great as Klobucher and Costigan and Pressly. So even though I wanted to reach students, I had to figure out how to do it all by myself. I couldn't even organize an in-house seminar for sharing techniques; nobody had time for it or cared enough. Some justified their resistance by claiming that all faculty members already knew how to teach. Gradually I began to think that the best tool for self-improvement would be to collect anonymous student feedback and correct my approach accordingly. But that's where I ran into a brick wall that said "NO TEACHING EVALUATIONS!"

Teaching evaluations, so common nowadays, were only very cautiously being introduced in the 1970s. From what I've written already I suppose it could be predicted that I'd lock horns over them with some people in my history department—and by "some people" I mean, especially, senior faculty members. Harold Schwartz had openly paraded his hostility when he sent me that nasty note suggesting that "dedicated teaching" might be folly, but in fact the majority of my older colleagues believed, in spite of lip service to the contrary, that publishing should be the department's only really true measure of quality—and also, be it noted, of merit pay increases. Rudy Buttlar, the Dean of Arts and Sciences, encouraged this by routinely identifying all faculty members simply by the number of their "pubs"—his shorthand term for publications. Reportedly he'd been kicked upstairs because as a science professor he'd been a complete flop.

Open warfare over teaching evaluations began in January 1975 with me contending against almost the entire department—a few younger faculty quietly supported me, but only passively. The struggle arose unexpectedly when the central administration proposed the establishment of Student Teaching Evaluations throughout the university—proposed it, and then, having done so without adequate preparation, sharply stepped back in reaction to apoplectic resistance from the various departments. Much of the bellowing came from "Full Bulls," senior professors. The administration then decided that evaluations could be "optional" rather than mandatory.

To me, refusing professors the opportunity to collect anonymous critiques from their students was like saying that none but cooks should judge the broth. I vigorously attacked that idea in the January department meeting called to discuss the issue. My position was that we all should submit to student evaluation every term, for every course we taught. But a host of bugbears was summoned up against my arguments: the students would be unfair; a good professor would get bad evaluations because he demanded too much work; students couldn't discern quality anyway. Those were all smokescreens. Really, the only good reason to oppose student evaluations was that sometimes they'd not be serious, like the time somewhat later when Prof. Ann Heiss's evaluation came back with only two words: "Great Tits." Apart from jocular irrelevance, unsigned hand-written student evaluations, scrupulously given in secrecy, and with equal care scrupulously conveyed under seal to the Chair of the department, should help a conscientious faculty member detect his own teaching weaknesses—and, not a small point, yield salary improvements if, over time, he or she received consistently high marks.

I continued to argue my case. Feeling the issue's importance, I allowed myself to become annoying. Before the faculty meeting in February I hand-ed out a lengthy proposal that included the following questions: "What about teaching, in relation to our other activities? Does our actual promo-tion policy either encourage or reward special effort in teaching? Isn't it as thoughtless to say that no meaningful distinctions can be made between levels of teaching as it would be to say that all 250-page books, or all 30-page articles, are of comparable quality? Is there really any reward at all for energies specially directed toward improvement of teaching? Does anyone in the department seriously believe that teaching excellence is even rele-vant, much less 'crucial,' to promotion?"

Such aggressive arguments from a relative newcomer awakened some of the more totally burned-out senior faculty to the existence of a black sheep in the fold. Augie Meier, the celebrated and very generously paid-for departmental hood ornament, stomped in to do an absolute flame-out at me in my own office, calling me "a revolutionary"—which to this man, our chronicler of Black History, was a bad word! Ultimately, however, the His-tory Department, feeling pressure from other departments less fossilized, caved to the use of student evaluations. Here are excerpts from a few of mine, all anonymous. (A teacher receives copies after the semester.)

> "He guided us through the material without being boring, and threw in interesting and funny anecdotes to keep the class enter-taining." "He was incredibly knowledgeable and knew how to ig-nite group discussions involving many participants." "He always wanted students to voice their opinions to get a good conversation going." "He was respectful of students—expecting hard work & ensuring that everyone had their chance to contribute to discus-sions." "He led his class in a dignified manner and respected stu-dent opinions." "He challenged us to think critically and study carefully." "This class required me to take a more abstract view and integrate knowledge from all schools of learning." "I had to work a lot harder in this class than others I am taking this semester. It was different from the Hist. of Civ. class that my friend is taking from another professor."

So much for the ridiculous argument that students would bridle at being worked hard, or that they were insensitive to the ways in which they were being taught. And I find it pleasant to add, after all that fuss over evaluations, that I later received the university's Distinguished Teaching Award. To me, though not to many of my colleagues, that was very important. I felt that by that recognition I entered the empyrean already inhabited by two of my educational heroes, Giovanni Costigan and Jim McAree. It figured as evidence that I'd done for some students what my own greatest teachers had done for me.

The teacher's satisfaction comes from showing students how to develop their skills. With many students I developed great personal relationships, and even now, 20 years after retirement, a handful keep in touch via Facebook and occasional emails. They and many of my grad students went on to successes employing higher-level skills. Among them were dozens of K-12 teachers, researchers and librarians in many states, journalists like the fine former editor of the Kent *Record-Courier*, Roger DiPaolo, Foreign Service officers and other U.S. government workers, and foreign-born officials in such faraway places as Nigeria, Pakistan, and India.

Receptive students value strenuous efforts to train them; a superior student will find value even in harsh criticism if delivered by a conscientious teacher. In critiquing my students' essays I was as conscientious and politely brutal as Costigan had been; in running discussions I even employed the Socratic method in large lecture halls, putting students on the spot; and in lecturing I always dug for more topical and provocative materials to inspire debate. But despite my piddling efforts in my own little workshop, the entire History Department's enrollments got ever smaller in the 70s. That steep decline embarrassed the whole department when President Golding rather annoyingly pointed it out in a public address in early 1979, fully quoted in the *Daily Kent Stater*.

But to me, never shy of taking an irregular position, my department's enrollment decline was an advantage, and I replied to President Golding in what became a very highly praised Guest Column in the same newspaper— it received letters of congratulation from faculty, administrators, and even a member of Congress. Here's the bit in which I observed that whereas, in 1970, my upper-division Victorian class had an overflow enrollment of 59 students, I now had, in 1979, only 22:

Now, I am able at the beginning of each term to meet individually with the student, discuss his personal research interests, help him clarify his ideas, prepare his bibliography and organize his paper. Another consequence of this meeting is that we begin to know each other as individuals. As a result, I think we both feel bound to do better work. And when the student turns in his paper at last, he turns in something original, something he has improved his mind on, something he can be proud of. He also knows, with some mixture of gratitude and fear, that I will spend an hour poring over and marking what he has written. Plagiarism has nearly ceased, and the papers are spectacularly better than in 1970. Today, the typical instructor thinks less about making himself famous and abandoning Kent, more about ways in which he can teach, help, and earn the respect of the people in his classroom. Fear is a powerful motive. No one wants to end up at last in a totally empty classroom, droning only to himself.

From this a perceptive reader will also see that by 1979 I'd begun to teach at least one of my courses exactly as I would have done if I'd been working in a small liberal arts college. Poor departmental teaching performance had helped me, at least, to achieve the kind of fulfillment I'd hoped for. I really loved that Victorian course, and by 1979 there was more to it than its books, discussions, office conferences and papers. I taught it in the spring, and so, with the weather warming, I regularly invited my students to come to a relaxed "Victorian Luncheon" in our backyard. As a joke, they were invited to adopt "Victorian names," so Bob Smith would become "Algie Worthington," Joe Doaks would become "Reggie Playfair," Mary Jones would become "Gwendolyn Moncrieff," and so on. With that established, and the group feeling merry, I'd serve iced tea and cucumber sandwiches made just the English way, and then for dessert, Victoria sponge cake, after which we'd all watch that hilarious 1952 film, starring Michael Redgrave and Dame Edith Evans, of Oscar Wilde's classic "Importance of Being Earnest." The whole event, an attempt to add something memorable to the Victorian course, was a kind of substitute for what I might have done if I'd spent those 30 years working in a more teacher-friendly environment.

My most sophisticated work was in the realm of Victorian studies, but with my heightened interest in innovative teaching I didn't confine myself to the subjects I'd been trained in, the history of Britain, European Intellectual History, and World History. In fact I think I made my biggest impact through two courses I simply cooked up because I saw a need for them, and thought they'd be fun.

First I dreamed up a course on World War II. I got it off the ground in 1977 and successfully continued it till I retired in 2000. There were lectures, discussions, films, reading assignments, three exams, and a mandatory formal report, double-spaced and at least five pages in length. That written report made my course one of the department's most popular offerings. The paper had to be, as I stated in my syllabus, *"based on one or more detailed interviews with someone who survived the war and was old enough then to understand their experience."* A bad job on it would sink any hope for a passing grade. The assignment forced students to do something they did for no other history course, that is, write a good paper after finding a suitable interviewee, prepare questions based on serious research, and set up lengthy interviews which they frequently tape-recorded to preserve the tone and details of the interview.

That writing assignment often resulted in unusual emotional as well as intellectual experiences for my students. Over the years, they found many different people to interview—soldiers, sailors, medics, pilots, ambulance-drivers, and so on, but also German soldiers, Holocaust survivors, Chinese-American immigrants, Ohio women who'd worked in munitions plants, scrap metal collectors, people from Mexican-American families whose parents had come in as wartime braceros.

A significant number of those interviews were conducted with the student's own older relatives, and not infrequently led to emotional breakthroughs that never would have occurred otherwise. The breakthroughs occurred on both sides, the interviewee emotionally revisiting memories that in some cases had been long repressed, and the student learning and writing history in an entirely new way, literally as "his" (or her) "story." I was surprised to find my assignment brokering new relationships between the younger generation and the older. One example will show exactly what I mean. Here's a paper from December, 1982, written by a student named Caroline Koran, who'd interviewed her uncle Chester:

> I anticipated a challenge in this interview from the beginning. I
> had to ask eleven times before he would give me a definite date and

time when we could speak. When I arrived he asked me to come back in a few hours, and proceeded to write down all he could remember. When I returned he handed me two small sheets of paper filled with basic information in the hope that it would suffice. After some persuasion and an agreement that I would not use my tape recorder, he agreed to discuss his memories. Reluctant and unsure, my uncle discussed his memories which still seem to haunt his thoughts after forty years of suppression.

Her uncle had been a Cleveland machinist. He signed up in 1943, was trained in Ohio and Oklahoma as a member of the 342nd Armored Field Artillery Battalion, was shipped to Marseilles in bitterly cold January 1944, then moved into southern Germany against heavy resistance. Ms. Koran continued: "The fighting was intense and costly. He recalled the blood-stained and sometimes deformed dead bodies being picked up by the truckload. His voice hinted of some hidden anger and his body tensed. Quietly he told me of a handsome 20-year-old friend, Orrin, who could no longer withstand the anxiety and stress and pressure. Orrin suddenly rushed madly toward a German tank only to become another casualty."

The girl's uncle went on to describe the failing German resistance, the flood into camp of very old and very young German deserters, the exhaustion of German fuel and supplies, the drunken celebration that he and his mates indulged in at the European war's end on May 8, 1945. And then Ms. Koran concluded as follows:

I have always been my uncle's favorite niece; it was because of our close relationship that he finally agreed to discuss the war. Our talk, though strained and unsettling, taught me much. Perhaps the most important thing I learned was somewhat distant from the true conversation. I left my uncle's house knowing our unique relationship was based on more than a little wide-eyed girl idolizing her uncle. Rather, he saw me as a mature woman able to understand his past difficulties and his individuality.

In 1979 I launched a similar course on the Vietnam War—in the late 70s there was growing student curiosity about it. It could have been launched by our U.S. specialists, but they declined—there were so many "pubs" to grind out for Dean Buttlar, such a need to address issues like why President Polk vetoed the Rivers and Harbors Act of 1846.

To teach that course for two decades was enlightening. It afforded a fixed vantage point from which to observe students' basic attitudes evolving from postwar dovishness in the late 70s to growing hawkishness during the Reagan years, the 80s, and then to nearly total ignorance about the war in the 90s. Really! By that time many students didn't even know that the U.S. had lost it. Their parents had shied away from discussing it, and their high school history teachers, fearful of controversy, hadn't ventured past the Truman Administration in their classroom studies.

And so, if those 1990s college students were any gauge, our citizenry entered the 21st century almost totally clueless about that tragic quagmire of death, expense, and humiliation. After every war, I think, people forget its pain and lessons, and return to more basic instincts of selfishness, aggression, and emotional thinking. Teaching that course, I actually saw that happening year by year. And so I was probably one of the least surprised people in the country when I saw that by 2003, the second year of the George W. Bush administration, it was almost impossible to restrain my countrymen against going off half-cocked into Iraq without examining facts or questioning the need for another disastrous invasion of another faraway country. It was the German philosopher G.W.F. Hegel who declared that "the thing we learn from history, is that we never learn anything from history."

⌒

My keen interest in teaching led me into K-12 classrooms when I became coordinator of the regional History Day competition held annually in the dozen counties surrounding Kent State. History Day, founded in Cleveland (at Case Western) in the 1970s and then expanded to the entire nation, was created in imitation of "Science Fairs" to promote and showcase historical study. It's been a huge national success. From 170 participants in 1974 it grew to more than half a million by 2020. KSU joined the program in 1984, with our History Department, meaning me, running it. That meant I began working with teachers throughout the area, organizing the annual event in the KSU Student Center, recruiting the faculty judges and conducting the awards ceremonies, and then tidying up the odds and ends left afterwards.

I performed that service for 16 years, till my retirement, and thoroughly enjoyed doing so. When I departed from KSU, Cathy Gorn, PhD, formerly my own student, who herself had advanced to become, in Washington D.C., the National Director of the entire program, sent me a beautiful letter of thanks and congratulations. I particularly appreciated her saying I'd been "a tremendous force for educational reform in Northeast Ohio; your leadership has been an inspiration to teachers. Because of your efforts to recognize and reward them, history education in your area has improved dramatically in the 'Newman era.'"

Running a History Day awards presentation, with, in background, two high school history teachers, and John Jameson, head of the KSU History Dept. in the 1990s

I said earlier that in my professional life I tried to imitate my mentors, Giovanni Costigan and Thomas J. Pressly. They were both, in different ways, great teachers, but another thing they had in common was a disinclination to attend history conferences, and in that I channeled them too. I was no good at the game of fitting in, moving up, and getting promoted. That was something you were supposed to pick up on the job, from a mentor if you could find one, or from gauging and profiting by the atmosphere of your department.

Unfortunately my department's atmosphere was pretty much an every-man-for-himself thing, not a scene of mentoring and working collaboratively, so although I did figure out for myself how to be a decent teacher, I never learned how to play the professional game. I disliked conferences,

I made no attempts to get onto panels, I didn't work on essay collections or meet editors or do anything to keep my name out there in the scholarly world. That was a serious weakness, which I trace in part to my gypsy childhood—the rootless moving-around that resulted, as I said earlier, in my tendency to become "a loner or a director, a go-it-alone guy or a supervisor."

But I didn't really care. And so it wasn't till 1988 that I made Full Professor, and that was after the publication, naturally, of a book. Yes, I did publish a book—actually, two, if you count that giant encyclopedia, *Britain in the Hanoverian Age, 1714-1837* (1997).

But the book I should mention, just to shield myself against the charge of "doing nothing but teaching," was *The Rise of English Nationalism: A Cultural History, 1740-1830* (1987). My manuscript threatened such a scaffolded tower of preconceived ideas that the top American specialist in my field, R. K. Webb, furiously rejected its publication! It's funny—his hostile written appraisal took me back to high school, when Warden Willie had glared at my unorthodoxy the same way Warden Webb now glared at my book. Webb was a former editor of the *American Historical Review*, an illustrious professor loaded with distinctions; as chief British History advisor to Oxford University Press he read my manuscript and angrily declared that "this book should never be published by Oxford!" He was having none of it!

Happily I did manage to fool some others:

"One of the most significant of this year's books . . . This account of the late 18th and early 19th centuries throws such a wholly new light upon the political and cultural life of the period that it illuminates obliquely our own." —Peter Ackroyd (chief book reviewer for the *London Times Literary Supplement* and a distinguished author)

"A brilliant piece of work . . . written in a striking and lively style and the material is skillfully orchestrated." —Kenneth Minogue (Professor of Political Science, London School of Economics)

"A brilliant explication . . . As a work in intellectual and cultural history, there is nothing like it. Engagingly written, highly provocative." —G. M. Straka (Professor of History, University of Wisconsin)

"His attempt to bring us face to face with our own national myths should provide some timely self-examination." —Roy Porter (Professor of Social History, University College, London)

"He brings together so many elements in a series of syntheses that nearly everything looks a bit different from what we previously thought it was. This is probably the highest form of scholarship attainable." —Leon Guilhamet (Professor of English Literature, City College of New York)

"One of the most exciting and engrossing studies I have read in years." —John N. Murrin (Professor of History, Princeton University)

"All future students will have to read and argue with it." —Kenneth O. Morgan (British historian, broadcaster, author)

"Well researched, richly suggestive, and of interest to students of English literature as well as to historians." —Linda Colley (Professor of History, Yale University)

"A bold synthetic work, full of interesting material and insights."
—John Brewer (Professor of History, Harvard University)

"This is a book I will keep, recommend to my colleagues and assign to my students; it ought to spark debate and provoke new lines of research on a number of questions. One could scarcely say anything more laudatory." —Thomas C. Kennedy (Professor of History, University of Arkansas)

Foreign exchange programs are a part of Academe, and I laugh as I recall my experience of the KSU summer-abroad program, the Oxford Summer Seminar. That program included a bus trip around Britain, visits to famous locations like Stonehenge and Stratford-upon-Avon, gawking at cathedrals and ruined abbeys, and then settling into St. Hilda's College in Oxford for a month's study under a few British academicians. The program had been in existence for some years when in 1973 the university asked me to take it over. I accepted, and 30 students, many of them survivors of my British history courses, signed up. I was to be Director, Ruth was styled 'Assistant Director,' and we brought Pete along because he'd expressed an interest in crumpets.

The program had been designed by the KSU Center for International and Comparative Programs, working with a study abroad outfit called CIEE. Unfortunately the pre-Oxford tour had been made so "affordable" that our accommodations were lousy. The first sign of this came after we landed at Heathrow and arrived at a shockingly ratty little dive, the Sovereign Hotel. The dead plants in Reception betokened what awaited in our rooms; I was glad they were lit with only 15-watt bulbs because I was afraid of what we'd see growing under the beds. My students, used to dorm life, were fine with the lodgings but close to rebellion after tasting the Sovereign's cuisine, which we'd already paid to consume for five days. The hotel served us ghastly meals—breakfast was baked beans and a piece of pork fat, toast optional, while dinner every night but one, for five nights, featured pressed turkey and something that looked like cabbage but smelled like fish and disinfectant. The one exception was the night when, for a change, we got pressed fish with cabbage that smelled like pressed turkey, with a double helping of baked beans.

Thus powered, we trotted around London, ogling Big Ben and Speaker's Corner between bathroom breaks. The weather was pleasant, but there were mishaps that earned me my Director's stripes. One student developed an impacted wisdom tooth and gobbled codeine tablets for a week till okayed to totter into a dentist's office; another needed an eyeglass repair after being rudely jostled by Japanese tourists in Westminster Abbey; and then of course there were those who wandered off and got lost, and those who didn't show up on time in the first place, and the ones with feminine emergencies, lost garments, blisters, body odor, sore feet, and two mysterious hickeys on the neck.

After London we began our 7-day bus tour, which also seemed to prove how shabbily our group had been treated by CIEE. The bus rattled like a barrel of castanets, our driver was gruff and truculent, our guide, though a very nice young man, was only that. He'd never guided a tour before and was only a high school graduate—which left me sitting up front with him, sharing his mike. But the experience wasn't all bad. One nice pre-arranged highlight was a tour of Windsor, followed by a meeting with the Mayor of Windsor and his wife, the Mayoress, followed by a glass of sherry in the Guildhall. We mingled with toffs!

A new low came when we reached the Lake District. We'd expected to stay for two nights in a decent hotel near Grange-over-Sands but instead were sent to Keswick and were there received by the individual responsible for this unwanted change in arrangements, a young lothario wearing trendy aviator glasses who produced a surprise list dividing our group into two separate hotels which he owned, ten miles apart. In a letter home I recounted what happened: "A young, rich and highly egotistical young man, a bit of a satyr, owned both hotels and obviously intended to prey on the girls in our group. We arrived at the first of the two hotels and found that the rooms there had been assigned, by the manager himself, one to me and Ruth, and all the others to 11 girls!—his idea being that 'Dr. Newman' would be, like Roy Wenger [my predecessor], a decrepit old fossil who would turn in at 6:30, leaving the girls (with no accompanying boys) to this Romeo, who had carefully planned a 'Folk Sing' for both nights in the intimate and cozy licensed bar within the hotel."

And of course *he* was the "Folk Singer"! The owner-lothario professed to be a musician of great fame and popularity, telling me he'd been signed for a tour, next year, to the U.S. for $80,000. My reaction: "What a crock! His voice was mediocre, his playing terrible, and his ruddy goatish face and ears went limp when he found that 'Dr. Newman,' far from decrepit, would not hear of such an odd hotel arrangement." I scrapped his room lists and insisted that the rooms in both hotels be divided equally, as they had been in other hotels, between pairs of girls and boys, and then I proceeded to stay up as late as everyone else in the 'Folk Sing' event to watch him like a hawk through both evenings!

The down side was that this left me totally unaware, for two nights running, of the locked bathroom tristes arranged by one of my less intellectual students, the handsome and, it seems, prodigiously virile Franco Laguardia, who, I learned later, was in fact, while pleading headaches for his absences from the 'Folk Sings,' inviting and enjoying oral sex from quite a surprisingly large number of the young scholars I was endeavoring to protect from the hotel owner! It was only later that I learned this, and in fact I learned it purely by accident, when, one late night in Oxford, I walked into a Gentleman's toilet and found Franco and Susan Olson in flagrante delicto oris.

Then the whole story of Franco's multiple conquests came out. He was a charmer, and it seems he'd actually begun serial auditions in the airplane restroom on the way to Europe! I've got to admit that I quite liked Franco—he was very proud of his Italian-American background, by the way, and we'd often exchange "buongiornos" and "ciaos." But I'd never given him credit as a quick worker, or indeed as any worker at all. Whatever became of him? Considering his early success rate, it wouldn't surprise me to learn that he ended up with many adherents falling to their knees in admiration.

The bus tour was a big success. There was slightly more culture than beer consumed along the way, which is all a study-abroad director can hope for. At last we pulled into Oxford University, where my students would be educated for a month in a variety of subjects—English government, diplomacy, educational practices, artistic and musical culture, and so on. I was in high hopes, imagining that I'd gotten through the worst part already. Unhappily, from the moment we arrived we were treated like gate-crashers by our host and contact man, a senior member of the university's Department of Education, John Francis, a frowning insufferable prig who also happened to be Chairman of the Oxfordshire Conservative Party!

He demonstrated his slim regard for his paying American guests by showing up two hours late—two hours after our group, tired from its travels, waiting to be assigned its rooms, arrived on time at St. Hilda's college.

He made no apology; instead, with his prim mustache and penetrating gaze he resembled a magistrate eyeing a gang of confessed felons. As if to confirm my fears, before assigning our rooms he began unpleasantly with a speech notably full of demands and prohibitions and stipulations, as though we were going to tear St. Hilda's to the ground! In a letter home I wrote that "I believe he expected a hayseed in charge of an army of savages, and was trying to browbeat us into line from the beginning. He's apparently used to bowing and scraping, smiling and lying; he acts like he's used to having his slightest suggestion taken as holy law. It was obvious from the first moment that he looked upon our group as 'lesser breeds without the law,' barbarians who'd be charmed to be fleeced and spat upon by dignitaries like himself."

Just arrived at Oxford University

Do I need to say I stood up to him? Furthermore, I do believe my students got their money's worth from the academic program. The lecturers were good enough, and the reading assignments well chosen. I found additional pleasure at meeting several well-known resident historians such as J. H. Plumb, Max Beloff, and Geoffrey Marshall. In fact Marshall even kindly invited Ruth and me to dine with him in his private chambers in Queen's College. This was, however, a very unfamiliar and somewhat strange situation for us, to be eating a nice dinner in that ancient wood-paneled chamber, just the three of us—or rather the four of us when you count our uniformed servant who not only helped us to the dishes but then stood there attentively by the wall as we continued to eat and chat. He had a pleasant face, he smelled slightly of cologne, he looked to be in his forties; I didn't even know his name. He stood no more than eight feet away as we sat there for more than an hour. It's as though he were a limo driver, but without plexiglass to wall him off.

Geoffrey Marshall, as we prattled on about the state of the world, acted as though the fellow was invisible. I, not comprehending how to acknowledge the man's presence while totally overlooking it, was confused. To ignore the fellow as a mere servant was expected: we were, after all, licensed poohbahs, discussing public affairs. But didn't he have opinions? Shouldn't I, as a small-town egalitarian from a breakaway democratic country, find some small way to include him in? I half-chose to do so, sometimes glancing or smiling at him while keeping up my side of the chit-chat. I thought I saw him smile back once or twice, silently acknowledging my glances, though for all I knew he might have been deaf as a post.

The whole episode taught me something new about what sociologists call "class consciousness." The room had been full of it, but it'd been experienced in very different ways by the Americans on one side, the Englishmen on the other. Yes, I was still learning, still trying to figure out the ways of the world, still trying to fix my own stupidity. It's never too late.

10

Pole Observer

WARSAW, POLAND, 1980S

Before writing this chapter, which I think might turn out to be my favorite, I've got to say something about a very painful subject, my separation and divorce from Ruth in 1978. I want to say I spent a dozen happy years with Ruth and don't regret a single one of them. She made me very happy; she had extraordinary qualities, she was intelligent, sympathetic, sociable, impressive. And she could be such fun. It should be obvious from what I wrote earlier that I deeply loved her. We had so many delightful times together, times I still treasure and can relive by returning to my diaries and photos.

But to do so is painful, and I don't make a practice of it. The fact is, we grew apart in Kent, then resentful, then willfully inattentive to maintaining our love, and then at last too mulishly stubborn to fix our problems the way we should have. We should have given counseling a chance. Instead, we stopped working at our marriage. And it's certainly no excuse, though I find it a very curious and perplexing fact, that while the national divorce rate absolutely skyrocketed in the 70s—statistically the all-time worst decade in history for American marriages—all three of us hired in 1970 (Balsama, Friedman, and me), together with two others (Kenney and Louis), and even my old friends Dave and Lizzy Davis, broke apart and got divorced.

I'm no sociologist, I can't explain that and won't try to, though I think there was something in the battle atmosphere of the 70s—there was a lot of battling going on. All I can do now as an old man is take responsibility for my own failures, which were many, and express my regret. I envy couples who stick together through thick and thin; their lives seem beautiful, and a reproach to mine. For what it's worth, I do believe my marriage might have survived, Ruth and I might have overcome our problems, if I'd taken that job in Canada, a very different place with a different group spirit and atmosphere. But of course I'll never know.

Up till the 1980s I didn't travel much; I mostly led a humdrum academic existence broken only by family trips to Washington State. Travel is, of course, a major fringe-benefit for college teachers, it's a special inheritance of educational workers ever since pioneer days. For me, *foreign* travel was a special asset. Teaching the histories of England, Europe, World Civilization, and 20th-century wars, it was of great value to have been, in some measure, an eye-witness to the people and places I was teaching about. What I learned from foreign travel I recycled to my students. And, to return to my original theme, travel is, I think, one of the shortest and best ways to fix all kinds of stupid.

A big opportunity came in 1988 when I was invited to teach behind the Iron Curtain. I accepted, and made the trip with my new roommate, Barbara Clements, another professional historian. Barbara taught at the University of Akron. She struck me as one of the brightest people I'd ever met. Raised in Richmond, a Phi Beta Kappa type at Westhampton College, she'd gone on to Duke, earned her doctorate, and begun an impressive career not only as an increasingly famous scholar but as a teacher, mentor, and even as president of the Ohio Academy of History—a proof of her smartness, popularity in the profession, and remarkable people skills. I must say I've never encountered another academic so well-read, so intimately acquainted with material in her own field, yet able to converse knowledgeably with, say, bird-watchers, and vulcanologists, demographers and medical practitioners. If she'd been at that Harvard party I described earlier, she might have put down half the twits I met there. Her only big fault is cosmetic. I don't blame her for being much smarter than I, but I think she should try harder to conceal it.

Her field was Modern Russia and the Soviet Union, so her professional expertise made her, in the eyes of the suspicious Communist governments of the 1980s, a "Soviet expert." No country in Eastern Europe, no "satellite" nation taking orders from Moscow, would let her enter and run around there, making notes, taking photos, conducting interviews. I, however, a specialist in Britain, had been offered a teaching post at the University of Warsaw for the Fall of 1988, and wanted to go. Could Barbara come too? The problem was that if she came as just herself, an unattached Soviet specialist, then this might inspire the Polish government to investigate who she was, misidentify her as a spy, and throw us out. Together we went to talk with Bob Clawson, KSU's manager of faculty exchanges. His advice was unequivocal: Tie the knot if you want to go without worries.

Being unmarried chums had worked so well, but we decided to risk it. "I will, if you will" lacks mystery, but it brought Barbara's mother, recovering from astonishment, from Virginia to wit-  ness the event. She, and Peter (who was then 15), and a few others, helped us cel- ebrate. We sat down to plan our trip and immediately hit upon the idea of visiting Western Europe before disappearing be- hind the Iron Curtain. Livia would come with us, return to Portland for school in September (Portland was where Ruth and her second husband lived), then fly to Warsaw with my parents at Christmas.

~

First we flew out to Washington to attend my dad's 76th birthday cel- ebration on July 24. That was a big outdoor party, attended by lots of peo- ple. Earlier he'd scared us with lung cancer, and everybody wanted to show him how much they cared. It was a great affair, and he expressed his humor and legendary hospitality in a way that made everyone happy. Barbara was by this time a family member, and, having lost her own dad when she was only nine, felt a special bond which he very genuinely reciprocated—he liked and admired her, and on family trips they'd sometimes poke around together like ancient buddies.

And this may be the place to mention that my own relations with him had greatly improved. He was now always cheerful when I was out West, and when I was in Ohio he'd add jocular postscripts to my mother's letters. We even began exchanging stupid presents, a sure sign of camaraderie. I remember an absurd pair of Hammacher Schlemmer bedroom slippers, "Night Mates," ugly stiff black things with small lights in their toes to help the wearer see where he was going when creeping in darkness to the bath- room. Chortling, I gave them to him as a birthday gift, he later rewrapped them and gave them back, then still later I returned them with a wisecracking card. Now, stubbing my wizened toes against bathroom doors, I miss them.

We set off on our grand adventure, visiting Athens, Rome, London and Paris. It was in Italy that we had our silliest experiences. When we visited St. Peter's Square in Rome we noticed a warning posted for tourists: it said that women with their arms uncovered would not be admitted to the Vatican Museum, and that males wearing shorts would be denied admittance also. We took note of that because, next day, we had a morning appointment for a guided tour of the museum; in late August it was hard to land such tours.

But we forgot all about that the next day as we hurriedly dressed, then dashed from our hotel to the bus that would take us to the museum. Halfway to the Vatican I suddenly realized, with a start, that Peter was wearing shorts! "You idiot!" I yelled, startling the Italian passengers. Peter's attire would keep us from entering the museum. But there was no time for griping. I had to find a way out of the predicament. Then I saw it. "Act retarded!" I yelled at him (that was an okay word back then). "Let your jaw hang, and look dazed! Look stupid!" He tweaked his everyday expression and looked like an imbecile.

Soon we reached our destination, and as we hurried from the bus I took his wrist, as though helping him along—he was nearly 16—and we proceeded in that fashion, with Barbara and Livia behind us, all the way to the entrance where we were to buy our tickets, and where I could see our guide in his pink shirt waiting for us. At that point I coached Peter to limp a little, too. We edged through the gate, with me paying our entrance fee and hastily saying, as a way to explain the young man's shorts, "He's slow. He's verr-ry slow." The Admissions guy nodded sympathetically, and we were in.

So the guide began our tour. I asked a passer-by to take a picture, and in it one can see Pete looking like a zombie. With our guide tuned to Pete's diminished intellect (I was still clutching his wrist), he conveyed his tourist information very carefully and verry slowwlly—so slowly that after about 15 minutes of this I prodded the guide to speed it up—"He's not THAT slow," I muttered, dropping Pete's wrist and striding more briskly toward the next exhibit. So the guide speeded up, and we began moving along like a more normal group.

It was only then that I perceived other males freely strolling here and there, totally unimpeded, wearing shorts. What the @#%&*!?? I'd gotten myself so uptight and worried about the dress code—but this was ITALY, for gosh sake! That warning sign, the day before, in St. Peter's Square, was meaningless. So it turned out that the biggest idiot in our party was, um, me.

To set in motion a different fiasco we rented a car and drove south on the E45, passing the famous abbey of Monte Cassino. We visited Pompeii and got pick-pocketed in Naples, but the highlight, if you can call it that, was dinner in a family-owned restaurant on a cliff overlooking the Bay of Naples. The place was nearly deserted, and the skulking family members who let us in looked more like peasant goat-herds than restaurateurs. I ordered a simple pasta dinner with, to share, something from the local catch.

The pasta was agreeable enough, but the fish wasn't—it was smaller than an anchovy. Oh well, the experience was what counted, no? So after dinner I pleasantly called for the check, and as we sat enjoying the view of the Bay, and waiting for a very long time in this nearly-empty restaurant, I began growing impatient and a little worried. Looking around, I could see, in the kitchen, the entire family of goat-herds, big ones and small ones, gathered around a table where the senior male, sucking on his pencil, was working out exactly how much he could get away with overcharging me! At last he came out and presented our bill—more than 50,000 lira, upwards of $60! I nearly fell off my chair! However, he cut our price in half after I jumped up all nasty-faced and loudly showed I knew the Italian word for "police," yelling it loudly several times, "Polizia!!!" I'd seen it on a bus placard.

We spent a great week in London, another in Paris, and then at last our wonderful West European travels came to an end. The approach of October meant it was time to go to work. We prepared to fly through the "Iron Curtain" to land in a different universe. We landed at Okęcie Airport outside Warsaw on the evening of September 26. We'd stay 15 weeks and learn more in person than we could have done in a lifetime of reading.

Poland has an illustrious history. It had defended Europe against the Turks, its monarchs had been admired and feared, its artists envied everywhere. Warsaw, Kraków, and Łódź were centers of culture and refinement. But Poland was a battleground between Germany and Russia, so there were tragic invasions and annexations. If the two bordering powers were to invade simultaneously, which would the Poles fight first? Their answer: "The Russians." Why? "Pleasure before business!" We found that while many Poles disliked Germans, they despised Russians as uncultured brutes.

Poland was the initial battleground of World War II when Germany invaded on September 1, 1939. The bordering powers then divided the country for six years, the Germans dominating till war's end in May, 1945. Poland suffered more deaths per capita than almost every other country. Thousands of its citizens, Jews and gentiles, were slaughtered; 700,000 died in Warsaw alone. Polish resistance produced even more misery. The brave attempt to throw off Nazi rule, the Warsaw Uprising of 1944, resulted in one of the most cruel and vengeful acts of modern history, the Nazis' intentional demolition of the entire "Old Town" of Warsaw. With dynamite they blew up the Royal Castle, the opera house, the archives and many palaces before retreating to Berlin. And meanwhile, just across the Vistula River that runs through Warsaw, the soldiers of the Red Army, directed by Stalin, sat on their hands. They deliberately permitted the Germans to complete those demolitions, the better to extinguish the Poles' fighting spirit and prepare them for Russian annexation when the Germans pulled out.

And so when we arrived in September 1988, we came to a victimized and impoverished country only recently pillaged again by its neighbors. Gallant Poland was desperately poor and had suffered indescribably. We came to an historic city, Warsaw, whose cemeteries and streets were full of memorials and tragic markers of slaughter and execution and heroic resistance. Poland was now a major Communist "satellite" whose regime was itself a vivid reminder of the country's endless suffering under foreigners. Forced to adopt an alien system, it was part of the broad strip of Russian-dominated states behind the Iron Curtain—East Germany, Poland, Hungary, Czechoslovakia, Romania, Bulgaria, Albania, Yugoslavia. In power was a pro-Russian dictator, Wojciech Jaruzelski, supported by the Polish Communist Party, the Army, and Soviet force if needed.

That system would tumble down later, but when we arrived the Communist regime seemed permanent to us, and it did also to the Poles we interacted with. Barbara, in a letter to her mother, wrote that "the mood of the people is awful. Everyone we've talked to is gloomy about the prospects for improvement. They don't think real change will be allowed." Communism was something Poles expected to live with for the rest of their lives. No one we met had any inkling that the whole system would collapse, that the Russian leader Gorbachev would usher in the breakup of the Soviet Union itself. That great eastern force still held the satellites in its paralyzing grip like a deadly spider.

~

We arrived in darkness that September night and were picked up by Krzystof Michałek ("Kchistoff Mihawek"), a smiling middle-aged character in strange clothing with a pencil mustache and somewhat shaky English. He was an historian at the university, and it was his job to show us around and assist us with our basic needs. We climbed into his car and proceeded through extremely dark streets in the city's outskirts. I was surprised by the darkness; even the bus stops were so dark I could barely make them out. We passed buildings that looked like shops, but there were no neon signs, no advertising to be seen, nothing to identify them. It dawned on me that night-time advertising is unnecessary in an economy where there's no competition; Pete got it right when he wrote his grandparents that "the government doesn't believe in advertising or any kind of decorations on buildings so the whole town is really ugly and boring to look at."

We reached a building constructed in the featureless style of the ugliest office buildings of the 1950s. That was Smyczkova ("Smeechkova"), a dormitory used by Warsaw University for important guests. The halls were so dim that we almost needed flashlights to find our room. Next morning I went onto our little balcony and noticed big white chunks of building styrofoam sticking out through the plaster and paint, and in a nearby courtyard I saw a mountain of dirty metal water pipes, looking as though the entire water system of an apartment house had been torn out and discarded.

Krzystof Michałek, our "Red Shepherd"

Later I found this to be a common sight. Throughout Warsaw all the water pipes in the buildings were, every five years, *jackhammered out of people's kitchens and bathrooms, and replaced with new pipes by squads of plumbers.* That's because of the corrosive chemicals and solids in the water supply. Unfortunately I didn't learn about that before drinking water from our own tap, so of course I soon grew sick with a sore throat. A doctor gave me the all-purpose medicine, garlic.

In our hallway I saw a young woman on her knees, using a scrub brush to clean the floor; her blond hair was obviously dyed and looked very coarse. We chatted, and Jagoda later became Peter's good friend and ice-skating buddy. Taking a taxi to the university, we were treated by its driver to a violent anti-government diatribe. He was thin, wiry, sixtyish. Hearing us talking in the back seat, he broke out his English. As we passed the offices of General Jaruzelski he flew into a rage and shook his fist at the "Red House, Red House"! He bitterly complained that even though he was a qualified engineer, for six years he'd been driving a cab, thanks to some government screwup. He was still yelling when we reached the gates of the University. They were heavily scaffolded, and I was later scornfully told they'd been "under repair" for decades.

Things brightened up at the American Studies Center where I met the director, Michał Bartnicki, and learned about my work assignment for the Fall Term. I would teach 18 students, once a week, under the authority of the English Language Department, and would be able to perform my duties in English—the students were proficient in it. What a sweet gig! Bartnitzki went on to explain that my pay would be in Polish Zlotys and that it was *strictly forbidden for anyone in Poland to work for, or be paid in, American dollars*. He spoke of dollars in hushed tones as though referencing something sacred, and suddenly I felt glad I had some.

My classroom at the University of Warsaw; top student Melanie Melcer at left

He handed me a salary advance, a paper bag full of Zlotys in huge denominations. The smallest bills were 200 Zlotys, the largest 20,000 Zlotys. Polish price inflation stood at 70%: the country's "soft" currency couldn't retain its value the way "hard" currencies of capitalist countries could, so Poland's constantly rising prices created desperate battles to exchange savings for dollars. Peter wittily summed things up by calling low-denomination bills "potties," because although nearly worthless to us, they'd be handy in toilet emergencies.

Krzystoff soon arrived to show us the city. While waiting for him, someone had confided that he was a member of the Communist Party. I began thinking of him as our "Red Shepherd," and, seeing that he was a good-humored fellow, I told him so. He laughed out loud—he was a congenial guy and a good sport. He told me he specialized in American History and that although he admired *Herbert Hoover* as a great man, his greatest idol was *John D. Rockefeller*. Our Red Shepherd was a big fan of American capitalists! He'd written four books about them and had another in the press. Flabbergasted, I asked how he'd managed to accomplish so much. He smiled and said, "Andrew Carnegie taught dat it vwass good do beginn one's career urlly in life, and I bigan studdying Ameriggan history and lit-eracher when I wass vary young."

As we drove through Warsaw, noting the features of ordinary life, I was struck by how dirty everything looked. There was trash lying around, the shop windows were unwashed—another sign of the absence of competi-tion? The sky was ugly too, it was sooty and full of pollutants. City buses and dump trucks spewed filthy particles from their tailpipes. Didn't the au-thorities care about such things? Was it because Poland was being milked to death by communists? I glanced at Krzystoff's Swiss watch.

And then I noted the scarcity of stop signs: drivers were unregulated except for being flagged by the occasional uniformed cop standing by a street—he'd hold up a little sign, small as a lollipop, if he wanted someone to pull over. The dirty sidewalks were used as parking spaces, and I also noted that Polish cars were filthy. Weren't there any car washes?

Stopping in the city's biggest park, it too looked filthy; there was dust on the tree leaves. The only birds I saw were black crows in large numbers, cawing noisily. Were they the only birds that could live in that air pollu-tion? Then I spotted a lone sparrow. It was dead. Crows were eating it. Everything seemed weird and darkly threatening. Would I find ordinary Poles depressed too?

We stopped at what Krzystoff said was a typical grocery store, to learn about shopping. We stood in line outside it for such a long time that I wondered whether there was something wrong inside, maybe an accident? But, seeing people just standing there patiently, I gathered that this was standard operating procedure. At last we were given a small wire basket, the sort you'd carry on your arm, and that was the signal for admittance—you couldn't enter without a basket, and you couldn't get a basket without waiting for it. Finally we were inside.

Next step? More waiting. Looking around, I found the place jammed with people, baskets on their arms, lining up here, lining up there, in front of half-empty glass display cases behind which stood totally bored-looking employees wearing aprons.

If you wanted to buy a certain article from a display case, you'd write that down on a slip of paper, then go to another line in the store. That's where you'd pay up. After waiting in that line, you'd show your slip of paper, hand over some Zlotys, get your slip stamped, then go back to the display case, where, after more waiting, you'd show your slip and get your article—if it hadn't been carried off already by somebody else! Shopping in Warsaw, I perceived, was not like walking into an American Safeway, where, oblivious to the miraculous abundance and freshness of everything, you'd zip around filling your cart.

I tried to figure out what I was looking at. Why did Polish shops hold so few goods, and why was there so much rigmarole attached to buying them? Then I began to see the light. This was a communist society, where human equality was the ideal. Well, that's great. Philosophers from Marx to Mao had hated the greed, unemployment, inequality and suffering of capitalist societies; they wanted equal shares for everyone. But equal shares of what? What would stimulate production when the government owned all the factories and farms?

When private "greed" was a no-no, when entrepreneurial cravings for profit and wealth were banished, then how could an economy generate enough stuff to make people happy? The sad truth is, it couldn't; in economics, selfishness can be a plus—it fulfills the "supply" side in the mechanism of supply and demand. I began to see that chronic shortages, endless waiting in line, and infuriating rigmarole were the only way to equalize consumption in a society unable to generate enough goods and services to make people happy. The result was misery shared equally.

Resuming our tour, we passed the Russian Embassy, a huge grey building not far from the American Embassy. There was nobody near the Russian, but at the American we saw an immense line. Krzystof said that people began lining up at five a.m. to acquire tourist visas for entering the U.S.—often to join the underground economy, earn precious dollars, and return to Poland later. Many, he said, had relatives with whom they'd stay while breaking American law (which forbids tourists from working in the U.S.); others might simply stay on illegally. He said the number of Poles living abroad, thirty million inhabiting "Polonia" (the countries of the world-wide Polish Diaspora), was about the same as the number actually living in Poland. Chicago, he noted, was as full of Poles as Warsaw!

Then came another shop very different from the first one. Its interior looked much nicer and brighter, and there were fewer people inside. This was a "dollar store" of a very unusual sort. Inside we found a long counter like one you might find in a fancy American jewelry store. Under glass, as though too precious to leave unprotected, were fancy tins of German ham, boxes of Belgian chocolates, American cigarettes, Scotch whiskey; and, arranged attractively behind the counter, Italian leather goods, English tweeds, Irish paisleys, French silk scarves. The store's attendants were nicely dressed and attentive, and due to the paucity of customers, there was no waiting.

This was one of Warsaw's "Pevexes." It too was government-owned, but it only accepted dollars for purchases; its mostly imported goods bore price tags in dollars. I found this paradoxical because the Pevex had to be paid in a currency which it was illegal to earn! I guessed that it catered to Communist Party members, but perhaps also to ordinary folk who might like to buy something luxurious *if* they could find the dollars to pay for it.

We stopped at the Forum Hotel, which Poles considered swanky, and sat down to tea and cakes. Idly perusing the dinner menu, I was astonished to see a four-course dinner of hors d'oeuvres, seafood, salad, roast duck, torts, ice cream and coffee for 3,000 Zlotys, or about $1.40 American! My brain reeling, we exited the hotel and found lurking outside a pair of shady-looking guys in grey parkas. They sidled up with wads of Zlotys in their fists and whispered, in English, "Change money, mister?" They wanted me to trade some of my dollars.

Krzystof, smiling, gently advised me against it, saying such activity was illegal, but noted that if I wanted to change my dollars into Zlotys—the only legal tender for any transaction outside a Pevex—I could certainly find friends, Poles with whom I'd grow intimate later, who'd "love to work with me on that." Everybody, it seemed, wanted greenbacks, "zielony" ("greens").

But that reminded me to ask him when we might expect to move from Smyczkova, our unpleasant academic dormitory, to better quarters—a two-bedroom flat, for example. He made an unhappy face. The problem was that housing was just as scarce as all other consumer goods, and, further, that landlords wanted to be paid in dollars; they wanted, in other words, to be paid under the table. So, since it would be illegal for me to pay rent in dollars, we'd need to wait a while for adequate housing.

Waiting, I saw, was big in Poland, very popular. Karl Marx, I began to think, was not just the Father of the Classless Society. Irreverently I began calling him the "Tata Czecach,"— The Father of Waiting. Marx was the patron saint of Standing in Line.

Continuing our tour, we circled the central business area, dominated by the towering Pałac ("Pawatz") Kultury, the huge but grotesque "Culture Palace" given to Warsaw by Stalin—some Poles laughingly told us later that its observation deck afforded the best view in Warsaw because that was the only location from which you couldn't see it! We drove through "Stare Miasto" ("Starry Meeyasto"), the colorful Warsaw Old Town that had been laboriously reconstructed after the Germans demolished it at the war's end; we had a look at the Ghetto Heroes Monument dedicated to the martyrs of the Jewish rising in 1943; we crossed the Swietokrzyski Bridge to take a better look at the Vistula with its barges and tugs; we moved out into suburban areas to look at the huge grey high-rise apartment complexes that surrounded the city, all of them identical, looking like giant, ugly fleets of battleships anchored on scrubby patches of grass.

As we drove near a church I saw its cemetery plastered with huge hand-made signs, and asked Krzystoff about it. He explained that it was a sort of impromptu shrine to an idealistic young anti-Communist Polish priest, Jerzy Popieluszko ("Yezhy Poppyushko"), who'd been beaten to death by government agents in 1984 for protecting Polish workers on strike, and helping Solidarity.

As we drove back to Smyczkova I saw, in the dusk, another very long line, a queue of Polish men waiting on a sidewalk to fill ordinary one-gallon plastic milk jugs with water from an underground natural well. The ordinary tap water, as I said earlier, would make you extremely sick if you drank it, so either you boiled it or joined one of these long lines for water that wouldn't hurt you. Later I myself joined such lines and waited hours to fill my own jugs. With nobody but Polish men near me I'd stand there in line, muttering my little joke, "Karl Marx, Tata Czechach," to see whether anybody got it. A few did.

Finally our tour of Warsaw came to an end. It was a day of discoveries, surprises, and a growing spirit of ironic chuckling and friendly amusement shared with our new guide and companion, our Red Shepherd. Krzystof understood our general perplexity because he'd been in the U.S. He didn't want to bad-mouth the circumstances of ordinary Polish life, but it interested him to observe our reactions, and he was almost as fully capable of laughing at the absurdity and contradictoriness of things as we were. We liked him, and he liked us; before long, he and I became very good friends. It was through him that I first began to see how many Poles overcame the limitations of their way of life.

⌒

Weeks later, Krzystof found another way to help us. He'd discovered an expatriate American couple, Anne and Fred Cook, who found us a comfortable apartment in their big grey apartment house, "Neseberska" (another suburban battleship), where we settled down and happily began our new life. Well, happily except for having to call the electrician twice, the telephone man twice, and the toilet man once, though he was drunk and stared more at Barbara than at the toilet.

For that apartment we paid monthly rent to Pani (Mrs.) Kobayashi, a Japanese woman, who, thanks to her friends the Cooks, kindly accepted our Zlotys along with a small green sweetener. I worried whether the communists running Housing would learn from those running The University that our rent arrangement was illegal, but our new Polish friends considered that hilarious: "One department of government bunglers never finds out what another one is doing!"

Next, a car. Krzystof took us to the tiny flat of Vitek Kosinski, a short, plump, smiling, energetic little man and his larger and plumper but very good-natured wife, Sofia, and their cute little eight-year-old daughter Julia, who, showing off her English, bade us "Good Morning" at eight p.m. Communication was highly iffy, but Vitek, so far as I could understand, was some kind of night watchman at a reform school, or else maybe a volunteer cheese donor at an armaments factory.

He had a dead-end job but was a real go-getter. He spoke no English but did know German, so although I'd flunked it twice I muddled through with kindergarten stuff like "Guten Abend" and "Ja" and "Nein" and "Auto" (pronounced "Ow-toe") and "Sehr Gut" and, of course, "Kindergarten," though finding opportunities to use that word was taxing. My favorite German word, though, was the one for "thing" (Ding), whose plural is "Dinge" (pronounced "dinguh"). I often attached it to English words as a suffix, hoping I'd be understood. So, for example, when I meant "bushes," I'd call them "bushen-dinguh," "bush-things." Pathetic, but there you are.

Sofia, the wife, knew a little French, so I told her I was "enchanté" to make her acquaintance, clicked my heels and kissed her hand in the approved Polish manner (I was getting good at that!), then offered "à votre santé" as she hauled out ceremonial biscuits and vodka. The mishmash of languages was laughable, although Barbara, managing in Russian, battled through. The other man in the room was introduced as Vitek's "little brother from Bialystok" (he was big as a bear), and it turned out that the car parked outside was his. So, accordingly, he and Krzystof and Vitek did all the car-talking; I, understanding nothing, handed over my paper bag full of Zlotys; we agreed to meet in 30 days to make a second payment; and then walked outside, got a short course in the car's mechanics, and drove back to Neseberska with the engine screaming like a machine shop.

Barbara and Pete with Vitek Kosinski

That was some car. With only 700 kilometers on its odometer, it was a Polish Fiat of the larger size, not the cheaper golf-cart size that most Polish drivers owned and hated. Although it was almost brand new, we found that the only thing that worked perfectly was the left turn signal. The car whined, it coughed, any random turtle had more acceleration, its brakes squealed like pigs getting slopped. Vitek's brother had taken it twice to mechanics and was told that all this was perfectly normal! I found I could barely shift its gears—it required all my strength to move from first to second, so sometimes I drove 15 miles at 12 miles an hour, not including rest stops. I've since learned from a car-fancying friend that even in Italy, where a better grade of Fiats is common, they're hated for their unreliability. "Fiat," he told me, is an acronym for "Fix It Again, Tony."

How appropriate, then, that our first daylight excursion in that car was a raid on the Polish state! More specifically, we conducted a brazen theft from one of the government's forests. Our co-conspirators were the Welbels ("Vellbells") and the Bugajs ("Boo-guys"), two blood-related families who became friends quite early in our stay.

The Welbels lived on the top floor of our apartment building, jammed into a tiny flat. We met them a day or two after renting our car when the whole family passed by in the corridor. The mother, Jola ("Yola"), was perhaps 45, stocky, blond with short hair, very Germanic-looking, with bright eyes and thickly accented English; she was extremely quick and naturally funny. She was a music psychologist and a fine violinist. Her husband, Stefan, was a psychiatrist; he smiled a lot and knew English also. He wore thick glasses and had the abstracted look of an academic philosopher—or of a father of four children, which is exactly the number he had; he also played the piano and was a skillful amateur sketch artist.

In fact the whole Welbel family was musical, artistic, creative. The son, Piotr, our son's age, was a math whiz and played the accordion, the older daughter, Marta, who was nimble and bright as a penny, played the recorder, her pudgy little sister, Basha, played the violin, and the shy little boy, Stash, played I forget what. The whole family lived four stories above us (there were no elevators) along with a mischievous white cat named Ramona (named, Jola told me, after the 1928 American song).

Jola Welbel

We met Ramona an hour later when we encountered the two girls lugging her past our door. Liking cats and missing our own, we invited the girls to leave Ramona with us for a while, to enjoy a saucer of milk and some petting. They did so, and before long Ramona was exploring the whole place. An hour or so later, Barbara decided to take a bath, and when she left the tub, Ramona, roaming a nearby countertop, spied the bathwater swirling down the drain and decided to attack it! So swiftly did she move that Barbara was unable to prevent her jumping into three-inch-deep water. And so, although we toweled her off, we had to take Ramona home quite damp. Of course this led to more pleasantries with Jola, who laughingly told us that Ramona did this at least twice a week in their own flat!

The Welbel family had acquired a tiny plot of land outside the city where they hoped to do a little landscaping, raise some shade trees, and start a garden. Promising a picnic, they invited us to see it. Coming along too were Jola's cousin, Tomasz Bugaj ("Tomash Boo-guy"), and his wife Alicja ("Aleetsia"), together with their children whose names I forget—just call them Tad Poles.

Tomasz and Alicja were, like their Welbel cousins, highly impressive individuals. Tomasz was handsome, about 35, with a little grey showing in his neatly trimmed hair and beard. He spoke perfect English, which was unsurprising because, having studied piano since childhood, he now traveled frequently outside the country as guest conductor from the Łódź Philharmonic Orchestra. He drove a Toyota—his eyes crinkled with mirth as he told me "Polish Fiats are very popular—with the Poles! Ha, ha!!!" He wore a tan English car coat, had an extremely pleasant manner, and laughed a lot, though with some bitterness, at life behind the Iron Curtain. He knew how hard it was to be Polish and happy at the same time, yet told me he would never emigrate, "for this is Poland, the land where the Poles belong, and who, leaving home behind, could be sure they were truly heading for richer lives?" His pretty, dark-haired wife Alicja was a concert pianist who specialized in Chopin: she played and taught in Żelazowa Wola, the village and birthplace of Frederic Chopin about 30 miles west of Warsaw.

Altogether, these two related families, the Welbels and Bugajs, were the most talented collection of people I've ever known. They not only invited us to join them, they treated us as friends. That alone made the whole Polish experience wonderful and memorable. And then, when my parents and Livia arrived at Christmastime, they widened their circle and opened their hearts even more, making everything so warm and musical and beautiful that none of us ever forgot it.

But, returning to that criminal afternoon: the purpose of our excursion was to plant trees on their barren plot of land. Where, I asked, were we to find saplings to plant? Jola pointed to the common land, the forest, nearby. Once I understood the plan, I organized it, and the eleven of us cooperated for three hours, sneaking into the woods in my big Fiat, digging up small trees and bushes, packing them into its trunk, weaving our way back to the Welbel plot under the eyes of inquisitive onlookers, and then replanting the trees as quickly as possible. "Ziss might zeem like ztealing," Jola remarked brightly (her smile was strong as sunlight—she was always ready to find the comic side of things), "But ze State belongs to everyone, so zees trees belong to no one, so zay are homeless and vee giff zem a home!"

Giving Bushes a New Home with Tomasz Bugaj.

I delighted in Jola's sense of humor and often tried to repay it. I remember how, two days before Thanksgiving, I went to a Pevex and bought a large Danish ham in a tin can, potentially the centerpiece of a large holiday dinner, and then got myself invited upstairs to the Welbels' flat with it hidden under my coat. Sitting on their sofa, drinking a cup of tea, I waited for my opportunity, then stuck it under the sofa when nobody was looking.

Turning conversation toward America's Thanksgiving, I told the Welbels all about our traditions, the turkey and gravy and dressing, and then related the cherished story about how Miles Standish and Wild Bill Hickock, thinking about food for the winter, had hidden all the smokehouse hams before inviting the Cherokees to come on over for Thanksgiving Dinner. "The Hiding of the Ham," I explained, had become one of the best-loved parts of the whole American holiday. Americans hid hams every November in unexpected places. But I cautioned that it was considered extremely bad manners, a rupture of civility, for anyone ever to mention the hiding, in hallowed memory of keeping the Indians in the dark and not giving them any ham.

The Welbels looked quizzical when I finished this ridiculous story, but I told it so soberly and with such reverential gravity that they refrained from questioning the monstrous selfishness of my pilgrim forefathers, and the conversation passed on to something else. Next day, Barbara and Pete and I went ahead with our Thanksgiving train trip to Prague, so we weren't in Warsaw when the Welbels found the ham. But they never mentioned it later.

~

It was wonderful to receive "care packages" from Kent containing things we couldn't find in Warsaw, such as decent toilet paper and shaving cream, or food articles like taco shells, salad dressing, and pancake syrup. Non-injurious toilet paper was impossible to find in Warsaw, and more significant items—apartments, telephones, car parts—were so scarce that people waited ten years without satisfaction. Krzystof, even with the privileges of Party membership, hadn't been able to procure a telephone; Stefan Welbel owned a small Polish Fiat but wryly explained it stood unused for years, lacking parts; Melanie Melcer, a good-humored student in my class at the university, smiled when talking about living in a storage space over a garage—she and her husband had no hope of finding an apartment. Indeed it was only by a stroke of luck that we ourselves were able to leave Smyczkova for a decent flat.

But although many things were scarce, others were plentiful—entertainment, for example, and education. Poland was poor in material items but not in intellectual, artistic or spiritual ones. Polish books, even illustrated art books, cost only pennies; we went to the Teatr Wielki ("Great Theater") two or three times a week, enjoying opera and ballet, sitting in the best seats near the orchestra pit, paying only 22 cents per ticket. Of course with dollars we had an advantage, but even so, to maintain Pete's education we paid excellent bilingual teachers, Leshak Sidz and Margaret Ryziak, to tutor him 12 hours a week in geometry and French; they both came from far away after working regular jobs, but refused the three dollars an hour I wanted to give them, calling it excessive. We hired Marek Sawaszkiewicz, *a coach of the Polish Davis Cup team*, to work with Peter three times a week to improve his tennis game, at the rate of two dollars an hour, and he wouldn't accept a penny more.

Coach Marek
Sawaszkiewicz

When winter arrived we found that the city's only indoor tennis court, used almost exclusively by Communist officials and foreign diplomats, was a place called "Mera." It was hidden away from ordinary view in a sunken area in a forest—the regime didn't want ordinary Poles to see this luxury enjoyed by the elite. I had to work hard to schedule court time there for Peter and Marek. My payment was arranged via a money-laundering scheme to buy, on behalf of the tennis court management, *400 German tennis balls*. (Remember, I couldn't directly pay dollars.) Polish tennis balls were terrible—even new ones went dead in an hour—but with credit for those German balls I was permitted to book a court for two hours, three times a week, *from twelve to two a.m.*—the Mera courts were in high demand. So we drove there, often through snow, in the dead of night. The court manager also tried to muscle me into writing "an invitation" to the U.S. for his son to go to Florida for professional lessons, but I pleaded inability to help. I didn't think of blackmailing him for better hours.

Pete's tennis coach, Marek, soon became another of our well-loved Polish friends. He was burly, red-haired, fiftyish, tough, and proud of his country—though certainly not of its automobiles! One day I asked him about eastern European cars. He laughed with contempt. He said there was a new "luxury" Polish Fiat, made at the factory that had produced mine, that had heat tapes in its rear window. The rear window was heated, he said, "Zo you can keep your HANDS WARM venn you PUSH it!" I asked him about other cars I'd seen in Poland: "What about the Russian Lada?" "Oh—veddy SLOWW!" "What about the East German Wartburg?" "Oh—veddy LOUD, NO STEERING!" "What about the East German Trabant?" "Oh—18 HORRSE POWER, veddy SMOKY as IRAK OIL WELL!!!?" "And the Romanian Dacia?" "Oh—NO PARTS, ze WORST KAR EVERR MADE!!!"

In our luggage we'd brought an unopened vacuum-packed tube of three Penn tennis balls. I handed it to Marek for Pete's first practice session and laughed at his pantomime when he opened it. He pried up its flip top, air suddenly whooshed, and, pressing his nose to it, he sucked in its fragrance as though it were the sweetest smell on Earth! I watched him coach Peter,

smoothly striking balls over the net at him (using his foreign-made rac-
quet, a French Rossignol), pausing now and then, exaggeratedly rolling his
wrist to act out the instruction, "More Row-TAY-shun, Peeder, more ro-
TAY-shun. Good! Oh, Oh, Oh, Ohh! Good! . . . Never Mind, Never Mind!
Now krosskort wiss ze backhand!"

On first meeting Marek I asked how much per hour he wanted: 3,500
Zlotys, or about $1.60. I insisted he accept more than that, and take it in
dollars. After my protests he finally accepted the princely sum of two dollars an hour, for three hour-and-a-half lessons per week. Peter received, for
nine dollars a week, instruction that you couldn't have bought in the U.S.
for less than two hundred!

And all this because the Poles were poor, their economy was a sham-
bles, and self-respecting people like Marek had to work extra hours at extra
jobs at ridiculous midnight hours if they wanted to go into a Pevex and buy
a can of Gillette shaving cream for $2.70, or a box of West German laundry
soap that wouldn't ruin their clothes, or a brand of French hair dye that
wouldn't turn their scalps orange in two days!

I said that Poland, as we found it, was economically poor but in many
ways so very rich and beautiful. Barbara, in a letter home, explained it in
her own way:

> Before we came here we were told that the compensation for all
> the ugliness was the warmth of the people, and we have certainly
> found people to be friendly. We have more social obligations now
> in a few weeks than we would have in 2 months in Kent. The Poles
> party a lot. I think they make up for all the crisis around them
> by cultivating friendships. The people here must depend on each
> other more than in the States for daily survival. I mean, if there's
> something good in the store, you don't buy one, you buy three and
> give one to each of your friends. And this builds closer relation-
> ships between people. So does the fact that most Poles are too poor
> to go out for entertainment, so they make their own entertainment
> with friends. So there's lots of warmth and hospitality, and that
> takes the edge off the difficulties and sadness of everything here
> for visitors.

Some people, like the Bugajs, were determined to laugh, to dwell in that Polish warmth and hospitality, and make the best of things. Tomasz, the talented orchestra conductor, could have emigrated with his family if he'd wanted to, but Poland, he declared, was "where the Poles belong." The depth of his feeling became more real to us when on All Saints Day we accompanied the Bugajs and Welbels to Warsaw's cemeteries, where, in cold and fog, amidst masses of candles, flowers, and people moving in silence, we visited the graves of their ancestors. We also saw those of martyred Polish heroes, and, in another cemetery, the graves of soldiers massacred by Germans during the Warsaw Uprising; and, even more heart-wrenching, the sad memorial to Katyn, where 15,000 Polish officers had been massacred by Russians in 1940.

When we returned to the warmth and happiness of Tomasz's home, Barbara said to him, "Coming to the cemetery every year gives you a chance to teach your children their history." To which he replied, "Yes, it is our strength." And then again he asked, or rather stated: "Could I really have a better life anywhere else?" Barbara, in an eloquent letter describing this exchange, concluded thus: "And we, who initially thought any Pole with the opportunity should get out of here, came to understand better what it is to belong to this place."

But what about that long line outside the American Embassy? There were other Poles who, having visited America, came away scarred. Jacek Hołówka ("Howovka"), a philosophy professor, was a specialist on Karl Marx (which was funny, because he hated him). I first met him at a party. He was small, bright, nervous, spoke nearly perfect English, and was married to another philosopher, Teresa, who was decidedly cold and unfriendly. They had two children, and Jacek, learning we had a son the same age as his, invited us for dinner, hoping the two boys could socialize. That seemed like a good idea, so we drove to their gloomy flat and sat down to an unglamorous meal served late by Teresa, who spent half an hour in her room after we arrived, not talking to us.

While Peter and young Tomasz went off to play games on the computer that the Hołowkas had purchased in the U.S., Jacek told us his story. In academic exchanges he had taught a semester at KSU, and, later, two years at Indiana University, bringing his family with him. The family's stays in the U.S. permanently altered their habits and satisfaction with life. Jacek, on the eve of returning to Warsaw from Indiana, had sent out more than 100 resumés to other schools, trying everything humanly possible to stay on in the U.S. and prepare the ground for permanent immigration. "But alas, there was no room for me," and so he and his wife and kids packed themselves onto a plane and returned to the motherland.

What a sad airplane ride that must have been. And now the man and his wife fought bitterly over the legacy of that experience. With us as his guests he sat there and grumbled and complained and laughed up his sleeve at the Polish life, and spoke in his flawless Midwestern-accented American English of his longing for the States, while his wife coldly announced that she and Jacek had a difference of opinion on that subject, and disclosed that she had just written a book on why she would *never, ever*, emigrate from Poland!

That book, I thought, must have been a coming-to-grips with the sad failure of her husband's attempts to transform them all into happy Americans. He blamed himself for failing with the job applications, she blamed him for screwing up their emotional life, and their children, I learned from Peter, blamed Poland for everything else. While playing, young Tomasz had told Pete that Warsaw was boring, there was nothing to do, he hated the place, and that one of the worst things was the filthiness. He'd shown Pete a school poster with a child standing in a scene of polluted air, with dying trees and vegetation all around, the legend reading simply "Nie!" (No!)

~

One morning the plumbers arrived and knocked at our door. Opening it, I found a man in a filthy workman's costume with a cigarette hanging from his lip, and a ridiculously tiny pair of welder's goggles pushed up on his brow. He handed me a slip of paper. Oh, no! We'd come to Poland the year our five-story concrete building was scheduled to have all its rusting water pipes jackhammered out and replaced!

At seven the next morning

I was wakened by Stefan Welbel ringing our doorbell. When I opened up, he held out the white cat Ramona and, with an imploring look, dropped her on our hallway and bolted back upstairs. Surmising that the pipe work had begun at the Welbels' and that Ramona was brought for fear she'd escape with their door open, I yelled after him to "please bring down the cat's potty box!" He shouted he'd bring it at once, so I sat down in my pajamas to wait. After half an hour I began trying to improvise; I'd take care of the problem myself. So I started wadding up torn newspaper for Ramona's bathroom needs.

But then, reflecting that we had no waterproof box to put them in, and becoming increasingly irritated at the delay, I started to stomp upstairs for the Welbel cat box when again dashing downstairs came Psychiatrist Welbel with little Stash, his four-year-old! Stash had to go wee-wee, and this was impossible because of their disconnected toilet. So Stash disappeared into our bathroom while I loudly petitioned for the cat box. Stefan, still looking dazed, was about to go for it when Stash reappeared and the two of them shot off again while I set out chasing Ramona, who'd hurtled out our open doorway.

It was a hard day for all concerned, even Ramona, who got splattered by the red wine bottle she broke in our storage room, and undoubtedly frustrated when relieving herself in our bathtub. The entire morning could have become a short movie with Stefan as clueless Stan Laurel and me as starting-to-boil Oliver Hardy.

A few days later the plumbers arrived at our own flat. Targeting our water pipes, they ear-deafeningly jackhammered the concrete around them in both floor and ceiling, used acetylene torches to cut them from our sinks, radiators, and toilet, and then deposited them outside in a growing mountain of bent rusted pipes, concrete chips, and foul asbestos batting. They also began excavating the grass patch outdoors, in order to change the underground pipes as well. Peter, in a letter, gave his reaction: "The goons, as we call them, are changing the pipes in our building. They woke me up at 7:00 with their incessant pounding. This has been happening for two weeks straight. There is a leak in the pipes in our area so they have been digging huge craters in our 'lawn' with derricks. There are five nice-sized holes in our 'lawn' and it looks like a WWI mine field."

In the true Eastern European spirit of sardonic amusement I began a photographic study of our outdoor mountain of pipes. I took pictures of them in morning and evening, with the sun setting on them, with dogs peeing on them, with the odd passerby sorting through them and helping himself to this or that scrap of iron. I even took pictures of them with the first snowfall of winter dimly glinting on their eerie skeletal outlines. Sometimes lonely crows sat on them, croaking their last hoarse chorus of the day. Yet over this ugly wreck as the gauzy sun went down you could sometimes hear, drifting through the fog, the sound of an oboe, the sweet solo voice of a violin played by a child.

~

When first renting our car from Vitek Kosinski and his family we'd handed over some Zlotys, partaken of ceremonial vodka and biscuits, and departed with the understanding that we'd do a repeat performance at seven p.m. exactly one month later. But when the day arrived, Barbara began wriggling out of going. She had writing to do, she said, so she couldn't participate in the handing-over of the loot and the ceremonial wafers and alcohol. Couldn't I go without her and make whatever small apologies might be necessary?

Peter, sizing up the situation, asked whether he couldn't stay home too and work on his French. So, although highly put out, I prepared to carry the ball and lie to Vitek about the others' indisposition. We had dinner as usual at 5:30, and, as Barbara had become something of a Soup Queen in Poland, I rather overdid the eating and stuffed myself to the gills. No matter, I thought, as I washed the dishes afterwards, belching pleasantly.

At six o'clock, Vitek arrived an hour too soon. There he was, full of smiles, waiting to be let in. He seemed to be all dressed up. I urged Barbara to jump into bed and pull the covers up over her clothes, so that when I let him in, I could gesture sadly at poor Pani Professor Barbara, so sick that she couldn't come to the handing-over-of-the-money! Vitek, when he spotted her, looked even more dumbfounded than when he'd caught sight of me in my grubby shrunken Polish pants and T-shirt. Was I supposed to dress up? His face fell still more when he saw Peter in his running suit, cracking his French textbook and regretting that he couldn't come, either.

Glaring at them both, I desperately cried "No matter! We'll be just as well off without them!" Hastily I changed my clothes, glaring with extra nastiness at Barbara because without her mediating in Russian I'd be a goner for communicating at the money-handing-over thing. We left in Kosinski's car with me clutching a large Polish-English dictionary like a flotation device in deep water.

Well, IMAGINE MY SURPRISE when Kosinski opened his apartment door! There stood his wife Sofia, dressed in fancy silks with ruffles, and little Julia ("Good Morning!") all bedecked too for the wonderful warm-hearted Amerikanskis who had been invited, though unbeknownst to them, to A FIVE-COURSE MEAL, EVERY DELICATE MORSEL OF IT HOME-MADE, WHICH WAS TO LAST UNTIL 11:45 THAT NIGHT!!!

I saw there'd been a serious misunderstanding. I pulled the longest possible face about the dreadful attack of galloping whatchacosis that had overcome the miserably bed-ridden Professor Pani Barbara and the so-sad-not-to-come young heir apparent. "But no matter!" I virtually shouted with gaiety, "I am here, and I am HUNGRY AS A BEAR!!! I'll eat for all of them!! Ha, Ha, Ha!!!"

Boy. Imagine what an ordeal it was. I tried to communicate with Vitek in German; Sofia, who knew no German, strained to catch every word and inclined her head like a puzzled cockatoo. I tried to eat up time by relating my story about how, driving Peter's friend Jagoda over to Smyczkova, I'd received my first traffic ticket from the police, who, having hidden behind bushes, caught me turning in the wrong direction and stuck me with a ten-thousand-Zloty ticket. My desperately tumbling words combined terrible Polish with ridiculously bad German and a word or two in Russian, and, where I could think of no word in any of those, I resorted to French which Sofia knew just a tiny bit, or to English which little Julia knew best among the three because she could count to six in it:

"Ja był eeetch do Smyczkova, wenn die POLITZEI sind AUSGEJUMP-PEN fom den BUSHEN-dinge, und sagt 'NEIN, NEIN, Sie konnen nicht seine SAMOHOT zu TURNen darum! Dlatego me dać EINE BILETY dziesięć tysięcy Zloty!!! Ha, Ha! Zabavna situacja, nicht?? Bardzo amusant, n'est pas?"

On their faces I saw puzzlement and exchanged looks of medical concern as I jumped from one topic to another, trying to look as large as I could as I sat in the middle of my side of the table which was set for six people. I not only had to eat for three, I had to be entertaining for three! I was alternately witty, grave, philosophical, and confiding, all the while thumbing madly from one place to another in the Polish-English dictionary, or handing it over to Kosinski when his German failed him.

And it only underlines how mortifying the whole situation was when I say that I had no idea at all of *how many courses of this meal I would have to eat!* The first tableful of food, I believed, was the sum of it until Sofia cleared away the dishes and brought out the *second* course. Imagine the tears of delight gushing to my eyes as I perceived that this was to be another full course, complete with salad and homemade beef stroganoff that Sofia had spent her meat coupons on! "Wunderbar! Ach, dass ist ZO GOOT!!! FANTASTYCZNE TONAĆ!!" I cried, while redoubling my kisses to the outstretched pinkies. It was only later that I learned this meant "Fantastic Lavatory," not "Great Cooking." I could have throttled Barbara when I got home.

The Kosinskis did at least get their really huge monthly jolt of American dollars, and they got another a month later. Soon Vitek started coming to Neseberska every time something new went wrong with the car. We'd conduct our diagnostic conversation in German. I'd say, "Die BLOWER dinge ist NEIN GUT. Er geht woooOOOOoooo un den er bleibt geshtoppen kaput! wooOOOooo, wooOOOooo." He'd scratch his head, then repeat: "wooooOOOOOOoooooo?" "Ja," I'd say, "Bardzo." He'd get out a wrench, murmuring reassuringly all the while, "kein Problem, kein Problem" (no problem, no problem).

Sooner or later he'd fix it, but on one occasion he couldn't. We believed the car's refusal to start came from a battery issue. "Kein Problem, kein Problem," he said. And then he said something like this: "Ja mussen ousgetaken den batterie vom KLEIN AUTO (meaning his own little car) und esgeben zu GROSS AUTO (meaning my rented car), und overnighten zu chargen up die GROSS batterie un den gibben es back zu you. Kein Problem."

So in the darkened parking lot he put up the hood of GROSS AUTO, then brought his KLEIN AUTO over to it, and got his frozen tools out of the trunk. I helped him unbolt and remove the one battery, then the other, and then exchange them. All the while he worked, with the puffs of steam from his breath curling up around him, and with his small pudgy hands moving this way and that—all the while, he muttered reassuringly, "Kein Problem, kein Problem."

So we exchanged the batteries, and then he invited me to get into the car and start it. Nothing. Absolutely zip. Not a sound. Dead as a doornail. Perceiving this, he suddenly lost his presence of mind and began wildly kicking the car's fenders, its tires, its bumpers, dancing crazily around the car and pounding on it with his frozen little fists, hollering an earful of obscenities in which I could only make out the words "Polski Fiat! Polski Fiat! Polski Fiat!!!"

And then, the fury subsiding, he became silent. He became thoughtful. He looked from the rented no-good big Fiat to his own little Fiat, which at least worked. "Klein auto ist gut? Klein auto ist gut? *IST KLEIN AUTO GUT?*" He'd found a solution. He'd give us his own golf-cart for however long it took to drag away and fix our GROSS AUTO. "Ja," I said, "klein auto ist gut." So for several days we used the small one, till GROSS AUTO whined its unreadiness to serve us again.

Spoofing Krzystof at my 50th Birthday Party

December brought the holidays, which, for me, begin on my birthday. That 1988 birthday was my 50th, one of the big roll-over events, so we decided to make it a big bash with all our Polish friends. It would be a dinner banquet in a fancy restaurant for 22 people, hang the cost. I also decided that while our invitations would stipulate no birthday presents, I'd surprise each guest with a customized gag gift.

So I went out into the mud, and cold, and polluted dark sky filling with snowflakes, determined to do some shopping. But I was often disappointed. I looked, for example, for a toy car, to give Vitek while telling a funny story about GROSS AUTO, and actually found one in a shop window. But when I went inside, grabbed the obligatory basket, and pointed at the car in the window, I was told "Nie Ma" ("Nyeh Mah")—"We don't have any." The car in the window was just for display—I couldn't purchase it. Well, maybe more toy cars were on order? Were more coming soon? The answer was "Nie Wiem" ("Nyeh Vyem")—"I don't know." So I'd ask, WHY don't you know? "DLACEGO?"("D-Lah-Cheggo")—"WHY?" And then, once again, "Nie Wiem"— "I don't know." These were, of course, State stores, government stores: the clerks didn't give a rat's ass whether they had toy cars or not—what was in it for them? Customer service? Pah! In four months I never once heard a "Have a Nice Day!"

Spoofing Jola

After every disappointing excursion I'd come home and blow off steam to Barbara and Pete. Fortunately, some gag gifts didn't require purchases. For example, Krzystof had once proudly informed me that the most wonderful dish in the world was "Bigos," which in fact is really regarded (google it) as the "Polish National Dish." But when I asked him, "What's in it?" he was evasive; in fact he didn't really know. Obviously he'd never cooked anything in his life. Bigos is a kind of hunter's stew. So as a gift I printed out, on gold-edged vellum, a bigos recipe with a picture of the stuff; then, for entertainment at the banquet, I told the story and handed it to him.

"Dlacego" = WHY?

That got a laugh—Barbara caught the reaction in a photo. She caught another of me and Jola. To "comfort and relax" Jola in her tiny, noisy, and always crowded flat, I gave her a large bottle of vodka and a sleep mask—another hearty laugh. There were American tennis balls for Marek, toilet paper hidden in a hat for Alicia, a square of parquet flooring for Melanie (in memory of her wish for an apartment), a ridiculous police commissioner's uniform for Jagoda (who'd been with me when I got that ticket).

To close the show, Barbara and Pete hatched their own hilarious surprise when they snuck up and thrust onto my head an absurd shopping basket, which they'd tricked out with a map of Warsaw and little signs reading "Nie Ma," "Nie Wiem," and "Dlacego." Bartnicki later posted a picture that shared the joke with the entire American Studies Center.

No sooner had we recovered from all this than my parents and Livia arrived at Okęcie Airport. They'd stay with us for ten days. I'd rented both Fiats and booked a room at the Solex Hotel, to enable all six of us to live and travel together comfortably. Then followed a dizzying profusion of events. There were memorable dinners, a trip upstairs to visit with the Cooks, a five-piece family concert at the Welbels', multiple visits to Teatr Wielki (*Fledermaus, Swan Lake*), a ladies' visit to a beauty shop for facials, a dinner at the Bugajs, a tennis lesson with Marek for Livia, a two-hour private Chopin concert in the flat of an old pianist whose husband had run off to France, a sales visit to our apartment by a silversmith bringing fine jewelry of amber and silver, a three-hour private lecture in our own flat by a Solidarity activist who'd learned his English in jail, a tour of Warsaw's monuments led by one of my best students, Melanie Melcer, plentiful street shopping at bazaars, and just general walking-around and sight-seeing.

Touring Warsaw with Melanie Melcer

And then, after all that, we piled aboard a freezing passenger train and rode 200 miles south to the ancient historic city of Kraków, where I'd arranged for a guide, Danuta Jamrozy, to show us Wawel Castle, Wawel Cathedral, the Cloth Hall, the Barbican, parading mummers and Christmas crèches—all before we bedded down in the Forum Hotel. Next afternoon, we took off in a rattling bus to Zakopane, a simple, small, quaint mountain village. Blanketed in snow, it was wonderfully picturesque, a charming nest for our family Christmas. I'd booked an entire floor of a four-story private home, a giant beautiful A-frame owned by Halina, a friendly woman and amazing cook. Next day, Christmas Eve, we went shopping in the village, then ate our way through her amazing traditional 12-dish Christmas Eve "Wigilia Supper." She must have spent weeks preparing it!

Zakopane, Southern Poland

At 11:30 we set off for the midnight service in the town church. Snowflakes fell and stars twinkled over its steeple. Already we could hear music—have you ever heard Polish Christmas music? Its beauty makes you ache. My mother recorded what she saw and heard: "Went to midnight mass, it was snowing lightly, sound of voices caroling through the darkness; the stone church was crowded; four priests conducting the service in Polish; I watched the lined, careworn faces devoutly singing carols and praying, and felt the deep faith of the worshipers who knelt to pray on cold stone floors; 'Midst Silent Night' was a most moving hymn." We were all deeply stirred. Barbara wrote that "at the end, the people crowded forward to form a central aisle, down which the priests passed, administering the host. I felt the beauty of the service. It was a wonderful, memorable night!"

On Christmas Day we lounged around, exchanged gifts, played poker, went walking in the snow, and then, next day, returned to Kraków. We enjoyed more celebration and music at Danuta's house—Mom played carols on their piano, and we sang to our hosts. At last we returned to Warsaw and then, on December 28, in the wee hours of the morning, took Liv and my parents to the airport for their flight home. There was a burst of laughter when my mother, peering into the darkness at the small terminal—it was the *only* terminal—asked the driver, "Is that Pan Am?" "Yah, Lady," responded Ryszard, our driver, with his sardonic chuckle, "That's Pan Am all right!"

We too, Barbara and Peter and I, departed from Okęcie some eleven days later; school would soon reopen in Ohio. I have a memory of myself climbing aboard the Pan Am plane that cold January day, buckling into my seat, and, as the plane began to taxi, hearing the pilot's voice on the PA system. He sounded like a Texan; probably he'd been in the Air Force. "Good Mornin', Ladies and Gentlemen, this is Cap'n Brown. We aim to make you happy and comfortable on your way to America. We up here on the flight deck, *we know that we're up here because you're back there!*"

Home Again! Capitalism! What an amazing thing! Good old Adam Smith! *They're up there because we're back here! They want us to have a nice day!*

11

Coming Full Circle

SINGAPORE, KENT, ELLENSBURG, 1990S

The 1990s saw me coming full circle. Of course I continued my teaching, sat on committees, ran History Day, and labored on that giant encyclopedia, *Britain in the Hanoverian Age, 1714-1837* (1997). Peter Stansky, my counterpart at Stanford, had asked me to take it on. Organizationally it imposed a monster task, as it required me to interview and recruit four sub-editors (specialists in politics, literature, the arts, the British Empire), then commission and edit 1,100 articles to make up a reference work of more than 600,000 words in a small-font volume of nearly 900 pages. The book, carrying articles by 250 specialists, now rests in most research libraries around the world. It's been savagely pirated for information now on the internet.

I was approaching 60, beginning to think about retirement, and this chapter seems like the right place in which to bring together many strands of my story.

I should begin by saying that the magical 1988 Christmas in Poland was just one in a series of warm Christmastime family get-togethers, annual events in which our far-flung family came together during the holidays. For a long while, for much of the 80's and 90's, there were nine of us, old and young—myself, Barbara, Pete, Liv, my dad Len, my mother Loree, my sister Lynn, her husband Tom, and their son Mike. Some of us lived in Ellensburg, others in Portland, others in Kent and New Jersey. We were an academic family, so, luckily, most of us were free to vacation during the holidays. Homing pigeons like many American families widely dispersed, we found ways to keep together, and the best way was by gathering at Christmas in the country home outside Ellensburg, Walnut Farm.

Every year the rituals were the same. In the great living room with its hanging silk rugs brought from Singapore we'd decorate the Christmas tree, pile our wrapped gifts under it, and hang for Santa our big red Christmas stockings, handmade by my mother. There'd be hearty welcomes and lengthy sharings of news as we stood, drinking, in the kitchen, and then we'd have friendly tête-à-têtes while pairing off to chat or play cards or help each other with secret little projects. Looking through the giant glass doors of the kitchen, we surveyed that familiar scene—the shivering hawthorn's boughs dusted with snow, the whitened lawn, the pond, the fences, the faraway fields, the low-lying eastern hills. Out the back door, in that cooler where I'd once kept my stash of Löwenbräu, there were shelves of wonderful home-canned peaches and apricots, pickles, dilly beans, homemade wine, potatoes in a box of sand.

On Christmas Eve we'd crack some crab as in ancient times, and laugh about Grandma Nellie feeding her cats. In the morning we'd open presents handed out by the kids, the adults chattering amid growing piles of gift-wrap. Funny hats, rubber noses, silly plastic spectacles with mustaches were donned in good humor. One time, we had a Dickensian Christmas Reading whose sentimentality was mocked by everybody who hadn't

thought of it first. As Christmas day progressed, with good kitchen smells filling the house, we'd get dressed up and sit down to a splendid late-afternoon feast. There'd be toasts to the Patriarch and Matriarch, there'd be more clever conversation, and after dinner there'd be walks on the snowbound road outside, football on TV, and penny-ante poker at the same table where my dad had once fooled me with BEER.

Some years, when there was little snow, there'd be family drives to Reecer Creek to look for Ellensburg blue agates, or to the Swauk where I'd first learned to ski, or up toward Lion Rock and Table Mountain, just to wander around, do something different, wait for somebody to find something interesting or say something funny. And then there'd be trips to White Pass, for skiing on the front side and the back, down Cascade or Holiday, Quail, Ptarmigan, Grouse, Paradise. Taking run after run, pausing for lunch, then riding back up the hill together in pairs, we'd laugh at people hot-dog-

ging it down the moun-
tain and vanishing into
snowdrifts, or being too
dumb to manage a rope
tow, or falling in piles as
they'd try to duck-walk
off the ramp at the top.
There at the top there'd
be the tightening of the
grip on the ski poles, the
dismount, the ripping
sounds of skis on ice,
then at last the exhilarat-

ing attack on the slope, skis slashing like knives in the snow to right and
left and right again. At day's end, after the last run, with the light fading,
there'd be the warmth of that snug condo, the trip to the heated open-air
pool with snowflakes drifting down, and finally the bed-time descent into
the quiet of the mountain night.

In summertime, Walnut Farm was again our family gathering-place.
Again we'd fly to Sea-Tac and be picked up by the jovial patriarch and babbling matriarch. Again there'd be embraces, catchings-up, drinks, snacks,
meals in the kitchen, everybody talking at once. We'd play "horse" on the
asphalt driveway, help with the lawn or pond, concoct practical jokes. Once

the three young'uns put on
a hilarious skit in the front
yard, mocking the adults.
We'd go to Wilson Creek or
the Yakima for fishing, we'd
drive to the Columbia River or Table Mountain, we'd
hang out at the cabin on
Lake Kachess, always chatting and babbling as a family
of talkers will do. We'd row
the ancient rowboat out onto
Lake Kachess, the mountains
around us, we'd troll slowly
for silvers, remembering my

dead granddad, reciting that ancient fishing incantation from long-ago days on Lake Sammamish—"'Bout Time to Catch a Fish," and "Sure Is!"

I remember that we turned my dad's 80th birthday, on July 24, 1992, into a surprise party. Invited were all his friends from the Valley and his relatives from west of the Cascades. They got advance plans to hide themselves, then show up at Walnut Farm at noon, precisely at the time he was scheduled to accompany Lynn into town "to buy a fishing license." While they were gone, folding chairs and prepared food would be set out in the yard, and then, when Lynn and my dad returned, we'd all jump out to surprise him.

But—not so fast! The plan required *managing him* all his birthday morning and, in particular, making sure he wasn't too sloppily dressed for it. We also had to ensure that he depart for town before his well-wishers arrived, and, of course, we had to keep him in good temper for the big hoop-de-doo. But he had his own agenda for the morning, and he could be stubborn.

Doubtless he assumed there'd be, at dinnertime, a cake and gifts as usual, but was that any reason why he, at age 80, a dawn-to-dusk worker all his life—was that any reason why he shouldn't spend the day in his grubbiest work clothes, balancing on a ladder by the giant maple trees out in the front yard, with a chain saw in his hands, lopping off their many suckering branches? Certainly not!

And so, when my mother, never entirely the soul of tact, went out into the front yard, hands on hips, at 11:30 a.m., to kick up a stink about the rags he'd dressed himself in, and about how disappointed the clerks at Bi-Mart would be if he showed up late for the fishing license, he got somewhat marvelously ticked off and incensed. *Why the devil clean up and hurry off to stupid Bi-Mart???* But she prevailed as she always did and off he went, grumbling, driving away with Lynn in the little white pickup.

Then the hordes descended and waited for him in the long, curling driveway, laughing at the story. I have pictures of his return. They show how delighted he was by the party, the friends, Livia's poem, the gag gift of the multi-purpose helmet Lynn and I had made for him (with twin feeders for gin and vermouth). And, of course, for his feet I'd gift-wrapped those adorable Night Mates.

Some summers, we took trips over the mountains to the "West Side." One year, 1994, we all drove up to Big Lake, near Mt. Vernon, and had a happy family reunion with all our relatives—Aunt Ruth, cousins Helen, Kay, Bill, and Claire—and returned to Ellensburg via Winthrop and the beautiful Methow Valley. During other summers there'd be salmon-fishing adventures at Sekiu or Neah Bay, with lots of togetherness, a few fish but more stories of fish that got away, and always my mother's tale of a certain king salmon that got bigger every time she told it.

There were sundry trips to Queets, Ruby Beach, Kalaloch and the Hoh Rain Forest, each with its ridiculous story—a utility bucket that marinated my tennis shoes in pee beneath an opened sewer pipe, my clumsy responsibility for a sanitary tsunami at an RV dump station. And yes, you're right, it was my fault for all those mechanical embarrassments. Didn't you know PHD stands for "Push Here, Dummy"?

Sometimes my little foursome took trips to Glen Ridge, N.J., to see my sister's family, where the same greetings would be exchanged and bonds renewed. Lynn lived there, not far from the highway where she and I, eating watermelon, had first traveled east many decades earlier. With her leading us we'd sally forth into Manhattan to see the sights, or we'd visit the schools where she taught, or take little excursions to Newark, or Montclair. Her husband Tom, my brother-in-law, also taught English at Montclair

State, and was not only an hilarious poet but the best raconteur in the family, and we had doubly amusing times when their son, my nephew, Michael Owen Benediktsson (now a professor at Hunter College), was around to entertain his cousins Pete and Liv.

On other occasions we'd drive from Kent to Virginia, where, in Richmond, we'd be entertained by Barbara's mother, Champe, and her sister, Winston. Barbara's mother was a woman of learning, grace, and humor. The first time we took Pete and Liv to meet her, I warned them that like all good southerners she was sensitive to breeding and kept a "Manners Trunk" for rude youngsters; they soon saw how absurd that was.

Our kids, on those trips, had great opportunities to see the nation's capital with all its monuments and museums, and Mount Vernon, and important sites of the Civil War. They had advantages such as I'd never imagined in my own youth; they saw the great eastern centers of American business, government, and history. They never guessed they'd both wind up living there, only minutes away from their dear aunt, my sister Lynn.

My mother, delighted by Poland, continued to plot big adventures to faraway places. For one thing, she wanted to return to Singapore to look for that wonderful mountaintop home on Bukit Timah, "Tin Hill," where she'd lived those glamorous prewar years. She designed a two-week itinerary to the Far East. My parents, Barbara, Pete and I flew from Sea-Tac and landed on Dec. 30, 1990, at Singapore's Changi Airport. While Christmas carols still strangely played in the 80-degree heat, we went to Le Meridien hotel, our base, a splendid place with a nine-floor atrium, glass elevators, and wonderful buffet-style breakfasts.

My parents were staggered by all the changes since our hasty departure in 1941, fleeing the Japanese Army. Even the famous "Merlion," half mermaid and half lion, the great mythic fountain that stands spouting water into the harbor, was a late invention, a city trademark invented by the tourist board. The metropolis seemed rich, luxurious, ultra-modern. True, the entire island of Singapore, though tiny, had always been one of the world's busiest ports, a major crossroads, prosperous and sophisticated. But now, 60 years later, the place was, to my parents, an unrecognizable mélange of old and new, combining Taoist shrines, Hindu temples, rubber factories, jade shops, and the venerable Raffles Hotel, with fleets of Mercedes and BMWs, McDonald's, mega-malls, electronics everywhere, and soaring ultra-modern hotels like the one we stayed in.

Our first outdoor adventure was charming. We went to the Tiong Bahru bird-singing corner, an open-air Sunday gathering place for bird-lovers. Bird-lovers in Asia are as common as dog-lovers in Appalachia. Singaporeans bring their pets in cages which they hang up high, and then they sip tea, admire others' birds, and let their own birds listen to, and learn from, others singing. We wandered through this Sunday School for songbirds, taking it all in, and then went by taxi to the top of Bukit Timah to look for the old dairy farm and sprawling villa with its tennis courts and "Jerry" swimming pool. All we found was a housing project called "Dairy Farm Estates."

We took a day trip into Malaysia, traveling by taxi across the Straits of Jahore, visiting the sultan's palace, and then riding up the long two-lane highway to the ancient city of Malacca. Along the way we saw strange homes—round shacks on stilts, to defeat snakes—and lots of cute Muslim schoolchildren near their madrasas, but our most curious discovery was a Chinese funeral shop for people preparing to bury their dead relatives. It featured small inflammable paper replicas of luxury goods—tiny Rolex watches, miniature BMWs, Motorola phones—to burn up during the funeral service, to ensure the deceased's happiness in Chinese heaven. You could buy fake American Express cards to burn up too, permitting your relative to charge things in the afterlife.

My mother, who during her earlier travels had outfoxed vendors from

Nairobi to Petticoat Lane, instructed us in the right shopping strategy: "Find an object you like, ask its price, look extremely sad and declare that 'that's more than I want to pay,' and walk away." The vendor, she said, would then come chasing after you, and you could haggle till at last you got the thing "for half price or better."

But before we could practice her strategy we were off to Changi Prison, where, during the war, many of my parents' friends had been held prisoner by the Japanese. Barbara, in her journal, noted that "Loree and Len were quite touched, for they had friends who died there, and they themselves might have, if they hadn't got out just in time." It was hard for older Americans to forget just how murderous and barbaric the Japanese occupation forces had been.

What I remember most about Singapore was our adventure one evening to an outdoor take-out food fair. I should point out that Singapore, so tropical, so clean and well-run, was a very popular destination for tourists: over the ages, the good people of Singapore had become very skilled at fleecing them. In restaurants this was often done on the pretext of "misunderstandings" about how much food had been ordered: a massive pile of it would be brought, along with a staggering bill.

My mother had heard that an outdoor "Food Centre" under the trees, in a park, was a good place to eat, so we went there. There were picnic benches under giant banyan trees, and stalls selling cooked food. The place was crowded with families, and there were pleasant smells of barbecue drifting around. The specialty, cooked and sold in every stall, was satay, which is a thin strip of meat, skewered and cooked over charcoal, then served on a platter with spicy peanut sauce. I ordered a platter of it from one stall, and while we waited for it, some fried rice and Tiger Beer from another. The latter came first, with the sort of bill you'd receive when buying a yacht. Barbara kept a trip diary in which she described what happened:

> Jerry got mad & argued with the guy over it; the auguries were not favorable for the satay still to come. After 20 minutes, during which Jerry and Len valiantly ate up the tasteless fried rice, and Len began to talk wistfully about McDonald's, the satay came, a huge pile of it, at least 60 sticks. Jerry's bonhomie and 'My-isn't-it-grand-to-be-here' spirit temporarily deserted him. He asked the price & the boy who had put this huge plate of satay in front of us said, "$30." Jerry got grim & said "No" or words to that effect,

"Half as much, $15 worth." After unsuccessful negotiations he got up from the table & went to tell the stall owner that either half of the satay went back or he would call the cops. That seemed to get their attention; they took half of it back. We then ate what was left, & it was pretty good.

I hadn't forgotten the lesson I'd learned at that goat-herder's restaurant overlooking the Bay of Naples.

The unforgettable highlight of the evening came when my mother and I, leaving our picnic table to look around, stopped at a table where some Asians were eating. A young woman and four kids were all eating satay, all drinking Coke. My mother, feeling genial and perhaps exceptionally mellow thanks to her large bottle of beer, had decided to test her half-remembered Malay on these nice natives. She'd try out her words and accents on them. How were they enjoying their meal? "Poco broppa tai tuan teeda oppa oppa?" The young mother looked puzzled. She seemed willing to help, but baffled. Mom tried again: "Poco broppa tai tuan teeda oppa oppa gorang?" The woman again looked at her, smiled hesitantly, and, pointing to herself, pinching her own shirt as if to identify herself, said, slowly, in perfect English, *"I don't understand you. I'm Japanese."*

My mother reacted instantly: "*YOU* DROVE US OUT OF HERE!!!" But then she added, feeling embarrassed, and laughing more gently (for the woman couldn't have been more than 30 years old), "But that was a long time ago. Never mind!" And with that we retreated to our table. My mother could be impulsive, but she had a good heart and could tolerate everything but cruelty.

Then we were off to Hong Kong. "Singapore is pretty, but Hong Kong is massive and powerful."—Barbara's trip diary. In a way, Hong Kong was as familiar as Manhattan, with skyscrapers, crowds of people, narrow streets, scores of neon signs, giant apartment blocks, shops of every kind. But it was otherworldly and strange too, with its outdoor markets and butcher shops full of still-living things jumping, crawling, crowing, cackling, swimming—soon to be somebody's meal.

And what about those drug stores?! We entered one and saw pharmacists measuring out quantities of toad oil, worm grass, edible swallow's nests, tiger balm, ground dog penis, shaved deer antlers, dried squirrel feces, ground blister beetles, and powdered centipedes. With patients handing them prescriptions, they opened big jars containing such compounds, measured out a spoonful or two, then mixed and wrapped them up for the patient to take home, brew in boiling water, and drink as tea.

We went to a Chinese opera where the performers wore fantastic colored costumes and magnificent ornamented headdresses, uttered unmelodious screeches in piercing falsetto (we couldn't tell males from females), and were occasionally interrupted by deafening clatters of gongs and clashing cymbals. Meanwhile the audience kept up a continual racket of conversation, freely walked in and out, loudly ate snacks, and then at the end, after more than two hours, walked out without a single "Bravo!" or even a "Mamahuhu.".

On one unforgettable night we rode a tram up to Victoria Peak and looked out over the entire city and harbor; I thought about the millions living there beneath the twinkling stars. I ate snake soup, I bargained for jade, I learned to distinguish Hong Kong dollars and cents, I bought a jacket for myself and a mandarin hat with a fake queue attached for my dad. Barbara was bilked of more than $70 U.S. by a fortune-telling Indian fakir in a red turban. On a high-powered jet-foil my folks took Pete to Macau, to gamble. We visited Kowloon and Stanley and Repulse Bay on water taxis; we learned a lot from a day-long guided tour of the Chinese Communist mainland, visiting the birthplace of Sun Yat Sen, walking through small villages, looking at little kids in schools, watching peasants drive water buffaloes through rice fields. "I'm so glad we came to this amazing place."—Barbara's diary.

At a dressmaker's shop my mother, wanting a raw silk suit, sat down beside the shop's owner to design the garment and haggle over what it would cost. The owner, an immaculately dressed Chinese gentleman with perfect English, was a smooth operator and a celebrated tailor. They sat together at a desk where he rapidly sketched different dress designs for her, modifying them with quick pencil strokes as he asked her about the width of the lapels she'd like, the length of the sleeves.

At last she was satisfied, and then came the hard part—how much would the suit cost? Two hundred dollars U.S., he said. "That's more than I want to pay," she said, reaching for her coat. "Oh, Lady," he said smoothly, "these clothes are not ready-to-wear, your suit will be hand-tailored exactly to your dimensions . . . . ." and then, slowly turning back to the penciled design, he began sketching a breast pocket, asking her, "Here, perhaps, a pocket?" She directed her attention back to the design, inclining her head to study it.

I could see that he'd won and that she'd pay the full $200. So did my dad, who was judging the action from a chair at the side of the room. His face all severe, he looked exactly like an American eagle—being skinned alive. I looked at him and laughed. He looked back at me, smiled grimly, and said, "Well, the more she spends on that thing, the less there'll be for you when I kick the bucket." Then we all laughed.

Earlier I described the night the two of them, sitting in his Ford on a hill near Pullman, decided to get hitched. Their marriage was on December 18, 1936. Sixty years later the family gathered at my sister's house in New Jersey to celebrate their diamond anniversary.

We sat around the big dinner table, feasted on prime rib, told stories, drank innumerable toasts, put on ridiculous paper hats, trotted out gag gifts. Lynn and Tom each read a funny poetic takeoff of Browning's 'How do I love thee?'—one of Lynn's lines, mimicking my mom, was "I even loved you when we were in jail" (a reference to a crazy event on their honeymoon), and Tom's last line, mimicking my dad, was "I even love you more than I love my tools."

Next morning, we all flew

off to "Orchid House" in Jamaica, a beautiful sprawling private home on the north coast, where we settled in for a week of fun and togetherness. We paddled in the small indoor pool, exchanged gifts, lounged around in our pajamas, played cards, told stories, walked the beach, bought crafts from the locals, ate wonderful meals prepared by the in-house kitchen staff. There were motor excursions to the Jamaican uplands, and to Ocho Rios, to climb the waterfall. My dad spoke for us all when he swore he "enjoyed it all, I love you and thanks so much for this memory."

That was the last Christmas for all nine of us together. Many years earlier, on a summer day, my dad had returned to Walnut Farm from a checkup in town and cheerily told Barbara, "Well, now I know what's gonna kill me!" That year he underwent surgeries for prostate and lung cancers, and, a few years later, for colon cancer. A decade later he had a midnight heart attack, took a few aspirins, characteristically sat waiting till morning, then drove to Ellensburg's hospital where he had a much more severe heart attack—the E.R. doctor brought him back to life with paddles.

He'd been lucky, but also he had his philosophy to support him. He had the healthy outlook of a medical man who'd witnessed and assisted so many births and deaths, seeing them as links in the great chain of being. He didn't fuss about his declining health when his cancer returned. In August 1997 he was picking huckleberries in the mountains, still enjoying life, but the end was coming. Receiving my mother's warnings, I flew to Sea-Tac several times, always grabbing a Whopper for him before arriving at Walnut Farm.

In one of our last conversations he observed how lucky he'd been earlier to outlive his lung cancer, and lamented that it was "too bad there was no euthanasia, he'd do it himself, make it easy on everybody." I told him "you'll always be my lead dog," and implored him, "How can I help you, Pop?" To which he slowly replied, with a sad grunt, "Help me die."

I helped him shower. He was sliding away fast, too feeble to climb into the tub. In my underwear, holding him under his armpits, I stepped into it, lifted him in, and supported him as the water sprayed on us, my mother soaping and rinsing him, toweling him off before we packed him back into bed.

Lynn had been regularly flying out to Washington too, and we were both there when he passed away. After a long flight I'd just arrived and gone to bed exhausted; later, deep in sleep, I heard her murmur, "Dad's gone." I woke up in a muddle, regained my senses; she repeated, "Dad's gone." I went to look. Soon the funeral people came and took him away.

It was still pitch-black out, three or four a.m. Lynn and I took a long walk down Tjossem Road together. Then in the dead of night, trying to drive away such sad memories of his suffering, we set about dismantling all the medical stuff in the house, ridding the place of its hospital aspect, restoring the home he'd loved. There was nothing else we could do.

It was November 12, my mother's birthday: on the day he died, aged 85, she turned 81. For dinner we went to El Charro, the Mexican restaurant, her favorite, to celebrate her birthday. Gamely she accepted the sombrero for the waiters' birthday serenade. She'd lost her life's companion, half her past had been ripped away, but she'd carry on, that was her nature. She was, as I said at the beginning, tough.

I wrote the obituary, telling my dad's life story and praising his ingenuity, industry, and honest dealing, ending it with my assurance that "he had lived, in truth, a wonderful life." We held a general celebration of his life, all his friends and relatives came, we carried his ashes to the Thorp Cemetery near the graves of his parents, uncles, and cousins, all shadowed by that great white monument commemorating the pioneering John Miles Newman. I fancy the Patriarch looked down with pride at his grandson's arrival.

Having refused a fancy urn at the funeral home, we buried his ashes in his old red metal toolbox, the one with the broken handle he'd replaced with a worn leather dog collar. He would've liked that. The makeshift urn was cheap, useful, far from new, and so very like him—we cheered ourselves by laughing about how *he* would have laughed at it. Here gone to dust was the handy farm boy who'd thought of making his wife a dressing gown from a parachute.

I confess we buried the toolbox on the wrong side of his grave marker, and I'm extremely hopeful our mistake will never be discovered. I certainly don't want to dig the old boy up just to move him three feet to the right place. My mother, who was sitting grave-side on a camp chair while we buried the toolbox, should have caught the mistake, but was busy contemplating the hills and Mt. Stuart. I just hope the nearby sprinkler we nicked doesn't need repairs till I'm out of here. If it does, somebody will experience a grave shock.

There were other mortal transitions that deeply affected me. Jim McAree, the Bellingham friend who'd stolen others' anecdotes, died in 1977 at the Capitol campus of Penn State. Tragically, he was only 55. McAree was one of those heaven-sent beings who make us laugh, whose wit helps us find entertainment in life's stupidity. We need more people like that.

Next to go was dear Gramlin, who died at 86. Falling ill, frightened of hospitals, she arrived at a nursing home where I came to see her. On my sad return flight to Ohio I remembered our last conversation. "I love you, dear old granny," I said, to which she replied, "I love you too, Jerry, with all my heart." Thank God I wasn't there for the funeral. My mother was appalled: "I didn't like what the mortician did to her. He put a padded bra on her, and built her up. She was flat-chested. He put make-up on her, and she'd never used much of that. She just looked like somebody I'd never seen before. I found it very hard." What an outrage. Yet the man probably thought he was just doing his job, comforting her family by prettying her up. What a world we live in.

The next to go was my great hero, Giovanni Costigan. He died in March, 1990, aged 85. The newspapers extolled his impact, and the *Seattle Times* quoted his comment, "I was born to teach—there was nothing else I could have done." But he was so much more than a teacher. He'd imbued thousands with values of tolerance and reason, he'd fought right-wing ignorance almost singlehandedly, and, in a famous 1971 debate attended by 10,000 people in UW's basketball arena, he'd mopped the floor with the supercilious William F. Buckley, the intellectual god of the Republican party. (The full two-hour debate, which drew a larger audience than the Sonics basketball game that night, can be enjoyed by googling "1971 Buckley vs. Costigan debate.")

And of course my sorrow was deepened by gratitude. In 1987 he wrote me that "long ago, even before you went to Bellingham, I discerned the quality of your mind and knew that it was more analytical and penetrating than my own, & I am happy that time has justified my prescience. It should be every teacher's hope that one day a pupil will surpass him, and for myself that hope has here been amply fulfilled." That's so like him. That man was a mountaintop giant of erudition and eloquence while I was but a pygmy on the plain, but even to the end he stuck to his teacher's mission of encouraging performance with compliments and praise. God rest his soul. I keep his picture on my wall to remind me of intellect, courage, and the nobility of the teaching profession.

Barbara's mother, Champe, died a year later in July 1991. Her life as an aging widow had not been easy. After her retirement from a job as a clerk at an insurance company, she'd lived alone, sustained by her church, contact with her two daughters, get-togethers with a few old friends, and the best bourbon she could afford. Toward the end, Barbara frequently visited her in Richmond, but had no more luck than the doctor in persuading her to stop damaging herself with smoking and a little too much alcohol. In the ICU she gripped Barbara's hand, held it hard for five minutes and smiled, but later slipped into a coma and passed away.

In a graveside service we buried her ashes in beautiful Hollywood Cemetery, overlooking the James River. The funeral home had delivered the ashes straight to the family plot—Barbara, though she and her sister had declined a fancy urn, hadn't known they'd arrive in a rude cardboard carton. At the sight of it, Champe's sister-in-law, Mary Lou, a bossy character whom Champe had disliked, picked a large magnolia blossom from a near-by tree and laid it on the carton, saying it looked much better that way.

Embarrassed by the cheap look of the thing, I went around after the service whispering that Barbara and her sister were heavily into ecology. Alice Cherry, Champe's oldest friend, declared that "Champe hated magnolias—they made her sneeze!" The good lady in the box, a connoisseur of irony, might have burst out laughing at how she'd been garnished for send-off. If there's a heaven, she's there among the angels, gently smiling. On a coaster I see a small bourbon-and-water.

～

The 90s saw other transformations. Most importantly, Pete and Liv were growing up and flying the nest. Livia graduated from high school in 1993. She'd always shown dramatic talent, and just before graduation she'd won a big Shakespeare competition for young actors and traveled to New York to perform in a national contest. We were proud of her, and came from Ohio to support her.

"Livia's performance at Lincoln Center was superb," I bragged to my diary. "Her Lady Anne ('Richard III') showed great creativity and imagination, and she had the house riveted. People nodded at each other as they applauded her performance. We were sure she'd be one of the 9 finalists!" But no. I knew some kind of fix was in when I learned that *a mute guy* was one of the finalists. "We saw him perform his part with much jumping around and twitching. A conference official read his part out loud for him while he twitched. It's all very well to help the handicapped, but I think Shakespeare would have considered it absurd."

Livia should have done her part in an iron lung. But there's been a lot of progress since 1993; last week I saw a one-legged Cambodian lumberjack playing the lead in the musical "Diary of Anne Frank." It was delightful.

Livia was resilient, as I emphasized in the letter I handed her after she performed. It began with the usual salutation, "Dear Dollingk!," then "HAPPY HIGH SCHOOL GRADUATION!!" After information about the new computer accompanying the letter, I continued as follows:

It's such a long time since you were my little girl. The other day I happened to find a picture of you when you were little. You were riding on a pony at a fair. Such a wan little child you were, with such a lovely but somehow ethereal and faraway smile, like a Victo-

rian portrait, a waif by Rosset-
ti. You had short hair, you were
wearing a dress and smiling into
the camera.

There were other pictures,
but they show you less little,
and less mine. You were becoming more and more your own
person. There were birthday
pictures in Ellensburg when, under the hawthorn tree, dappled
in sunlight, you were Queen for
the day; pictures in Glen Ridge
and New York, with the city and
the Hudson behind us; pictures
at the cabin, the condo, skiing,
and in Europe; and, the one I
love best, the one with you wearing Barbara's bathrobe and your
dyed hair is sticking out all over your skullcap and you have that
devilish expression on your face, and are twirling your thumbs in
mid-air!!!

All those pictures mark the passage of time now gone. Your
youth and adolescence are over. You're grown up and can be entirely your own boss. I expect to see you blossom into a wonderfully
interesting woman. I have faith that you'll have a most interesting
life, a fulfilling life. You aren't easily satisfied, and it isn't going to
be an easy life. You'll have more hard knocks than you want. But
you have a good heart, you have spirit, and you have that wonderful thing, persistence. Persistence can *make* reality. So let the game
of your life begin. It'll be a great show. Break a leg, kiddo! I'll be
pulling for you!!! I love you. Dod xxxooo

She went on to college at NYU, became a professional actress and
comedian, then later a mainstay receptionist at a prestigious New York
law firm. She did indeed experience hard knocks but turned out just as I'd
predicted, with courage, brains, spirit, and an excellent heart. Maybe best
of all, she remains as funny as she'd been as a one-year-old tot laughing
through her chocolate birthday cake.

Next year, 1994, Pete graduated from the College of Wooster in Ohio. I wrote him a letter too, which also summed things up. Here's a little of it:

> My recollections of you go back to the day you were born. I fell quite in love with you at first sight, and the truth is that in spite of everything, no matter how wickedly you color-crayoned the house when you were four, or disobediently purchased turtles against my express wishes when you were six, or vilely tormented your poor sister almost to death when you were nine, or abused the lawnmower when you were six-teen, or disregarded my advice during any of that time, I have never been able to dislike you nearly as much as I should, or nurse a grievance against your neglect of me, for more than a day or two, and that was mostly acting anyway. I've had far more pleasure from your life than pain, and you've been one of my continuing sources of delight. May it always be so. May you not fuck up is my prayer.
>
> So all you need now to make you happy is money, a job, a girl, a car, a place to live, and a kid more or less like you. Not till you become a father will you understand fully what I mean, because the love of a man for his son is something that cannot easily be put into words. But that kind of love, whether the son deserves it or not, will stand more strain, I think, than any other kind on earth. It's partly because men are lonely, they are the lonely ones. Women may come and go, but a man's son will always be that, just as a son's father will never be anything else but that, his father.

I proceeded to give him "a final list of pieces of advice." There were 50 of them. Here, renumbered, are a few. 1. Keep a diary. 2. Eat more fish. 3. Vote against incumbents. 4. Never forget that the majority is almost always wrong. 5. Learn when to tell a woman to come off it. 6. Remember your grandfather. 7. Remember your grandmother. 8. Insist on evidence even from yourself. 9. More rotation! 10. Remember how long life is, and how things may change. 11. Write an angry letter when you're mad, but don't send it. 12. Don't be petty, and learn to forgive and forget. 13. Keep in mind that half of all mankind is alive today. 14. Shun personal vanity as unmanly. 15. Think critically, and resist intellectual fads. 16. Take up some form of artistic self-expression, and stick with it. 17. Change oil regularly. 18. Take a plumber's helper on sleepovers.

Other transitions? As I approach the end it may be time to recall my basic theme and do some summing-up. I've taken "Fixing Stupid" as my motif, and in the first few chapters I scrutinized my youthful stupidity and tried to laugh at it. In the chapters covering my education and early career I focused more on others' stupidity and my earnest but sometimes obnoxious efforts to fix that too. And so now, addressing my later life as a professor, what can I say? How was I doing as I approached old age?

I guess I can only give myself a C, maybe at most a C+, at fixing my own stupidity. Although I thought myself a strong supporter of human rights, I failed for too long to see the need to update my opinions about homosexuality and women's liberation. My mind had been shaped in the early 1960s, and although that made me suspicious of authority, and a strenuous opponent of chauvinism, war, and irrationality, it didn't protect me against other prejudices. No, I wasn't racist, I favored civil rights in every way possible, I defended affirmative action; that wasn't my blind spot. Really, all I can say is that in the later 1980s and 1990s came social movements I wasn't yet quite ready for.

Yes, I was getting to be an old man, but that's no good excuse. I was too slow to see the anguish and discrimination that fueled the ever-bigger and more gaudily outrageous Gay Pride marches with their legions of men flaunting makeup and jewelry and phony wigs and eyelashes. I was never a bigoted opponent, I was just too neutral and slow to realize that this proclaimed a basic question of human rights, and to act supportively. It wasn't till shortly after Y2K (the year 2000), that I fully saw my error, and that was with help from younger and better people than I, my own relatives.

As to women's rights, although generally a warm supporter I was inexcusably slow to endorse the crusade for women's equal employment when I saw it crushing highly qualified men. The KSU History Department began hiring female faculty members in the later 1980s, and it's no wonder that once in, they set about cleaning house from top to bottom. In the 90s I saw males' job applications shoved to the back of the files, never even considered, as our staff balance shifted dramatically in favor of new female hires.

There was, in particular, a fine candidate, a man with first-rate scholarship on Germany, but also, more important to me, a glowing record as a teacher, for whom I fought hard and built a coalition of supporters; but although the faculty voted narrowly in his favor, my female colleagues went off and torpedoed his chances with the Dean. I considered that terribly unjust, not realizing that injustice can really be an overdue rebalancing of the scales, and that ultimately a much greater degree of fairness will result. There too I was slow to see my own stupidity, even though, as with the gay issue, I eventually fixed it.

There's one issue on which I remained aggressively fuddy-duddy, and I refuse to fix it even now. Something that soured me in the 90s was the new mantra about how people in general, and KSU undergrads in particular, should not be made to "feel uncomfortable" about anything they were being taught. Call it old-fashioned, but the job of universities, as I saw it, and still do, was not to make students feel "more comfortable." Instead it's to teach them to think clearly even if this means stampeding their sacred cows—*in fact, making them feel uncomfortable was, in my opinion, good, not bad!* I see it as a measure of educational success. I fear that that same "comfort" standard may still today infect higher education, spreading perhaps through something they call "cancel culture." Should Harvard's Latin motto, "Veritas" (Truth), be traded in for "Sospitas" (Safety)?

A highly memorable example of that "comfort" standard arrived in 1997 when two students, sisters, leveraged a claim that they'd been made to feel "uncomfortable" into a refund of their tuition for a world history course. It had happened, they said, in a classroom. In fact they were flunking that course, they rarely attended its lectures or quiz sections, but, missing the official deadline for permissible withdrawal, they accused their professor of making them feel "uncomfortable" when, *lecturing to a classroom holding 140 students,* he illustrated a lecture by quoting some pretendedly offensive passages from *Gilgamesh* and *The Song of Solomon.*

Before a second-rate Campus Ombudsman he vigorously defended himself against the absurdity of his "sexual harassment case," but the apparatchik Ombudsman merely remarked, against piles of evidence and other students' testimony provided by the professor, that "on the one hand, they say such-and-such, and on the other, you say such-and-such," with the result that the university, intimidated by fear of public opinion lest the case reach the newspapers, quietly refunded the two students' tuition and left the indignant professor unsupported with that blot on his reputation.

It was only after the American Association of University Professors launched an investigation, found the complaint entirely frivolous, purged the files and vindicated the professor, that the case ended. That maligned professor, increasingly at sea in new intellectual fashions, and a little soured by changing standards even in his own department, was a holder of the university's Distinguished Teaching Award. That professor was me.

It was time to pack it in. The year 2000 (Y2K) brought my last months in the saddle. Y2K's arrival at midnight on Dec. 31, 1999, caused a global flurry of consternation because of a computer flaw, the "Millennium Bug," which, it was feared, would suddenly freeze up banks, power stations, and transportation centers everywhere. But that was a tempest in a teapot, and the new century rolled on without interruption.

Left to right: Barry Beer, Me, Vic Papacosma, Glee Wilson, John Jameson

My Kent colleagues arranged a surprise party to send us off. The Wilsons invited us to lunch at a roadhouse more than half an hour's drive from Kent; they said they'd meet us there. When we arrived, all our best pals popped up to surprise us, and we were indeed astonished and delighted to see them. It was a great occasion and I was quite touched. After drinks and a fine meal there were speeches and toasts. My colleague Barry Beer stood up and offered a little speech to conclude the festivities. It was a lovely testimonial from a man I'd always admired. Everyone laughed and applauded, confirming that he'd caught some essential truths. I asked if he'd share his notes, give me a copy of them. Here they are:

THE TRUTH ABOUT GERALD NEWMAN: APRIL 2000

Was always his own man. I may have been the first colleague who didn't impress this young Harvard PhD very much; but I wasn't the last. Regarded as unreliable by chairs, Whitney and Graves. He might ask embarrassing questions or state the naked truth. No team player. Sometimes completely off the wall. Always used too many big words. But he often said what others wouldn't. Fearless: provost best known for his wig, or Brenda Colley. [These are references to attacks I'd made on people with big reputations.] Scholarship always under-estimated. May not have written as much as others, but no one did work of higher quality. Had the misfortune to serve during an era when the big raises always went to the university professors. We will not see the likes of GN again. Unfortunate truth. Profession has changed—not always for the better. As he enters retirement, I can assure him that I shall not be far behind. And among the best memories that I will take with me will be recollections of being his colleague.

That was very generous, and when Barry stepped down in 2001 I flew back from Washington to attend his own retirement party.

Barbara and I sold our house in Kent, packed our belongings and pets into a moving van, and headed out to the Northwest, to Ellensburg. My mother, diagnosed with ovarian cancer, was waiting for us with open arms. After arriving and moving into our new house, we attended Pete's wedding in Seattle to Tina Kelley, a wonderful woman he'd managed to snag while he was working there.

Tina at that time was a freelance writer, often submitting news articles to the big eastern newspapers. She was brilliant, charming, vivacious, beautiful, outdoorsy, everything a parent could possibly want in a mate for his son and a terrific addition to his own family, and she reached out to Barbara and me in warm-hearted ways that would have melted glaciers. She was a gem. How'd he do it??? I'm reminded of my dad's rustic expression: "Even a blind hog gets an acorn now and then." But that's a joke, I do love my boy and think him a match even for the matchless Tina.

Their wedding was a grand affair on a houseboat on Lake Union, and an entire boat-load of friends and relatives attended it. The June day was brilliantly sunny, the bride's parents had come from New Jersey, Ruth came from Oregon, Barbara and I brought my mother, I sobbed as the couple exchanged their vows, Livia sang a song, there was a live band, the food was wonderful. Before long the happy couple would produce my first grandchild, Katherine Isabel Newman. There'd be another one three years later, Andrew Lyle Kelley Newman. My retirement years were now perfectly launched.

12

The End Times

ELLENSBURG AND TUCSON, 2000-2021

Barbara left the University of Akron, and I left Kent State University, at the end of spring semester, 2000. We moved to my old hometown in Ellensburg, Washington, and began a quieter existence. My first priority was to help my mother during her battle with cancer. We helped her sell and move from Walnut Farm to Hearthstone, a retirement home. She let me hover over her, I visited her daily, for many weeks I interviewed her about her life; I typed up the results and printed out her autobiography, "Memories of My Life" (2002). I gave it to all her relatives and the Local History section of the town's public Library.

We tried to help her have some fun during those last years. We took her to Seattle to watch the Mariners play, we took drives into the hills, she let me push her around outdoors in a wheelchair when she could walk no more. Imitating Gramlin, who, driving her car alongside, had exercised her dog Targi by running him up and down Bull Road, we did the same with Mom's wonderfully affectionate little dog, Otis. She made up zany stories about Otis the way she'd made up stories about my bear, Pooh; she complained that Otis liked the Yankees and spent too much time drinking bourbon and eating crackers. She delighted in Lynn's visits from New Jersey and anticipated her phone calls every day.

She played bridge and was considered a leader of "the inmates," as she

303

impishly called others in the home. Doing her morning crossword puzzles, she'd wake me up at six a.m. to ask roughly, with no sweetener or foreplay, "WHAT'S THE CAPITAL OF ZIMBABWE???" With her make-the-best-of-things attitude and her genuine interest in the Hearthstone staff, she became one of their favorites. To the end, she enjoyed what little life she had left. A week before she died, she requested an appointment at the optom-etrist's—that's how little she saw it coming. But she faced her decline with courage and resignation just as my father had, and when at last her time came, and I tensely asked her as she lay on her deathbed what I could do for her, she replied, "STAND ON YOUR HEAD!" I didn't know whether she was joking, or annoyed at my question. She had no hope for an afterlife, said she'd "like to go join Len," and passed away in October, 2003, at 86. With her departure I lost the best supporter I ever had, and the best and most forgiving friend.

As this is a memoir of my own life, I suppose I should conclude by briefly describing what I've done since I retired—after all, that's one-fourth of my entire lifetime. But there was no clear purpose to my life anymore; like other retirees I was just a random thrill-seeker. Of course we made new friends in Ellensburg, and also, to keep us company, we continued to own small dogs—after Bounder, then Duffy, then adorable twin papillons Lilly and Louie, and now another pair of papillons, Teddy and Molly, wonderful pets all; and we also owned cats to keep the dogs in line, Mai Tai and Yow-lice, and Buttons and Bigger (so named because she always was).

With Moose Mack at Thorp Mill Fund Raiser

As to public activities, well, naturally we supported our town, and Central Washington University, and the annual county fair and Ellensburg Rodeo. I related earlier how much I love my little town and the Kittitas Valley. And I followed my forebears by taking part in various local causes. In 2001 I was recruited to be a board member of the Thorp Mill Town Historic Association, which oversees, cares for, and runs tours of the oldest wooden structure in the county, the 1882 grist mill whose "mill race," its water-power source, runs through what was once my great-grandfather's property. In its activities I played a part for many years, helping, for example, to build its important connection with the University, which now supports much of its activity.

Also, I became Chair of the Lake Kachess Cabinowners Association, in which capacity I served a long while and helped guide its acquisition from the Department of Ecology of all-important water rights for that group. In addition, I became a board member of the Willow Glen Homeowners' Association, which governed the 28 residences in our area, and played a part in updating its codes and supervising this and that. Barbara and I helped build an organization, Citizens Against Sprawl, through which community leaders attempted with partial success to stop the evisceration of lovely downtown Ellensburg by curtailing the building of new shopping malls on its outskirts. These were all just the sort of activities you might expect from retired academics, "tree-huggers," tweedy L.L. Bean types—though actually we don't own a stitch of the stuff.

For recreation and culture we daily walked trails in the Kittitas Valley, I fished from a pontoon boat, we went huckleberry-picking, we read, we watched edifying stuff on PBS. I wrote more volumes of my diaries, and, for my grandchildren, two unpublished children's books about laughable calamities that befell an absurd family of beavers. In 2012 Barbara finished (under her then pen name Barbara Evans Clements) her magisterial *History of Women in Russia From Earliest Times to the Present*, a brilliant book, and, only last year, writing as Barbara Newman, her family history, another typically beautiful piece of research and writing, *My People, The Story of a Virginia Family* (2020). All her works, by the way, are findable on Amazon.

Barbara slaved in our flower garden, making it such a showplace that I began thinking of charging admission to see it. My own new hobbies included ping-pong (which, for an old man getting blinder by the day, I'm pretty good at), and photography in a club (naturally I had to be its president), and jewelry-making—I had fun making hundreds of jewelry sets from gemstones and beads, handing them to acquaintances who couldn't politely refuse them, and I also gave many others to charities that would accept almost anything to sell at fund-raisers. I croaked harmoniously for 20 years in men's choruses—the Singing Hills Barbershop Chorus in El-lensburg, and the Rincon Country Gentlemen in Tucson.

With Harry Matlin and Andy Piacsek

For the Ellensburg group's public shows I wrote what were generously called hilarious scripts that bound all the songs together, and for one I even flew Livia out to Ellensburg as a star comedian to play "Bossy Lou" in a ridiculous musical situation-comedy of Irish music. That was before my mother died in 2003, so she was able to attend and sit laughing in her wheelchair there in the front row of the Morgan Junior High The-atre—where, so many decades earlier, she'd laughed at me playing Shake-speare's expiring Pyramus. She saw, as she'd expected, that her favorite granddaughter, who'd often performed on stages in New York City, was an absolute riot. That made me very happy.

We supported many charities, including the Children of Chernobyl, founded after the famous 1986 nuclear disaster that showered radioactiv-ity all over Belarus. Its original purpose was to provide medical relief to children affected by that contamination, but gradually it became also a summer-abroad program that resulted in small groups of kids visiting and staying for weeks with welcoming families before returning to Belarus. It was in that capacity that Barbara and I, for a dozen summers, became a "host family" for Belarusian kids, and that was, when all's said and done, probably the best thing we did for anyone during all our retirement. We remain in close touch with four of our young Belarusian friends, whom we love like family members.

Every retired couple hopes to travel, and luckily our health held out long enough to visit a few remote parts of the world, and to fly east annually to visit family—as in 2006, when my nephew Michael Benediktsson married his sweetheart, Kate Slevin. I said earlier that our son Peter, an entrepreneur and all-round good guy, married a fine woman in 2000, the writer-poet Tina Kelley, and that they produced two appurtenances, our grandchildren Kate (born in 2001) and Drew (born in 2004). Both have lived up to their grandparental heritage but we think so much jail time excessive for teenagers,

Mt. Rainier, Me, Pete

and consider uniformed supervision unnecessary—well, okay, I'm joking, actually they are absolutely wonderful kids and we love them to pieces.

Our talented left-wing daughter Livia thinks she's saving the planet by remaining childless, but we believe it's going to the dogs anyway and wish we could have seen what droll trolls might have tripped down the yellow brick road behind her. The Benediktssons in Glen Ridge, N.J., my sister Lynn and brother-in-law Tom (both retired academics too, as you'd know if you haven't been skipping chapters to reach this exciting climax), hold grand parties, write witty poetry, and, among many meritorious volunteer projects, shovel out turkey-and-dressing for poor folks at Thanksgiving. We met them just a month ago at the Museum of Modern Art in Manhattan when we were all still being extremely cautious about COVID-19.

Kate and Drew

As for me, all through all this last phase of my life I remained as left-wing as ever—and also, I might add, as all my educated relatives. We're a real hotbed of what Spiro Agnew, Nixon's Vice President, stigmatized as "radiclibs," and, to dyed-in-the-wool Republicans, we're very scary and should probably be made to live in exile. I marched in downtown Ellensburg against the American invasion of Iraq in 2003 and spoke against it in that gazebo on Pearl Street. I read Obama's *Dreams from My Father* in 2007, greatly admired the man, and voted for him twice, in 2008 and 2012. I admired his eloquence, thoughtfulness, and personal qualities, and liked most of his policies except his failure to fight the Syrian dictator Bashar al-Assad, a failure that led to the disastrous exodus of Syrian refugees and helped fuel mass migration to Europe and the unwelcome rise of populism there.

The English philosopher-politician John Stuart Mill called the Tories "the stupid party," and the U.S. parallel is obvious. During Obama's presidency I saw the Republicans' ignorance and cynicism growing. In 2011 the "birther" campaign was launched by Donald Trump, claiming that Obama was of foreign birth—the popularity of that alone should been a warning about the party's capture by stupid people.

And not just stupid, but violent. On the Republican fringe, extremist groups mushroomed—militias, the KKK, Q-Anon, Proud Boys, the Oath Keepers. The Republicans were no longer the party of Lincoln, Teddy Roosevelt, Eisenhower, Reagan, the Bushes. I watched their populist Tea Party movement with disgust, condemned their opposition to Obama's healthcare legislation, despised their efforts through the Citizens United decision (2010) to turn political power into a purchasable commodity, was revolted by their spineless submission to the NRA and their unwillingness to halt massacres in America's schools. On top of all this came their maneuvering to repress the Black vote and pack the federal appeals courts and Supreme Court with their hard-right nominees.

With Livia

I continued trying to fix stupid. As I'd done so many times earlier when appalled by something totally idiotic, I spoke out in the newspaper. For example, after Thanksgiving one year I attacked Jimmie Applegate, the top philosopher of the Kittitas County Republican Party, ridiculing him for publicly criticizing, in a Guest Column, Barack Obama's *failure to mention "God" before the third paragraph of his Thanksgiving Proclamation!* Yes, that was his complaint! So, I demanded, "at what point should American public officials be sure to get the word God into their speeches?" Should Obama, just to make sure, give God a big thumbs-up in every first sentence? Maybe, I thought, God "wished we'd just shut up and concentrate harder on being decent people!"

Donald Trump, of course, followed Obama into the White House. His presidency came after Obama's like road apples after a horse parade. After losing the popular vote in November 2016 by three million ballots, he'd won in the antediluvian electoral college, a leftover from the good old days when public hanging and wife-beating were all the rage. The Russians openly admitted cheating for him.

With Lynn and Tom at MOMA in early 2021, half-masked against Covid-19

From the beginning I considered Trump so ignorant, undignified, and brutal, such a lifetime cheater and all-round despicable human being, that I and all the rest of my family gave money and worked hard to defeat him in the 2020 election. I even spent 13 hours on election day as a Democratic poll watcher, determined to prevent pro-Trump election intimidation at the precinct to which the Democratic Party assigned me. Like a hawk I watched every red hat, including those in the fire station next door.

The aftermath of that election, which Joe Biden won by more than seven million votes, saw an avalanche of right-wing lies and a riled-up Trumpian mob's effort to reverse the public's choice with violence in the Capitol on January 6, 2021. Now it would appear that the entire Republican party, led by unprincipled cowards, has decided to endorse Trump's ridiculous claim that he won the election. If you digested my comments about historical myths (Chapter 7), you'll see that this claim is extremely dangerous for our country's future. Talk about jihadi stupidity.

Barbara and I bought a Winnebago RV in 2007 and began wintering in

Tucson, where the weath-
er is warm from October
to May. Getting older,
we decided in 2018 to
downsize from our house
in Ellensburg and move
to Tucson permanently.
Here we live in a small
house overlooking the
desert and the beautiful
Rincon and Santa Catali-
na mountain ranges. We
do all the usual old-peo-
ple stuff and even run a
few local things. We'll

Our Home in Tucson

never forget the Kittitas Valley, and we return there every spring to tend
those many Newman graves in the Thorp Cemetery. I always begin with
those of my parents. I suppose I'll go there at some point to join them.
Many years ago my mother, by way of an odd birthday present, gave us
the deed to the plot right next to theirs; but aren't there warnings against
moving in with parents?

Anyway, right now, it appears, I'm healthy, and happily writing the last
words of these confessions.

Giving an Illustrated Talk about Killings in History

~

Looking back over it all? I've been very lucky, I've had a very lucky life. I escaped dying young, and outlived most of the people who wish I hadn't. I haven't yet discovered what will kill me—so far, I'm not living under that shadow either.

Around the world and throughout human history, whole populations have been born in unpleasant circumstances, some in hell-holes and dens of misery, many with lives shortened by disease, war, and violence, many more burdened with discrimination, and the vast majority, if employed, working at tedious jobs with no scope for creativity or personal growth. I, on the other hand, born white and male in the 1930s as an American, as a young citizen of the greatest and most powerful industrial democracy in the world, had none of that to worry about. Unlike most of historical humanity, I began unburdened and began to grow under miraculously favorable circumstances. My childhood woes were nothing, my adolescent torments mere trifles. I've been so lucky.

Jerry Newman has been alive for more than one-third of the entire history of the United States, and that has been the golden third, better than what preceded it, and very likely better than what lies ahead. Raised and feeling secure in a loving family, I acquired a little courage and resourcefulness from contemplating my pioneering ancestors, I developed discipline, a work ethic, and a few skills from my parents and grandparents, I had the pleasure of being the only brother of a caring and talented sister, I had a few nearly life-long friendships. I flourished under the encouragement and criticism of exceptional teachers to whom I'm so imperishably indebted; I'll never forget them.

Luck is so important to happiness, and I was beyond lucky. I never worried much about support, or money, or staying on the straight and narrow; I wasn't terrorized as a child by a knife-wielding step-dad, my family wasn't ruined by debt or inherited illnesses, my granny didn't sell drugs from her car.

Looking for some way to launch myself, I caught a ride in a profession, the American college teaching profession, that was just then in its Golden Age. Encircled by competent people, I helped to advance the work of an excellent university. In my classrooms, the most important place, I was my own boss, free to do almost anything I wanted to, equipped to make a small original contribution to world knowledge, take on new teaching projects, travel the globe. My two children, born healthy, with brains, sunny dispositions, and overflowing talent, brightened my days with love and laughter. Inept at marriage, I found at last my soulmate who, delighting me every day, has now shared half my 82 years of work and play, bringing me joy through her unfailing wit, understanding, and care.

Throughout it all, succeeding networks of friends and well-wishing companions and family members helped to keep me afloat. I had my trusty pen and inner eye to help keep me honest and, when necessary, guilty and repentant. Despite many stumbles and regrets, I matured, had a few accomplishments, helped perhaps a few thousand students along the way, became a better husband and dad, and, I hope, a not entirely ridiculous granddad.

I had my innings, I had my fun, I had some good, hearty laughs. I was extraordinarily lucky. Now, at this point, although carried on hips and knees yearning for the boneyard, and with my skin nearly ruined by the Ellensburg sun, I see nothing but blue skies ahead.

And finally? To go back to where I started: Whatever happens, I feel confident about a continuing supply of maverick professors. At some point I think they'll fix stupid once and for all.

Made in the USA
Middletown, DE
31 December 2021

57368022R00191